# The Philosophy of a Thought

## Written by
## Lyn Petit`

PublishAmerica
Baltimore

ISBN: 1-4241-8496-7
PUBLISHED BY PUBLISHAMERICA, LLLP
www.publishamerica.com
Baltimore

Printed in the United States of America

I would like to lovingly dedicate this book and all that it holds to my Dad, for creating our mum and for putting up with me.

To our mum, for helping to create us and make us into the people we are going to be and for putting up with us.

To our elders, for guiding our parents.

To Lady Bubbles and her mum, for making all of this possible and for bursting mine.

To Lady Gail, for opening up her heart to me and surrounding me with good churchgoing people from her life. Thank you for all your help with the corrections and the late nights, too.

To the mates who left and are still here, remember, where there is a will there's a way.

And most of all to our mum for having the strength, courage and perseverance to bring me into her reality and for helping me to find mine. For loving us, holding us and helping us to build our wings to fly and come back home to you. I love you all deeply.

GF

# Foreword

I have learned in life that before you can ever begin to have a philosophy of any kind, be it your own or some one else's, it has to start with a single thought. This thought has to be so great that it causes you to think about it, and then the more you think about it the more the thought can lead to a conclusion. This conclusion causes you to think even further past the original thought and before you know what is going on you have yourself an epiphany. Now, epiphanies are great because it causes the original thought to split; now you start all over, only this time you have to figure out two different thoughts and the only way to do that is to make your brain go in opposite directions at the same time. Think of it this way, you are having a private debate inside your own mind and you have to be unbiased when both parties come to the table to present their case. (Do you think your mind can do that?)

Picture it this way: you are having an argument with your conscience over a thought you once agreed with! Known truth, it really is a lot of fun getting your mind to believe you think just the opposite of what you just thought. Why would anyone want to play games with their own mind like that?

Simple, I would prefer to play head games with myself then have someone play one on me without my knowledge; also, it keeps your mind sharp in thinking how the other side might think about something. When you can do this subconsciously with anything that you think about or see, you will have taught yourself how to look at life clearly and will have gained wisdom in the process.

When you can see both sides as clear as a rain drop you will hold fast to your philosophies because you know in your heart of hearts that they are more than just another one-sided opinion.

Philosophies are pure facts from both sides that allow you to reach your own conclusions. The difference between the two? One will answer your question, the other will not. If this confuses you please do not feel left out, I was just as confused at first when I thought about all of this. The great thing about all of this is I learned a tremendous deal about not only the philosophies of life, but also the people that lead them.

I hope that something helps you in the following pages and that by the end it makes you think about your own philosophies.

# Contents

Chapter One Getting Back to the Basics from the Beginning ..................... 9
Chapter Two Learning How to Clean out Your Karma! ........................... 43
Chapter Three What to Do with All of This! ........................................... 81
Chapter Four The Elders ...................................................................... 122
Chapter Five "You Can Learn Something New Every Day" .................. 165
Chapter Six What If? ............................................................................ 176
Chapter Seven The Metaphysical Realm of Pure Thought and the Philo-
    sophical Side of Life. ..................................................................... 224
Chapter Eight The Bright Side of Life ................................................. 255
Chapter Nine Your Wit's End! .............................................................. 291

# Chapter One
# Getting Back to the Basics from the Beginning

Have you ever had so many ideas and thoughts inside your mind that you did not know what to do with them? You try to put them down on paper and all you come up with is a lot more things to keep up with. I always wondered why our brains never came with a secretary until I looked inside my mind and saw how I kept things! I do believe they would have fired me.

I would always wonder about the strangest things in life and the thing that got me was it would always make more sense to me with what I came up with than what I was told. When I would have one of these epiphanies I would always say, "Would it not be more logical..." and after I explained my thought about the subject they would agree in astonishment, which would always make me laugh.

They would tell us things like potatoes have eyes and corn has ears and they were fine with this arrangement. For some reason this did not set well with my brain. I finally had an idea and it went like this: "Would it not be more logical for the potatoes to have ears and the corn to have eyes. Think about it, if a potato opens their eyes, they will get dirt in them and the way the wind blows how could you hear a thing from way up there. If they traded, the potato could use its ears to listen to vibration and the corn could use its eyes to tell the potatoes what they did not hear." The thing that gets me is that after all that thinking I went through to come up with that rational solution the only reply I received was, "You're too smart for your own good." Now just what is that supposed to mean?

I was in school when I came up with what I thought was a reasonable suggestion and I said it to a teacher, was it not their goal in life to see that I was made smarter? I have to admit that I did go out of my way to drive them crazy with the things I would think about. The way I saw it was they gave me things to think about so why should I be the only one with homework. They asked us questions so why not have the same respect and ask those questions back to them in a slightly different way. Basically, they made me use my brain so why not make them use theirs!

"If a tree falls in a forest and no one is around, does it make a sound?" The teachers were all trying to prove this statement one way or another to us when I handed in my paper. "It is not the sound it makes when it falls but the silence it leaves when it's gone?" Known truth, my teachers all treated me as if I was a freak of nature after that. (They act like they have never heard the answer before.) Oh, I will not lie to you I knew my mind was going in that direction long before they ever called me that. I just had to find new ways of keeping it there and that is where the fun began.

I always enjoyed not thinking or being like everyone else. To me being called a freak is an honorable title and I want to hold onto it for life. People have come and gone in my life but no one has ever left with my freak of nature title. (Some of them will try to convince you that they never challenged me for it and they're right they never did. They just wanted me to surrender it and be like everyone else. Ha. I have come too far to turn back now!)

I learned that you have to use your mind in order to decipher between logic and reality. I rather enjoy being more logical then being realistic. I have also learned that more people prefer being realistic than being logical and you know what my thoughts are about that, "Where is the logical thinking in their reality?"

Basically, the definition of reality is not being able to see past what is in front of you even if its just a smoke screen, logic is having the ability to see the out come first, we just cannot see what is in front of us. I guess another way to look at it would be are you far sighted or near sighted or are you one of those gifted people who can see both ways?

Think about it for a moment in your own mind if you will. In reality, we are all told many things growing up that everyone else is told no matter what country you are from. The logic about what you are told however is not always there. Reality: "Just one more bite, just one more bite." The logic: The bowl contains a whole lot more than just one more bite. Now if you combine the two you end up with people who could have loads of problems in math class!

In reality, everyone does it the same way and always has since time began. Does that mean that logically everyone did it correctly from the start all this time? Do you not think that you could improve just a little or is your way of doing things that perfect? (Careful how you answer that one.)

All of us are told real young not to eat apple seeds because it will cause an apple tree to grow in our stomach. Logically, what kid would not want their own apple tree? Think about it, you are lying in bed, get a little hungry, instead of having to get up you just pull an apple off one of your branches and your feet never had to touch the floor! I never cared where the roots were going to come out at I just wanted my very own apple tree. You know what the people who are realistic left out; that seeds grow in dirt and dung that is right you heard dirt and dung. Now, logically if they had told me that from the start I would not have spent years thinking I was a lousy farmer at such a young age. I also would not have gone to the extremes that I did to get those seeds to grow. Let me tell you I was not one who gave up after a few dozen or so tries either. I would sneak out away from everyone, pull my trousers down, face my bum to the sun so that they would have a chance to grow and do you know what I received in return? Nothing, not even an odd tan, those realistic liars leave facts out that are needed. Getting the sun to shine on them was just one of the things I would try when I was younger, you can use your own imagination to figure out the rest of my failed bizarre attempts and they were all bizarre now that I think about it!

The things that realistic people say has always thrown me off and you can tell that they more than believe what they are saying and hope that you have just enough lack of sense to buy into their reality.

How many times have you heard, "Your being a smart ass?" If in life we are told that, everything has an opposite; love is the opposite of loathing, day is the opposite of night then how in the world is smart-ass the opposite of dumb ass? What? You being smart is making an ass out of the person you are talking to, whose fault is that and why should you stop being smart because they are too lazy to be anything other than a dumb ass. Correct me if I am mistaken but between the two would you not rather be the smart one then the dumb one? Moreover, why do they both end in ass, would it not be more logical to match the two where they are coming from.

Smart means that you are using your head and since your brain is located in that region why would you not say something like, "Your brain is being smart again," or try something truthful like, "You figuring something out that I cannot even though I asked you for your help is causing me to feel overwhelming daft (stupid) and I do not like it one bit. Instead of being grateful that you helped me out (when nobody else would), I would much rather have preferred you to be a dumb ass so that we could be stuck in the same rut together. Now you went and shagged everything because I was going to use the fact that I could not figure it out to get out of doing it. Now I have to figure some other way out of it. Thanks a hell of a lot." They then will walk off hoping that you will feel bad for using your head when they could not. Known truth, they're good at making you feel like you have done something wrong, I know because I use to fall for it myself every time. Combine the two and you come up with a lot of dumb ass people convincing smart brained people that they were stupid for helping them in the first place.

The dumb ass one I can understand. If your head is not screwed on your shoulders then you have to store it some place, you would be surprised at what all you can keep stored up your bum but I will talk about that later. I just know that your head can be up your own bum for years and you not even know it. How do I know this because I discovered a new disease and after running tests on myself, I found I suffer from it personally. The disease is called; Tunnel Bum Vision and it causes you to have your head not only up your own bum but you cannot tell if you are looking at things the way they truly are or if you have your facts bum backwards. People who suffer from it might not even know that they are or that they can carry the gene and pass it on to others not just loved ones.

How many times have you seen someone walking around being moody and instead of asking, "What is wrong, is there anything I can do to help? Do you just need someone to talk with?" You instead whisper to whoever will listen and you ask them, "I wonder what is up their bum!" I cannot tell you how many times I have asked the same thing until I realized I walked around the same way sometimes! Could something be up my bum that I was not aware of? When was it placed up there, why and who would do such a thing? This was definitely something I was going to have to look into, but I was going to have to do it in secret you understand. There was something to this logic vs. reality thing and your head being up your bum. The more I thought about the differences, the more I would find differences to compare. The more moments past in my life the deeper my thinking would go. Then I had heard an expression that would change my life forever over time.

In reality, we have all heard the expression that it takes a village to raise a child. Logically, no one ever investigates who these villagers are or what is in their true nature. I mean would you want a child to be raised by a village of nothing but thieves, whores, liars, cheaters and predators? I hope that both realistically and logically, you would say, "No," but how many of us were raised in that same village, we just lived in different huts? If you were raised in this type of village, can you move away? If you were not can you keep yourself out of one? The answer is yes if you were raised in one but it's called escaping not leaving. Yes, you can also keep yourself out of one but you have to know what you are looking for. You have to play it cool either way because if they suspect you found a way out, they will hit the lock down button then you pretty much shagged yourself unless you can learn from your mistakes.

See, I was raised in a village just like the one above until I learned you could be traded up and taken in! Mine however came with one elder who later learned about the villagers he lived with but by then it was to late. Several were all five, were proud of what they were never going to amount to, and broke you down into feeling the same. I learned all about the way they think, move, operate, and use people to cover up for them. Known truth I was glad that I was raised in this type of village, oh not while I was living there Lord no! I wished so many times that Dad in Heaven would let me grow a tail so that I could cover my bum up when any of them were around. Logically that tail thing is a great idea; realistically however they would all know why I was wearing it and know that I was onto them.

The reason that I am glad that I was raised among those types of villagers is you can learn first hand how they manipulate and what their M.O. patterns to using people are. Some times you have to live amongst your enemies to learn who you truly are so that when you leave you will know who you never were or want to be.

I know that I am not a thief, oh sure, I did once or twice when I was a kid but that is where I ended my outlaw days. I did not want to be known as the candy bar bandit, sticky fingers if you will. I do not care too much for lying because no one laughs afterwards. I can tell you a story that will make you laugh your bum off though. I know that it says in the Commandments not to lie but my thoughts about that are Dad does not care if we lie to our enemies, give them false information and misdirect them. I mean if someone is trying to hurt you then why would you want to tell him or her how and what your weakness are? (Remember it is just a thought I have been working on.) Lying to your loved ones or keeping things from them for whatever reason on the other hand is not good. You may think that they are better off not knowing but who are you really trying to protect and cover? Known truth, the younger the mind of a child is the easier it is for them to adjust. The longer you wait the greater the chance you risk of someone else telling them first and you will never make up for not being the one they should have heard it from. Kids act out because something is not right in their lives and too many people try and tell them that they are too young to understand. Anyone being told that would be frustrated; apparently, if they asked they want to know. Age is just a number and has no bearing on one's mental stability or maturity, after all look at all the immature babies in politics and running corporations!

Turning someone's life upside down just because you can does not give you the right to. Realistically you think that they do not know, but logically they know that you are the one keeping the secret from them, they just cannot find the proof.

No good can come from it. My mum says that it is better to be honest, get it out in the open and deal with it from there before it gets out of hand. In addition, if someone else goes to telling them they can say, "I know, they told me already," thus taking away their means of causing problems. I love quoting my mum about some of the things she passes onto me but since I am new to all this wisdom stuff of hers I do not always get it correct the first couple of times or so. A great example would be the time we worked together and I yelled really loud to someone, "Well my mummy says that you should learn how to play with yourself before anyone else will play with you. No wait, My mummy says that you have to learn how to play with others before you can learn to play with yourself. No, that is not it either. You have to play with yourself while waiting for others to play with you? No, you have to learn to play with others because in the end you will be playing with just yourself? No, well, my mum did say something and as soon as I figure out what she said I will be getting back to you." I turned around to walk off when guess who was standing right behind me, my mum. "Mum, what did you tell me again?" She had the most incredible look of astonishment on her face when she replied, "I have no idea what I told you after all that kid." A long, long while after that she tells me, "I said you have to learn how to like yourself before anyone else will like you."

"Oh, I was kind of off there just a little huh?" She just laughs, for a long time though. Oh yes, I can make my mum laugh when my thoughts get something more than incorrect. The thing that makes her laugh is that I just cannot seam to put it down, no I have to run in a circle while spinning my wheels. There are times when she feels sympathy for me and tells me to get my foot off the gas! Who would have thought that the answer was just that simple?

There is something about my mum that keeps me more then level headed and at the same time, she will repair my wings when I need it. Every time I make an error in judgment I get to receive two lessons from the same mistake. She will ask me what I learned and I will tell her in detail and then she will tell me what I should have learned! She has never made me feel daft or laughed at the wrong time. I call her my mum but she belongs to my sisters and brother as well, oh plus my dad. My mum never cared that I came from a whoring, thieving, lying predator, known truth she never even asked about my background. If you think it is because she did not care you could not be more wrong. My mum never asked me about my past because she could tell that it was hell the first time I went through it, plus she knew how bad I was hurting even though I told myself I never felt a thing. To me, she is a true real mum, not one that just spits out babies and thinks it should mean something.

I was more than set in my ways when my mum took me out of the world and put me in her life. I was ready to knock anyone out if they messed with me and stomp a hole in them if they messed with my mum now. (She called me her little tornado when I would fire up if that tells you anything.) I guess she could tell that I had a demon inside of me from birth that would not let go of me. Every time the word mum was mentioned, it would send me into an unknown rampage. I was donated and I had been fine with that fact until she came along. The adjustment was not easy on either part, I fought her without realizing it and she was more than patient to put up with it.

She knows that I am who I am because I had to be in order to make it this far. She is also smart enough to know that I never wanted to be half of what they made me turn into. I learned that if you want something bad enough or whole-heartedly enough you will change not only your ways but also what was instilled inside your nature. I wanted my mum and everything that comes with her but I had to learn to open up and throw everything else away. Now some people have no problem in the world telling others their life story but that is the thing; they tell everyone the same story. To me it is like they're stuck and cannot figure out how to move on to different opportunities. You also have people like me in the world that will never look back for any reason. There is a black hole back there that we escaped from that almost took our life so why revisit it? I learned through several loved ones why you need to go back and fill in the holes, to keep you from falling into them later, or to keep others from using them as their own personal traps of despair for you.

One of my mates told me something while I was going through all this mental adjustment. He said that a child is never the same when someone puts their hands on them in any way. I wanted to tell him that "they" turn out just fine but something inside of me agreed with him even though I did not understand why. I was thinking about what he said when he continued. "You have to be extremely strong willed, have a strong mind and come out to the right people in order to completely overcome what they did to you."

"Did to me? I have never had anything bad happen to me and why does everyone say something to that effect now?"

What was in my past meant nothing to me, to them I was a grave mistake although logically I do not believe that I should have been the one to pay for it but realistically I was the only one who paid. I mean I had nothing to do with being born; I just arrived on the scene and never would have thought that something was amiss. I was made to feel less because nobody knew for sure how I came to be. The lies had started out too thick for anyone to see through them and known truth nobody even cared. I was the one who was punished for being an evil mistake and was always told that I would never amount to anything. (This coming from the same people who could not count past one more bite!) I learned to be numb to them mentally, physically, physiologically and spiritually. I had to be because I did not want anything from those villagers; the cost was always everything for less than a sliver. I had learned so much about them that I actually thought I was one of them, that is why when my mum took me home to her heart I would only look through the window. I did not want my evilness to pour into it because she was the only one who took me in and treated me better then anyone else ever had.

My mum has always been so good to me since the day she picked me out that I never wanted to hurt her. I thought that if I opened up and remembered what all I had been through that it would hurt her in some way and it would be my fault. The only thing that I would ever give my mum to hold was my hand, because I thought that my heart was black and I knew that she deserved better.

When someone loves you unconditionally, that is exactly what they mean; unconditionally, those are the only ones you want in your life too let me tell you. The others will always have at least one condition to start off with for you to follow in order for them to act as if they care.

My mum never told me that the only way I could ever be one of her kids is if I came scar free. She never questioned me about my past to see if it would set well with the other family members. She just took me in, let me know that I was going to receive the same treatment as the rest of her kids and that was that. She informed me that I was not above being disciplined or beneath being loved and it did not matter to her how long I had been living on my own either. She means what she says too let me tell you because shortly after I became

16

one of her kids I got into trouble with (of all people) her and she grounded me. One week of no TV and I had to go a month without giving her a gift. The TV part was hard but the no gift thing was worse. How many of you have ever bought your mum a gift just because you thought that she would like it? (If you are one of these types of kids' maybe, you could talk to my mum and explain it because I did a lousy job of it hence the grounding!) Moreover, I had to go home and tell my flat-mate when I got in from work that I was grounded and why. She was really sweet about going into another room to laugh and helped make sure that I stuck to my grounding. She even added on an extra two days just to be safe with my mum. She fixed the chair so that I could stay in the living room with her and not see the TV through the mirrors, now that is a true mate. Anyone else would have said, "She will never know, I will not tell her." Now my version of what happened is that my mum grounded me because I have an exceedingly horrific speech impediment and could not say the word gift without that stupid "s" leaking out the side of my mouth. When you ask my mum why she felt the need to ground me she will tell you that she did indeed give me three chances to correct my lie and I just could not get it right. I tried, oh, let me tell you I tried (to cover it up) to believe what I was saying was true so that it would come out right.

I learned that I would turn against myself faster than the speed of light, even go as far as telling on myself when it comes to my mum. My eyes will look at her and go, "Yes, she did something that you should ask her about." My brain will tell her things before my mouth knows it was even opened, and to make matters even worse my mouth tells her things before my brain can put a stop to it. Now that is some kind of power to have over your kid when they will rat themselves out to you before you even have to ask. My mum is great at being consistent too because she laughs every time I tell on myself. All I can do is just stand there after words thinking, "I cannot believe that I am not on my own side, was I not involved in coming up with a believable story? What happened?" My mum is what happened!

I know that a great deal of people get adopted but you see, I was in my twenties when my mum wanted me and grounded me too. (See, if there is hope for a village baby like me, then there is hope for all of us to find a real life loving family.) If that were not enough of a Heaven sent Gift I look just like her. I never noticed how much I did until a mate took a picture of us standing side by side looking down at the same thing. I look just like my real mummy (her) and that is the picture I carry around in my wallet. (The one village babies arrived through is called the egg donor.) A lady saw the picture and told me

17

that I could never get away with telling people that I was adopted because I look exactly like my mum and realistically I really do. (I look like her in the face that is, in the height department from where I stand my mum appears to be about 78 meters high!) I never said a word, all I did was grin from ear to ear because hearing that meant the world to me. I went from being called rubbish and scum to being compared to the most gorgeous Angel in the choir. What the lady said never went near my head; it went straight to my heart where it belongs. Everyone knows that only babies are adopted, when they're no longer babies they know that they're part of the unwanted group. Everyone likes puppies but nobody wants a dog type thing but what they do not know is that we can be retrained.

People pray for miracles each and every day, but when one comes their way they're totally obvious to it or they dismiss it while they pray for another one. They prefer smoke screens because you can get away with not seeing what is truly there; I know logically it does not make sense to me either. These are the same ones who scream for something different, then go out of their way to make it just like everything else. The day the word Mum passed my lips, I knew I was given the greatest miracle a kid of any age could ever ask for. I was finally getting to go home to a mum's heart and all the love that it can hold, her heart is freakishly huge too. See, I never thought that age made you anything, smarter, better, wiser or more mature. What you are inside has nothing to do with the number of years you have been around. I have seen "Adults" throw some of the biggest tit fits you have ever seen as they tell you to grow up.

My mum knew in her heart that I was going through life bum backwards and she understood why. I still had the heart of a child but the mind of an elder, which is not a good combination in reality but logically I never noticed its devastating effects. My mum did and so did another mate of mine that I met shortly after my mum adopted me. She pops in and out of my life and unbelievably is a lot more strange than I am she just denies it. O.K. that might not be a fair thing to say so I will let you decide who would you consider being the strangest? One: somebody who just comes this way, or two: someone who acts that way? See, I agree.

This story becomes even stranger as paths cross; lives intermingle, straight laced met down to earth and the one connection to them all? An out of this world little freak of nature who never thought anything like this could ever happen outside the movie theatre!

Logically, none of this was suppose to happen to anybody much less

18

somebody like me but in reality it did and I am here to tell you that I feel more like a somebody now then I ever have in my entire life. I feel loved and know what it means, I feel accepted to the point that I know I belong and it does not cost a thing. All of us crave the same things in life, love, a sense of purpose and wanting to be more than just who we are. Why are we here, and what is the meaning of life? Thanks to the people who came in and out of my life, I learned the answers. Thanks to the ones who stayed, I learned not just why I am here but why I want to stay.

See, there is a hidden greatness about each of us that is so unique it takes someone good to find it and bring it out. To a certain point, we are all shy in our own way. I can talk to anyone about anything unless I like them then I either say something daft or I just smile at them all the time while silently having a smooth conversation with them inside my head. (I know that I am by far the only one who has ever done that.) I have always watched people ever since I can remember and we all have a clumsiness about us that is highly comical and yet still innocent. What I do not understand is why everyone goes to the extremes that they do to hide it. I know so that others do not make fun of them, but who cares. The best people in the world are the ones that can make you laugh after you have been through hell.

Remember hearing that the entire world is a stage and we are all playing a mere role? What happened to that feeling of being anything at anytime? Now everyone is told to act their age, to grow up and (get this) act like an adult. These people are the audience members who did not want to take their turn at being on stage. They only want to heckle and criticize you for having the courage to do something that scares them. I love that life is a stage, you have different scenes, different characters. You can have a lead role, or just be there to support your fellow cast members. You can have a love scene, or a dramatic moment with others. Life is about playing your role to the best of your ability and finding more adventurous roles to play. You do not want to be type cast while you are on stage because it is always changing so change with it. I get tired of always being the serious one or the funny one, mix and match for your mood.

Once you sit in the audience that is where you will always find yourself, that is if you come to the show at all. Why would you want to watch someone else play the part you were meant for or that you could play right along side of? Could it be that you are jealous because you see someone in the role you tried out for, if that is the case do not tell me that that is the only theatre in town. Everyone that you meet has access to a stage so look around and have fun.

Everyone watches someone else play the role of a hero, when that role was meant for all of us to play at some point in our lives. What scares some of us into idly sitting by and causes others to jump up and take action?

If you ask me it has everything to do with your childhood however it was instilled in you. Some kids are told that if someone is bothering them to run and go get an adult. Logically, doing this will have a lasting effect and not one that is good. Why would you tell them to run when they're the ones that need help? Making them run causes them to become winded and then they cannot get the story out, plus it makes them become weak over time. The more they run and get help the more they become dependant on it. This can become dangerous because they might end up running into that village I was talking about earlier. I know because that is what happened to me. I broke out of the one that I was born in and ran straight into the back yard of another just on the other side.

Why would you tell your child to be weak in front of the one who wants to hurt them? Do you not realize that it gives the other side full power as well as control? I know that I have watched a lot of different people raise kids and on some of them all I could think was Thank-you for not being the one I came out of either. They want their kids to feel less than anyone else because this is the only way they can feel powerful themselves. In addition, how many times has a kid run to an "adult" tried to tell them what was going on and they do not believe them in the first place? Why, because they were not on the scene. To make it worse they take the side of the one hurting you without looking into it because it is easier. The same kids who were taught to run eventually grow up to play the same role repeatedly, that of a victim when they were meant to play the hero at least once in their life. Why would you want to cheat a child out of what is rightfully theirs because you turn yours down?

They learn so much about the role until it becomes a part of them and to me the only ones who deserve to play the role of a coward are the evil people. Too often the good one is made to look bad while the bad ones always take the credit. Then at the end you find out who the bad guys really were but it is too late to give the good one any recognition. The play is over, the audience dispersed and the house lights have been turned out. The end, now another production has set up in its place. Did you take something from it with you, like learning from your mistakes?

Some kids are told that if someone is bothering them to stand their ground and make the bully back down so that everyone can see the coward for who they really are. The sad thing about these people is that they get a bad rap from the runners. Due to the fact that they did not run then in the runners eyes they are the bully because they made someone cower to them. The runner does not see that logically because they stood their ground this will not happen again. All they want to do is run and tell someone and that is usually when another bad person comes on the scene to "protect" them. Bad people never work alone, there is always at least two because someone has to be the watcher. The watcher has to keep an eye out for you and tell their partner when you are coming and what your weaknesses are. They cannot act worth a hoot if you really watch them but they can smell. They can smell a runner because they reek of fear, terror, shock and dismay and they welcome the runner with open arms to a never ending dark trap of being everyone's prey.

Then there are the ones who are told to protect only other people in need. To jump to someone's defense without thinking what the cost to them might be. The only problem with this is they are also told to suck it up when they are the ones in pain or need help. These people talk through their eyes but only for a moment. Blink and they will deny what you saw.

In reality all these types of kids grow up into something. Logically you should have a right to defend yourself against anyone and if you cannot then you should be able to stand there, yell for help so that aid can come to you. If everyone would do this for not only themselves but for each other then when help arrived there would be a Calvary heading your way. Talk about personal back up. The way it is now is if you yell for help everyone stands around waiting for someone else to answer the curtain call. Then they get mad because people are thanking you instead of them. If you did not earn it then you should not be entitled to it. If you earned being a hero for a moment in time then you should learn what it feels like and then let someone else have the spotlight. To many times childish people take the stage and hog the spot light when there is really no reason to other than they are just being selfish. If you really look there is nothing going on but a childish temper tantrum going nowhere and you can see that all the time.

Why do some people feel the need to intentionally mislead young minds because they can? If you ask me, that is the most ignorant reason to do such a thing to an innocent child. They do not know any better but you however do. You can mislead in numerous ways, but to lead correctly takes a steady path.

I went through all of these stages at some point in my life. I started out standing my ground, then was told to protect everyone else first. I was then forced down into being a part time runner. I would stand my ground on certain things and leave before anyone noticed I needed any real help.

I swore to myself that when I was in my own charge no one for any reason would get up on me ever again. The problem was after a while I was going after anything that moved and if there was nothing there I would shadow box to keep on my toes. This is the stage I was on when my mum entered and asked if I wanted to perform in her theatre and on her stage. I felt like I was going to Carnegie Hall and had a lifetime backstage pass. My mum is classy, down to earth and believes highly in her support group of family. I have never had a support group before, all I kept thinking was what do you do, and how do you act?

You would think that I would have jumped at the offer, but leaving everything that you have ever been taught behind, all at once? I do not mind starting over, Lord knows how many times I have done so before, but this time was different. This part was going to cost me everything including who I was. No not because she told me it was going to but because I could feel that it was. To be someone completely different from myself, why and for what reason? If people did not like who I was then they were free to piss off and that included me. I mean I never asked people to change for me because I accepted them as they came. Why can they not have the same respect for me? If later on I learned that I did not like them then I would piss off, easy as that. I have always been able to cut ties the same way they were cut with me, without blinking an eye and moving on. I learned that some ties are not cut, they're simply buried.

I did not want to hurt my mum by telling her that I could not be a part of her life any more because I did not know how. I had been in the dark for so long that the light coming from her was killing me and I could not see a thing. I could not find it in me to reach out to her; the hell I had been born into had indeed consumed me without my knowledge and took total control of my mind. I fought all of my life to help other people and I knew that I was about to have to stand up for myself, I just never realized against how many people. Basically, I just stopped caring about everything that had to do with myself, it got to be to much and then before I knew what happened it grew dangerously worse and because I closed my eyes to everything, I could not see the point it had reached. Good thing that the people who love you are a light house themselves so that they can see in the dark to find you.

Known truth, there were a couple of things that I liked about myself but there were loads more that tipped the scale in the other direction. I no longer liked who I had become. I had no control over my temper, my thoughts or myself any more and I no longer cared if the bad people won because deep inside of me I knew I was one of them. (I just did not want this side to win.) I had to be, it would explain so many things, like why I was having such a power struggle inside myself. I had both good and bad inside of me and because I had more bad people in my life then ever before they were only bringing out that side of me.

When I lived in the village the only time I would hear the word God is when they were using it to break me. I was told that God loves his children and would not let anything happen to them and since they were allowed to do this to me I must not be one of his. I was told lots of ignorant things along those lines but that one stuck hard and I never realized it. To throw the Commandments up in a baby's face just to destroy them is ruthless but there are people who will do such a thing. "See God gives His children mums and dads to love and honour, do you have one? No, well I guess that is proof enough," even though they constantly reminded of this. I accepted this as fact and went through life trying to make up for being born pure evil. I did not care if anyone got up on me because I knew that I deserved it. The thing about people is that you never know who are watchers like you, and why they are watching you. I watch because I find people interesting others watch for weakness and a way in.

When you are surrounded there is something inside of you that knows the end is near and I felt it coming up fast but I was not scared nor did I move. I had told myself all those years that they never got to me and to face my past would mean the end of who I knew I was. I had always been loyal to myself, I trusted me over anyone else until my mum. What do you do when you find out that your own mind has betrayed you? You find out why.

One of my mates who lived down the street from me came into my mind and life thick when this was going on. She was not like my mum in ways; she wanted to know all about my past. (Maybe she wanted research for a role she was about to play I do not know.)The more she dug into my past the more I unknowingly helped her. I wanted to be close to both my mum and mate because everyone else in my life had either left or I pushed them away. She could tell that I was miserable without my mum but I had stayed away too long to ever hope of coming back. I believed that in order to save face you do not show your face. (Did I have that one way off or what?)

These two ladies would change me in different ways far beyond my own thought process and way past the norm. One would force my past to the surface and then leave like all the others, the other would stay and help me pick up only the pieces I needed. The strange thing is that they both had this way of taking care of you without making you feel bad for it but their agendas were completely different.

The more I struggled with the memories in my head the more her and her son would stay and help me through it. I watched how loving she was to him and how much they needed one another. They had times with each other, good, bad and different but they had them together. The closer I got to the both of them the more I felt myself doing the same thing to them that I did my mum. I kept them at arms length because I did not want to hurt them in any way and I learned that this can hurt worse than pushing someone completely away.

Why do we push the ones that love us away and keep those that want to hurt us as close as possible? I think that it has everything to do with the saying, "Keep your friends close and your enemies closer." I do believe they are the same people, what throws everyone off is that you are led to believe that they are looking for two different kinds of people. Then when they duck all you see are the people you love to take your frustrations out on. Why would you want your enemies any where near you for that matter, so that they're close enough to eaves drop? To me the same people who say that it takes a village came up with this enemies closer thing so that you do not catch on that your living deep inside their lair.

Logically, where does this put the ones who care about you, realistically it puts them no where near you and that is what the bad ones want. If you keep good people away from each other then they become easier targets. United are the bad ones divided are the good ones but together the good ones can make them fall. See, I also think that these are the same people who came up with the phrase; if it walks like a duck, talks like a duck to cover up then it must be a wolf in sheep's clothing or a devil in disguise. How many people do you know that walk around acting bad, tell people they're scum so that you know that they're scum? Wolves in sheep's clothing and they hunt in dangerous packs.

Everything that I had been told was coming up a lie and my life was about to be flipped upside down again. The more my mate and her son would get close to me the more I found myself backing away until I hit a corner. Now normally I would come out swinging but I really found my heart learning to care about her and her family. I knew that if I did not allow my mum to get close to me I was not going to allow anyone else either. The cycle was about to come full circle again only this time it was going to break and turn into a cross road. The scary thing is that I knew this, the fear was would I know it when it was happening?

I had so many learning disabilities growing up but I never thought that thinking was one of them. People in my life were starting to tell me that I thought too much and that would cause me to think even more. Why would people not want you to think about what you just talked about? When you feel your brain going one way and your life going the opposite direction it will make you snap and that is just what I did. I snapped at everybody including myself.

I remember what caused it to, I was watching a talk show with a mate and the guest on there was just like me. She was born out of wedlock and was the last to know. The more the show went on the more outraged I kept becoming at the egg donor. I could tell by her eyes that she did not give a toss about that kid she brought into the world but wanted everyone else to think differently. She wanted the world to think of her as this perfect person who never does any wrong and lives by the good book. The more that female opened her mouth the more I wanted to go through that screen and take her on myself. The kid was asked if there was anything that she would like to say to her egg donor and instead of being open to the pain her kid was in, she made the gesture of, "Bring it on."

I went ballistic after that, her kid just opened her heart in front of the world and all she could do was be cold and cruel to her like always only she disguised it as humour. The egg donor does nothing but put her down for everything that she does and keeps her kid feeling bad about herself because of all the nit picking then blames the kid. After the show had ended she still never went up to her kid and put her arms around her but she wants the world to think that she is a perfect human being in every way. I wanted so badly to stand in her kids place and take this female on for her because she was not in the state of mind to be defending herself. In addition no kid should have to protect themselves against the people who created them, nor from the other villagers for that matter. I think that people who want their kids raised in a village are just looking for free baby-sitters and do not care what they teach them as long as they're out of their hair.

I learned so much about a lot of things after watching that show. I learned that people like that make sure you are not in the right fame of mind before they strike, that I indeed had the same type of egg donor only I was free from all of them, I just had to learn how to let go of the hate they had caused.

There was something about that talk show that would not leave me alone though. My mind kept going places that my heart was not allowed to go. What could possibly be so bad up there, never ask your mind that unless you really want to know the answer because it will let it go.

I felt like my mates were having to baby-sit me and I did not like that one bit. I have always taken care of myself, I may not have done the best job in the world but it was only me. I was nobody important, at least not to me anyway. I know what my mum said about liking yourself but it did not sink in as you may have noticed. Do you always like yourself every moment? If you were honest and said no then you did not listen to her either so there. (This is where I should stick my tongue out but I will not.) Everything that I did had some tie to my past now. When my mate down the street and I would talk, I would tell her the conclusions that I had reached. (She would either agree or secretly roll her eyes.) She was always easy to talk with and was learning just how my thought process works. The things that we would do together sometimes would cause a thunder of laughter and not just for us. She pushed me around in a shopping cart one time, and not just a regular cart but the ones that have a car on them. You do not know how long I have waited for someone to say yes to pushing me in one of those. Every time we were together laughter was somewhere near. There for a while the only word that would come out of our mouths was unass. "I unassed a lot of things today." We would came up with loads of things together, we discovered that if you turn the light on, take the skeletons out of your closet, put meat on their bones you can give them a proper burial. We also discovered that the nerves everyone seams to hit are really pieces of a big button and if you figure out how to put it all together you will be the only one with your finger on it. Now instead of everyone pushing little pieces of your nerves you can look them right in the eye and tell them that if they do not leave you be you can and will hit the thing yourself and then only Heaven can help them. It is a great feeling to have your own finger on your own button or at least know where it is now.

How do you go about cleaning out your mental closet, well in my own experience I needed someone to help me dig? Never dig in your own past when you are alone, the reason is you do not know how deep you have actually dug until you find that you cannot get out. This will make you so freaking depressed that you can tend to give up when you do not have to. Misery does not love company it needs it. When you or someone you know is depressed, they need someone good close to them more than ever. Mainly to protect them from the vultures circling around them but to make them realize they have already been through it. Remember there is safety in numbers and you can help pull each other back out. In addition, keep in mind that when you dig you will not just be uncovering dirt but a tremendous amount of dung will be mixed in with it, you know to help keep it growing. (This is where I should have planted that bloody apple seed come to think of it!!) Now how is that possible, logically the best place to grow them would be up your bum all things considered but realistically the hole with the best dung is in your mind? Well who would have thought that logic was not always the best way to look at things and that reality is sometimes the best possibility? (I know that you think that you read that earlier but I erased it before it went to print. OK, so I am not right in the head but I told you that up front. Would you have admitted any of that to others?)

The more you dig the closer you are to the core of how this all started. My mate kept making me go all the way back through my childhood and I will be the first to admit that the more I uncovered the easier it became. Digging up my past was a walk in the park, opening Pandora's Boxes however, was a walk in the dark. How was I supposed to know that when I turned the light on in the closet that I had my eyes closed! Keep in mind that I just kept storing things up here, I never looked through any of it.

I had so many thoughts racing around inside my head that I could no longer sleep and I no longer wanted to talk with anyone because they were adding to the things I was thinking about. The thing with being autistic is that **everything** gets in and I do mean everything, my head was over flowing as it was. To add to this I am also dyslexic, colour-blind and as you may remember suffer severely from tunnel bum vision. When people come to me with their problems or worries I try to figure things out logically for them but because realistically I had my own problems both trains collided hard and everything got jumbled together. I could no longer figure out if I was logically looking at their problems or realistically if they were mine or if the two were backwards? To make matters worse I somehow got locked inside my own mind and forgot to leave the door open! You would think that since it is your own mind that you would not be terrified but I know how my imagination can run wild, especially when it gets scared.

I learned a valuable lesson though; fear is just that; it is all in your mind. You are not a by-product of your mind you are a product of your mind, heart, body and soul. This makes up your spirit, when one is out of alignment the rest follow. I once believed what I was told until I discovered that they had lied about everything. This caused me to have to rethink all that I was taught and change my mind about everything. This is by far an easy thing to do for a mind that is set. If you tell someone that they are daft then they will believe you because they trust your judgment over their own. If you believe that you are smart then you can go further in your mind and therefore in your life. I was always told that I was daft and I believed them, until one day a mate told me he thought I was smart. What was the difference between the two, oh just a thought. The difference between who we are and who we can be is something as simple as a joining of positive thoughts. Could changing our minds be that easy? Well, it depends do you have a good relationship with your mind? You may laugh but not everyone is on speaking terms with any part of their own being. The voice inside your head is suppose to be your conscience you know and is the voice of reason when you are being or about to be unreasonable. Depending on what I am about to do I can hear my mum in my head over my own conscience, this will make you feel out numbered so just straighten up while you are given the chance. I learned that I have been somewhat more than unreasonable at times with my mind, just when it came to me that is. The talks that my mum and I have together now have helped me to change my mind about myself and about everything the villagers told me were true.

From what I learned it wanted to change its mind about us years ago but since I am more than stubborn and hard headed getting through to me was not going to be easy. I learned that I thought that I was untrustworthy instead of figuring out that I was just taught incorrectly. I had to unass all previous thoughts and ignore all the preconceived notions that I had about myself because they were never mine. I had been given the chance of a lifetime and I was not about to screw it up for any reason…. I hoped anyway. The cycle could only be broken if I snapped the first link in it and that was in my mind.

"Those who do not learn from their past are condemned to repeat it" (until they get it right). If you look at your life from as far back as you can remember does a lot of it appear the same? Do not think about the people just think about the situations for what they were. If it does then you're on a loop and you need to learn why. I learned that throughout my life that the few good ones never stayed, they always ran off (I guess to go get help then by the time they returned I could not be found.) See, no good can come from running if you're alone. Someone should stay just in case the situation changes and it always does; this way when help arrives they can be brought up to speed. Remember that keeping good people in your loop is great. Keeping your life in a loop is self destructive and people come with that. To make it worse other people can be self destructive themselves.

I learned that I let people control my life because I did not care any more and that can get you hurt because once someone has or thinks they have control over your life they are not always willing to just let go. They believe that you are an indentured servant and since you let them in you belong to them. Now keep in mind that this is a village's motto. You know what I learned through my mum and another loving parent, that it does not take a village to raise a child, it takes a family. I also learned that just because you're born in a village does not mean that you have to stay in one. There are people looking for ones to love all the time, they just get boggled down in their own village and cannot find you either. (That is why you yourself have to learn how to be a light.)

How many of you have ever thought, "I cannot be related to these people." What happens if you are correct, no I do not mean through DNA or blood but I mean spiritually. Have you ever met someone for the first time and felt like you have known them forever, but the people related to you feel more like strangers? We tell kids all the time not to talk to strangers but never really get more specific than that. We do not teach them what to look for as far as hidden dangers inside ones own group. What happens to us between the time we are born and the time that we go home? A stranger to me is anyone that I think will hurt me; everyone else is either a member of my family or a mate. I learned that I knew more strangers than anyone else combined and that there are more strangers willing to take the place of your entire family if you allow them to.

Think about the great things about being a kid; out of the mouths of babes, that kid has so much energy, animals and babies have the greatest instincts. A kid can never see past you when they're into you and will go out of their way to impress you. They never hold a grudge because they're forgiving, and are not scared to try new things. They do not see you for your possessions or care what your job title is, they just like you. They want to come over to see and hang out with you for no other reason except that they like you. How do we go from this to turning into adults who no longer want to come out and play?

Remember when you were a kid and would go over to the neighbours to play, or just moved in and the kids are the first to make contact while the adults hide inside protecting their secrets while peeking out the window. Why in the world would you tell a kid to grow up and stop looking at life with innocent eyes, Lord knows that they see things in their proper perspective? Why are we in a hurry to make people as miserable as what we have become? Why would we not find a way to hold fast to what we believe in instead of letting others do our thinking for us? When kids go out to play they do not ask adults what games they should come up with, they just make stuff up as they go. Kids do not lack imagination, adults bury it and act like they have never been a kid before and therefore have never done anything wrong.

I cannot tell you just how many times I have been told that I needed to grow up, get a life, act my age and become just like everyone else in the world, a robot if you will. Why, I do not want to walk around like a know it all, I do not want to be tied to a lifestyle that I cannot afford and if I were to act an age all I could ever be is just a number! I enjoy the fact that I am more than a number. Plus everyone knows that when you become an adult you loose your hearing completely, because every kid will tell you that adults do not listen unless their own lips are moving.

"I want to give my kid everything that I never had," and instead of really looking at what they never had they just go out and buy things thinking this will fill the void inside of all of them. What you never had was respect that your opinion mattered because you took the time to form it yourself. Hugs when you were hurt, needed love or just to make your world a better place. How about giving them a way to communicate with you instead of the non-communication way that you were given? How about giving them a place where they can feel safe to screw up and grow into better people because of it instead of being reprimanded for every little move they make? How about giving them things like common courtesy, common sense, your time and legs to stand on? How about allowing them to be kids for as long as possible because childhood ends abruptly from what I understand? Let them grow up in their own time so that they can feel their legs, and smell the roses. We are in such a hurry for them to make something out of themselves that we do not care if they are not ready. Why is that, so that you have a better view of the fall?

Why can we not be happy when someone else makes it just a little further than where we are, why are you comparing your life to someone else's anyway? Some people will tell you that they want their kid to go further than they did and at the same time they are sabotaging them every step of the way. What do they say when they get caught, "I was doing this to make you stronger, this is for your own good?" Depending on how hard headed you are, this will either do one of two things to you; it will either break you completely or make you strong enough to get out. Those that have a strong mind will learn to break free and those that choose to let others do their thinking for them will stay forever broken and in a dark world of constant hurt.

When someone close to us warns us about something or someone why are we so fast to dismiss them as trying to pull the wool over our eyes but when a stranger tells them that we are full of it they are believed over us? Our records show that we have caused you no ill-will of any kind or brought harm to you in any way and yet you still decide that someone you just met is more trustworthy. Could it be that deep down none of us trust the ones we are told to because they live under that same family umbrella? I cannot tell you just how many times I have heard people say that because they have feelings for someone then that means they trust them. I think that the way we are taught to trust or not to trust has everything to do with how we are brought up.

I never trusted any of the people in the village because I would hear what they would say about one another, how they would give their word when they just broke it with someone else not but ten minutes ago. I would hear them say that they promised that they would never do it again even though this is their hundredth offence for the same crime. Kids are not lab experiments that have gone wrong, they all start out the same way the difference is how we teach or do not teach them. Stop leaving it up to others or to themselves because you may not like the final results.

We tell kids to start thinking for themselves and then knock them when they show initiative or give their thoughts about the matter. We tell kids that if they need help to ask for it and then when they do we tell them that they are smart enough to figure it out on their own and send them on their way. We teach them one thing and tell them another then wonder why they do not listen. We yell and throw things trying to get them to listen and then get upset when they learn to communicate the same way.

Kids do not judge and yet an adult is more than quick with that response. We are so quick to judge others and look down at them because it is so much easier then looking at ourselves. A kid does not have a past they are just living life every day and to an adult that is the only thing that matters to them. How much pain have you been put through? A kid does not want to see their mates in pain and after they talk, will make them laugh. To me our past is just that ours and does not belong to anyone else just because they want to know something that is none of their business. These same people will tell you that you have no right to ask them about theirs though. Our past does not make us who we are, it was only meant to be a stepping stone into something greater.

I sometimes wonder if these people were asking me questions to later hurt me or if they wanted to know how I had dealt with things. Known truth I had not dealt with it and that is why I was ready to throw my hands up and fight anytime someone knocked on that door. I did not like the people in that village and therefore saw no reason to ever talk about them no matter what the circumstances were. If I talk about my family or mates now, it is to tell a funny story or because they are the ones that I learned something from. If I do not like someone then I doubt they will ever make me laugh so there is no reason to talk about them. Were we not all supposed to be taught that if you can not say something good then do not say anything at all?

I learned that there is a group of people out there that are rare but they do exist, they are called grown-ups. This is the group that my mum is in because she is still way too young to be called an elder. Oh she has the wisdom and the maturity but she has not lived life yet either. She will even tell you that she is still learning things and applying the wisdom that is past down to her. Now grown ups I like because they're still a kid at heart and when something comes up they just take care of it. They see things from more than one view and give advice accordingly. I now have a family full of grownups and it is helping me to grow up correctly as well. I never thought that it would happen in my life time believe me. I thought that I was going to stay screwed up forever or that there was no hope for change.

My mum knew that I was born an adult and knew that I not only had a chip on my shoulder but that I had a big tub of dip on the other side to go with it. I wanted to be close to my family without snapping because something else was on my mind. I wanted my mum but I was so full of loathing that I never minded the bad people in my life because I could take it out on at least one of them but then it got to the point that all I could think about was the past.

I knew that I needed help and the best people to help you through things are your family and mates, (not friends they laugh and point when you fall then gossip about it later.) I went to four different mates who put me in touch with two others and when it was all said and done I went back to my mum. I am more than grateful believe me. I learned that I should have stayed all along because she would have ended everything right quick and not made me suffer.

When my trains collided everything in my head got knocked around and this caused me to become so overwhelmingly confused about everything. I felt like I was in a different dimension and everyone around me sounded muffled and blurred into the back ground. I felt something all around me but did not know what. All of my senses were going haywire and I could not think straight any more and that scared me until I felt like I was paralyzed with the fear of not being able to think for myself. I felt like I was in one of those nightmares where you go to scream and nothing comes out. You go to run and you're moving in slow motion.

The weird thing is that something in the house I was living at kept knocking me in the head. They must have known how hard headed I am because they did it four times. I called the one who lives down the street one day and asked her to come and check on me because I had three gashes in my head and did not know how they occurred. I just thought that I was confused before but now I am completely dinged out of my mind. I could not figure out for the life of me why this was happening to me, the more I would talk with Dad in Heaven the worse everything seemed to be getting. I then remembered something and understood why he would come after me of all people with a vengeance; I had forgotten that I was not one of His kids. This was payback for something that I did earlier in my life and now it was coming up to take a chunk out of my bum. I felt more then bent over and since my head was out of my bum a little I could see it heading right for me.

See, I was so tired of hearing that I was not one of his kids that I made it my decision so that it was easier to swallow. I went outside where nobody could hear and God and I got into it big time that day. "You do not want me well I do not want you how do you like hearing that. Hurts when you think that someone wants you and then you find out that it was all just a sick game. Now you know how I feel but the joke is on you because I do not even like these people so you screwed you up. That is right you screwed up, you should have given me people I wanted to care about instead of ones I loath. See if you would have done it that way then those not caring would bother me but it does not. I will never ask you for anything ever again since all I asked for was a real mum and you could not even get that right. I will leave you alone from here on out. Honour thy mum and thy father, what a joke if you do not have one."

I was one pissed off little kid let me tell you and I wanted nothing to do with any of their kind because they can all fool you. I was asked why I did not attend church and I would always reply that I was not on the list and walked off. I wanted to be though but I would never say it out loud. God was not going to know that He hurt my feelings.

Everyone wanted to know what my beef was with God but I never would tell them because that was between Him and me and nobody else's business. He knew why I was pissed at the world, I only thought that I did but He knew for sure what my reasons were. I was little and would always forget.

I went on a lot of journey's and adventures and was always knee deep in something but that did not stop me. I wanted more out of life then being around bad people all the time. I thought that if I kept changing the people in my life that it would not give them time to shag me. Boy was I mistaken, that just gives more people more opportunities and they all know that they have to act fast before you leave again. I started looking at people differently and wondered why I was always in the same rut. I kept walking right into another village after escaping from one just a second ago. Years of planning another escape, one second to ruin it!

Why did I feel the need to stay in with the bad people when I knew that I could not stand them? I had to learn what was at the core. I wanted to know, I wanted control over myself because I learned that I never had it to begin with. I had also spent my life over compensating, not knowing why and it was time to stop. It was time to relearn everything and this time I had the right people in my life to help speed things along. You do have to be extremely careful going back in your own mind because if someone were in your group that wants to sabotage you now would be the time.

I noticed something odd about doing this though, I was correct when I said that I never felt what they had done to me and that is what I had blocked out. I never allowed that part of me to be exposed and used my thoughts, mind, imagination and everything else that was up there to keep it from getting through. I had held everything in for so long that I could no longer carry the load, it was excessively heavy for even me and I did not know what to do with it. I wanted to put it down but it had become a part of me. When I had carried it on my back I never noticed the weight but when it went out in front, I realized it was keeping me from my mum and the rest of my family. I would only allow myself to feel when it felt good and everything else went inside the bag that I would get to later. You know how that goes, the to do list board, only I had so many of them that I had to start carrying them around in a huge bag.

I learned that sometimes when people ask, "What is in the bag, (a.k.a. your past)" they merely want you to open it so that they can throw their trash in it as well. I wish that I had learned this earlier because I would have kept the bag closed more often but at least I did learn it. I also learned that bottled up feelings really reek when you let them ferment because they do not go away until after they come out. This is a valuable lesson to learn because we were given feelings to use, you either use them when they arrive or they will use you in and over time.

I realized what my mates were talking about when they kept telling me to let it go. I was finding out the answers that I was looking for I just did not like how they were coming out. I wanted to deal with things my way but I guess my brain knew that I never intended to ever go through that bag. I knew what was in there so why bother? I learned the reason why you bother is simply to empty the bag of all it contents.

I had some elders adopt me for a moment while I was trying to figure out how to get back to my mum. You really do have to make sure you pick the right ones out for yourself or your kid because they really do play a vital role. They are the ones who help to shape a spiritual mind and with it, the way they think about themselves. The more I kept telling them that I was an evil little bastard the more they kept getting pissed off. "See if I was not an evil little bastard then you would not be getting pissed right now would you?" I know that a great deal of people want to hear that they are good people but I was not going to fall into that group. Talk about slamming heads over something and neither one of us was going to budge over this one.

They were trying to tell me that nothing of what I went through was my fault and I did not want to hear that, I needed something else from them but neither one of us could figure out what that was.

My other mate could not understand how anyone could do that to their own kid, someone they're supposed to love and protect. The thing about his kid is he went through hell with his egg donor too only he had his dad to protect him at times. He also kept asking me how his son could stay tied to someone who was continuously cruel to him. I could not understand it either but I knew that one would lead into the other and it went along the same lines as mine. The only difference is that I was no longer tied to any of them physically, but I was beginning to realize I was still mentally and that is what kept me pissed off because it was keeping me from going home to my family.

Everyone that I knew had some kind of abuse that they either had gone through or was going through it now. Instead of thinking about their problems, I was feeling their pain or at least had a better understanding of where it was coming from. I have never felt before and this was harder than anything I had gone through mentally. Feelings are so much different from thinking about thoughts. After I am done thinking I can for the most part stop, feelings keep going on even when you sleep. Then another lie popped into my head; "Sticks and stones may break my bones but names will never hurt me." Whoever came up with that saying was definitely trying to cover up a big hurt because words are a double-edged razor sharp sword. They can make you or break you and they do not even have to come from you. A thought consists of words; I am smart, a good hearted person and you feel like you are until your mind knows that it is. I am daft, I was spawn through a devil adult and you feel like it until your mind knows that it is.

I learned that some people talk through whatever part that leads their life. There are also those who are gifted enough to talk through more than one like my mum that is why I listen to her more than ever now. I have always lived life through my head and when I talk that is the part that I lead with. I watched how each one of my mates would talk with me, how some would use soft words because they were leading with their hearts and some just came right out and say what was on their mind regardless of how the words felt to you. Some of them could not understand where I was coming from because they never had to walk down that road; others knew that road all too well but had not worked theirs out either so did not want to walk with me down mine. Too bad I forgot to tell them that misery needs company if nothing else to keep them calm.

I felt like the more I helped them the more I would find what I was looking for. I now had to care because there was a connection that had to do with all of us. One mate had a kid almost like me but his kid had one good parent but the tie is still not severed and I still could not wrap my head around that one.

I am the type that if you hurt me I was out of there and I did not believe in giving you a second chance to do it again. I then remembered something that everyone has said to someone at some point in time. "Well you know that they are family and you do not turn your back on family." Why does a person get to stay in your life because they hide behind a word? They are correct when they say not to turn your back on these people because you really should keep your eyes open when they are around to see what they are up to if nothing else.

"Well, she is your egg donor, he is your brother, they're my kid," why does that matter? If the people are abusive in any way then it will never be a healthy environment to stay in and I do not care whom they are related to. Bad people have to come out of somebody do they not? I cannot understand why someone who has never been in a place like that can tell you to stay because of this or that reason. Do they thrive off your pain or does your life being in turmoil make theirs look that much better? There are some people who cannot just get out because of the danger, there are some that want to get out but nobody else wants to get involved. There are some that get out but never tell a soul in fear of being thrown back in, I cannot blame them because I learned that I used to be one of them.

If everyone stopped hiding or feeling bad about what they lived through then we would learn that deep inside there are many out there like my mum, you and me. We lived through it is the point and came out stronger because of it no matter who wants to make you feel bad. There are people who want to do you harm, then there are people who want to make sure that no harm comes to you and then there are people who do not care either way. Those people will ride the fence about everything that comes their way so that they are never found wrong about anything. They also have a great number of splinters up their bum from spinning on the fence so you might want to stay clear of these people most of all. They say one thing and then deny they ever said a word, until you come out correct, then, they were behind you all the way without pot shots.

Everyone received something from that nasty bag except for my family. Some mates received all the feelings of how did I go from there to here, one mate received all the this is what a kid feels when the pain comes from someone close to them. One mate had to keep me from leaving and still another received the blunt of all of my feelings because she would just not let it be. I was pissed off and I knew I was but I still could not figure out why until my mates son and I had a massive brain fart together, that was funny. He is one of the coolest mates to hang out with, and I like the fact that he thinks for himself. The funny thing is that we had that brain fart at the same time, about the same thing and both of us laughed after the embarrassment had past.

The sad thing is that he was the only one I felt comfortable around because he did not want anything from me. We would hang out, talk, play, laugh and figure out things just as mates are supposed to. He accepted me for who I was without implying change one in there. The adults that surrounded me all said, "I like you but could you not be so well, you know, you or maybe if you just stopped doing this one thing. Oh, just one more thing if you would not hold onto your beliefs so tightly that would be a big help in changing you too." When you do not change for them then they throw a childish tit fit and just as they did when they were little, "Well then I do not like you any more." Good because you are being so unbelievable ugly right now and you think that you can manipulate me with that kindergarten dung! Go find someone else who will buy into your just do this one thing for me and then learn it was everything about you that they did not like.

He never tried to get over on me, take control of my house or slick something out of me. When one of my mates past away he put his arm around me and let me cry on his shoulder and when I told him how I felt he said things to make me feel better not worse. Now tell me that kids no matter what their age make better mates then adults. When he needed me I was there for him too, but I was there in the way that he needed me to be. I have seen to many adults say that they will help but want to control the help that they give to you, and you will stay forever obligated to them. When mates help mates it is, "No worries. I know that if things were different you would have been there for me so D'nada." D'nada means no thanks are necessary. (We all should start saying D'nada more often instead of making others feel forever indentured over what turns out to be nothing.)

The more I kept thinking about everyone else's problems or questions the closer I was coming to the centre of my mind where this all started from. See when you spend your life taking notes sometimes you forget to go back and look at the old paper work. I had come across a memo that I wrote to myself a long time ago; Wanted to take up for myself but was not allowed, to make matters worse I was in a room full of people who would not stand up for me either. I remembered who I wanted to defend myself against that day; it was the egg donor itself. When that memory snapped into place, the rage came out in full.

I wanted to defend myself against her because we both knew that the loathing was mutual, no kid should ever have to feel that way. They should have protected me and they were the ones attacking me. Then it hit me why I overcompensate by defending others the way I do, to make up for all the times when no one would defend me. They would turn their backs and that made it all right to them. I have always jumped up to defend someone or help them out but cowered when it came to defending myself. The more I thought about why I became this way the more I would fill with rage again until I just started shaking.

Now when my mates saw what I was doing for therapy not all of them agreed with it but it was my problem and this was helping me. I had a punching bag hung out in the garage and I would picture all of them and just go to wailing on it bare knuckled. I do not know if you have ever just play hit one of these things before but there is a reason that boxers wrap their hands, because unless you are really pissed when you hit this thing directly you can dislocate your knuckles. I did it three times to myself when I was hitting it being all calm. My mate came over one time and saw me going after it, he could tell that I was just about tired so he went in the house and waited for me. When I came in he asked what pissed me off and for the first time I was so winded I could not remember what triggered me, I just knew that it was out of my system and therefore not in my home.

Now the couple of mates that did not like the idea of me punching on a punching bag to get it out of my system soon changed their mind when I went to using them instead. "See, when I get the overwhelming feeling out of my system I can come back inside and discuss it like a normal human being instead of an irate maniac. You are also missing the fact that a punching bag is meant to be hit, that is what they are made for." Their reply, "Well I know but it just seems barbaric if you ask me." I so wanted to tell them that I did not ask them but I would have missed the point. Why did they want me to keep all of this stored up or were they expecting me to be weak when it hit? I was the one being barbaric because I was hitting a bag but the people who did this to me were not because they used a child instead. Good-night what kind of people was I hanging out with?

I spent about six or seven months going out to the garage and wailing that bag for hours on end until I felt better. I would picture opening up my closet door reaching in, pulling them out, and just going to town on them. I would mentally tell them what I had been holding onto for years because it belonged to them and not to the ones I loved. I was big enough to defend myself against all of them now and none of them could stop me just as I could not stop them. When I came in all the trash was left outside and I noticed that my place was becoming a bit more peaceful. My mind was relaxing to the point that I could think once again only now it was about improving things not holding onto something. I learned that I can go through a brick wall when I am pissed off, but when I have a cool head I will take the time to look for the door. (Less wear and tear on your body and mind too!)

I was actually getting to repair the damage they had caused all those years ago. All I ever wanted to do was defend myself against them and in my mind, I finally got that chance, the monkey slid down my back and took the dip with him. The biggest part was gone. If you have ever stood up to a bully or even a mental ghost for that matter then you know the feeling I am talking about and you should teach others. If you have not then you definitely should try it sometime because it feels so unbelievable fantastic. Standing up for yourself also improves your posture because your head will be held up. You really do feel free and that whatever bondage they had on you at one time is no longer there, not even a trace. All this time I was running from a smoke screen while praying for a miracle I could not see. Logic had crossed over into reality when my train collided.

I left long ago but carried everything with me so that I would not ever forget and go down that road with anyone for any reason. The problem is that all I had learned was how to leave, not what to leave behind or how to stay out of someone else's village. I have become an excellent escape artist but I have yet to master the art of not reappearing in a different hut. Known truth, aside from outside appearances all people are either good, bad, evil or fence riders.

When you were growing up someone was either a good kid or a bad kid, now adults hide behind words such as, "Well, they have good intentions," or "I was just trying to be nice." Why do you have to try to be nice? To me the people that say things like that do so because it really is not in their nature to be anything other than nasty. "I was just trying to be funny." They all say this right after saying something they know was going to come out cruel. The thing that bothers me the most about this is why others tolerate being talked to like that. I have done my share of putting up with it because I was always told, "Well that is just how they are. What can you do about it?" Then when you say something you are the one put in your place instead of them. Someone has finally had enough and goes to do something about it and everyone has a fit. "You do not want to get them mad," no if you are going to say anything tell the truth. They have over time become too inflated for anyone close to them to put a stop to it. Why is it that they get to be the way they are but you have to change everything about yourself to please them?

Why is it that some childish babies get to stay that way while others have to make an allowance for them? To make it worse the childish ones are more likely to be in charge of others. I know that I have worked with my share of them. They act like they are still in school and scold their fellow co-workers as if they are naughty little children instead of human beings trying to make a living. They allow their little clique to stand around and gossip while they get paid and you are stuck doing the assignment and carrying the full load. They have to stay in a pack and if you will notice they always go after someone when they are alone because they are cowards by themselves. The way you take care of this is two ways; First you have to start standing up for yourself even on the little things because that is where they begin. Second you have to stick together with others just like yourself and start taking your own lead throughout your life.

I was always told that just because someone is bigger than me does not make them correct and I agree. I have disagreed with plenty of people in authority because they were abusing theirs to whatever degree they could get away with. I was told by my grandfather that criminals come in different disguises so do not be fooled by a uniform. If you cannot respect the person in it then their position is not worth respecting. Why, because no matter what their title or status is in life when you get right down to it everyone is a human being or they are suppose to be anyway. What changed, simply their mind set. Now if everyone would embrace the David in all of us then all the worlds Goliath's would cease to exist and then the meek would indeed inherit the earth.

Everything in life goes back to the beginning, be it in time, your mind, your childhood or a single thought. Everything, including your Karma.

When I got the name "Scientific Experiment," the other half of that story was this bloke was getting a Coke and heard me talking about my new name and that it makes sense about me being from another planet and all when he came flying up to the counter yelling, "I heard about that, your kind coming to live here among us disguised as humans and I do not think that it is right."

"Why, if we come in peace and love, what could it hurt? You would have love that is out of this world and it would be untouchable to humans!" I of course laughed.

"Well, they say that men are from Mars and women are from Venus," and no joking he looks me up and down and then goes, "and you do not look like you're from either one, so what planet do you come from?"

The cashier was stunned that he said that but without missing a beat I just told him, "Well, unlike you humans who are told not only where, when, time but to whom you are born to, we have to figure all those things out for ourselves, otherwise we can not go on. And well, near as I can tell from everything that has been going on since an earthling and I uncovered the word unass together, and what has been coming out of my backside since then, I do believe I come from a small planet called: My Anus."

He looked at me all serious and went, "Don't you mean Uranus?"

"That is what I said, My Anus. Only one person can come out of My Anus then what is left gets flushed into the universe. We are then taken to and placed inside the backside of Uranus where it shoots us out from there to several other planets. Millions to choose from, but you only have enough gas for one landing. We arrive on whatever planet through a powerful but not earth shattering… fart if you will. The saying, 'Do not hold your breath,' does not apply to us. If

41

you land wrong, which I found out that I did, your head can stay lodged inside your home planet forever. I just so happen to land on Earth where peace and love are dying and my mission from back home was to learn how to create more before I get recycled again. From my size you can tell that I have been recycled many times."

He threw the money on the counter and stormed off. I could not stop laughing, the cashier looked at me, "I can not believe you!"

"Oh, what, because I said you humans instead of including myself?"

"No, because you said all of that off the top of your head and then talked about a mission. See, I told my mum that you were from a lot further away then England and now I have proof because of what you just said."

Everyone in the store was laughing when they got out to their cars. See, that word unass is powerful and now we know why. It cleans you out. Kind of like that brain fart I had not too long ago.

# Chapter Two
# Learning How to Clean out Your Karma!

We have all been told in reality that what goes around comes around and do unto others as you would have them do unto you. They mix these two together and come up with something to believe in called Karma. Now this has always made me wonder for two reasons, first we are told to believe in it and if you look at the word believe, there is a lie right in the middle of it. (Be\Lie/ ve. Somewhat hard to believe if you ask me but there it is!)

The second reason is that logically this cannot be all there is to Karma. I like many others have never done half of what is done to me so there has to be something more here than meets the eye. I am held accountable for my actions but I have learned that not everyone is like that. How is their Karma clean when they crap over everyone and everything in there life and I get the dung when it hits the fan? Could I just be at the wrong place at the wrong time or does this once again have to do with your birth? I think it has everything to do with your birth and this is how I have come to draw that conclusion.

If your Karma is kept clean for you as a baby until you can manage it yourself then what comes around will usually be pretty good. If someone started using your Karma as their personal toilet then later on turned it into a public one what comes back is never going to smell sweet. The logic in all of this is that no matter what yours may be we all need to learn to flush everything even if it is just out of courtesy for ourselves.

Our lives are set up just like our bodies, we consume and digest but not all of us let the rest of nature take its course. Either we hold it in for some reason or we just keep sitting on the toilet letting it all come out and wonder why it is over flowing. I know that it may seem graphic to explain it that way but you need to think of your problems and life just like that. Karma is your soul and you need to start cleaning out your heart, body, soul and mind. Flushing out your system gives it time to repair what it needs to and not have to go through a lot of excrement just to get close.

Take your mind for example, you were told things and even though they hurt your feelings, you still hold onto them. The reason they still hurt is that the wrong body part is holding onto it. Give it to your heart, let it feel that they were using your heart as a toilet and get rid of it. The same applies to your heart, if something is bothering it more then likely its because the mind was suppose to think of what it needed from it and then flush the rest. Does this work for your body? Well when something is troubling your mind and heart does it not tend to make you sick starting with your stomach? All this no doubt will leave your spirit feeling bleu and that in turn leaves your soul in utter turmoil because it cannot get close enough to care for any of it.

You have to go through every part yourself and take only what you need and let the rest return back to the soil. Think about it this way, if your mind consumes knowledge and digests that into facts and you start storing the waste eventually you are going to have fertilizer for brains. (I have proof that this can happen and I will include it at the end.) The way this occurs is that you keep only the dung and after a while you have to start letting go of facts just to make room. I know this for sure because more than 99% of what I was told was just that….manure.

Cleaning out your mind leaves room for more thoughts to flow, and it makes room for more knowledge. What does thinking clearly, flushing, Karma and your birth have to do with each other? If someone started using your Karma as a village toilet and you were never taught to flush then no wonder you cannot think clearly. If your life is not flowing find the clog, I did and once I fixed the problems everything else took care of itself for the most part. I guess in a strange way my spirit had become constipated and me holding everything in was the cause. I also learned that a great deal of what was in there was not even mine, it belonged to the villagers. I learned that they stored their bad Karma for as long as they could in with mine and put it in the one place I would have never thought to look, up my own bum. See, I told you that something was up there and that I would find out just what it was. I knew that I walked around as if there had been something up there for a long time but I was too scared to look. I did not want to get my hands dirty I guess.

When everything started coming out of my ears I knew my system was in deep dung and I had to find the plug and pull it. Yes, I will be the first to admit that this was a strange place to keep a plug but maybe I put it there as a kid when I was trying to come up with that tail thing who knows. This has also made me wonder if two things cannot be crossed to match. Having a plug would cause you to have a strong bum due to the fact that you cannot hold onto it with your hands; this in turn causes people to start getting up on your bum because they see how strong it has become. Why, because they see how much crap you can and will go through to get to the other side and while you are cleaning off your boots they jump off and take your place for the reward. (They could even be in your work place, imagine that!)

See, when I was little I never would look at my own bum, not even in a mirror because I thought that one bum cheek was the size of the world because of how many people I could get up on it all at once. Now I know that they just did not want their feet or hands to get dirty or they were just lazy. I also have a feeling that if I could have grown that tree they probably would have stolen all my apples when I was sleeping anyway. I also wonder if they tell us about the seed thing because they know some of us will try and that is what causes the clog in the first place? (No, I have not lost my mind; I was just letting it wander off without adult supervision is all.)

My clog started when I was told that I was an evil little bastard and come to find out it was them all along. They piled things on top of it like I was daft and never would amount to anything just to keep me terrified from digging. I guess they did not think that I was smart enough to pull my head out of my own bum and take a look for myself! Known truth, I believed everything they said about me and now I am cautious about what I believe. Why do we listen to the people who are mean and cruel to us over someone who pays us a compliment or gives us credit? They are paying us a real compliment for a service we have already preformed; the people that hurt us make us pay out the bum for a slap in the face made to sound like a compliment. We are taught by the wrong ones who to keep close and now that my mum has taken the time to re teach me I cannot believe just how much I had all wrong.

See, I no longer mind the bad people waiting for me at the docks any more because even my mum and the family will tell you that I spend all my time out at mental sea anyway and only come in to see them or when I need to talk to my mum about what I just thought about. I can now by pass all the villagers when I come into port because I have a family that comes to pick me up and takes my bags for me while we catch up. I always thought that real families were just fairy tales mixed with lies but now I know that a real family sees you straight through from beginning to end and then starts all over again.

No matter what I go through my family is there for me in everyway. Everything that was wrong with me they helped to fix and not make the problem benefit them in someway. See when you go to cleaning out your Karma you need loved ones to surround you because what comes out is not going to be good and Lord knows that this is the wrong time for anyone to walk in.

I will explain it with the original weird thought that started all of this. I have always heard about keeping up with the Joneses and noticed that the people that did were tired and miserable because they had acquired all this stuff but could not enjoy it. The people who could not were miserable because they were being made to feel left out in a world they could not afford. My thought about all of this was instead of trying to keep up why not just stop and turn around to the person next to us and say, "I know that all of us walk around like we have something up our bum because we do. If you trust me enough to bend over I will pull whatever is just right there out and start the flow." Now you have to trust them because they could just cram theirs up there when you're not looking and then run off.

If everyone does it correctly then everything that has been held in for so long will start to come out. When this happens and it will happen, you can either stand in one spot and after awhile be knee deep in it once again. This makes you feel relived but does not get you anywhere further in life. The best thing to do when your Karma starts flowing is move; do not stand in the same spot because you do not want to re track it back into your life. When I say move I mean out of the rut you are in mentally or spiritually. If the saying holds true that someone's else's trash is someone else's treasure, maybe someone's else's bad Karma holds pieces of someone else's missing puzzle piece? I think that this is more realistic then being told that before you can judge someone you have to walk a mile in their shoes.

Logically you are not ever going to walk that same mile because you will not be taking the same steps that they did. I know that others would not want to walk a mile in my shoes because their feet would never fit and neither would them judging me. First off we are not suppose to be judging others for whatever reason but people are still willing to pay a high price to throw that first stone. You can say that you would have done things differently but the fact is you were not under those same circumstances and everyone responds to life differently because of what they have been through and the way they were brought up.

You can have a better understanding of that mile as they walk you along through it but someone else's life is not for us to judge for any reason. All we can do about life is live it, learn from it and help others as we go along. The more we hold onto bad things the more they become a part of our hidden being and that alone will keep the rest of you from shining inside. Karma is all about the flow of things and the thoughts that hold them in. The deeper you dig inside yourself and expose your true nature the better understanding you will have about how you came to be who you were and now are. You have to do this if you really want to know if that is who you want to be.

Remember when I told you that you could store a tremendous amount of things up your own bum and not know it? If I would have known how much storage was up there all along I could have saved myself a lot of lost luggage at the air port. I would have never have to rent a U-Haul truck just put it all up there, drive to the new place and unload. I know you might feel like laughing but you just wait until you try it for yourself. All the things that make you feel bad have to be stored somewhere do they not and when that gets full what do you think happens to the over flow?

Now if you think that cutting yourself off from everyone will solve your dilemma I have proven that it actually makes things worse. The reason being is you become so isolated inside that you become desperate for just a little conversation and this will make you settle for anyone. If you learn to balance yourself first just like you did when you were a baby you will become more selective in what you consider stable. If you watch a baby being left alone to walk they first learn to pull themselves up, then they balance but before they take their first step, they find something stable to hold onto.

Karma is life lessons from baby steps; look how many times a baby's nappy is changed throughout the day learning how to pull themselves up on their own. When they are not changed, do they not become extremely cranky and you wonder why adults are walking around as they do? Everyone forgets to go back to the beginning because they just want the reward of walking and being independent. Everything in life has to be learned the same way you have always learned from beginning to end and then you do it all over again. What happens when you leave a step out? You do more then stumble; you learn to never get back up again because you get scared of being hurt. The odd thing is that a baby gets hurt more than a grown-up or adult ever will yet they never stop trying, they are persistent in every form of the word. Why, I think it is because they forget about the pain and just remember what they were after. Oh, they get shook up but that never seems to stop them especially if they have been reassured.

The funny thing is babies are never told to act their age, grow up and be an adult and if you ever watch a baby, they will do some of the funniest things to get you to laughing at them. Now why can a baby make you feel good but then when they stop drooling they have to loose their innocence too? They do not care who makes them laugh or holds them dear they just want to be a part of life. We teach kids to pull away as they grow up from one another and even have them taking pledges to keep them in separate lines. I think babies are the most intelligent creatures when they're born and we as a whole make them ignorant as they go.

Think about it, a baby is into everything and does not shy away from new people or things. Now if they do not like someone you need to listen because they were not brainwashed to believe anyone is good or bad, they just know what they feel from Dad in Heaven. We go from that to being scared of everyone except for the ones we should be scared of and never listen to our own built in warning system. We teach them to cower and to fear instead of overcoming it and instill ours inside of them as well. Babies have a good time with each other and you never hear them gossip, cut each other down or become pissed off at the smallest of things. When they gripe it is out of a real need and we put a stop to this why? Now we have a great deal of whiners and you do it for me babies to contend with in the real world. How do you change all this, by cleaning out your own Karma so that you can start feeling life through the same instincts you were given as a baby.

I noticed that when I started this whole process of unassing what was up my own bum, I began to feel better about myself in every way. I was the type of person who has believed that I was Rosemary's baby and now I was beginning to change my mind about myself from the bottom up. To me this had become a game of "What else is up there?" The more I dug the more I noticed I was actually moving forward in reality but logically I knew that I was at a stand still because of where my head was still located. Despite contrary belief this is a rather awkward position to find yourself in when you go out in public. The funny thing is I did go out in public this way and made more people laugh then ever before and it felt amazingly great.

I was going to get to the root of my Karma when I discovered there is not one, only a centre and at that centre was my true being. I was just about to yell,

"See, I told you so," when I felt like I was looking into the wrong mirror. Everything that I have been pulling out could not have led me to this. Let me tell you that looking at your true nature from this point of view is not easy and I was not about to buy this manure at any price. I had come too far to go back now but this mirror has to be up the wrong bum. I knew who would tell me the truth, my mum. I am just thankful that from where I was calling from that she could hear me and that long distance charges do not apply when you're up there.

The thing about real mums is that they are going to tell you the truth even if it hurts. My mum told me why she adopted me because she saw a good kid inside of me. She said lots of other things to me that night too but they are personal and they were for my heart only but the fact is she said that I was a good kid. If you have ever been made to feel small in any way you know how good it can feel when that weight is taken off your shoulders. Imagine how fantastic it feels to have the last shackle removed for good. See my mum is all about good, Higher Authority and everything about being light in a dark world so I knew that she would not lie to me, even as much as I wanted her to just then. She is also not the type to tell you what you want to hear no matter how it makes you feel. To me that is one of her most admirable qualities.

Why would I want her to lie, because that was the last of it? Now everything they had ever told or said about me was proven a lie. I was never anything they said or wanted me to be. The more we talked the more I found I could not stop crying and I just wanted my mum to make me feel better for the first time ever. I knew that I was given a second chance at a new life and it started with her. My mum made me her kid a long time ago but that night I was to become what I had always dreamed of, a kid who is truly loved and protected by their mum.

There is a bond that is formed at birth be it good or bad and you can either keep the one you have or trade it for something far greater. I wanted someone who wanted me instead of settling for what I was given. There is a reason that we are given two parents because we get something past down from each of them. Being born a bastard is one thing being born all alone is another. I do not know what is worse; to be born alone or to be born into family and still feel that way. The way I was born I had to look for each of them and even though the journey was hell I sure do like the fact that you can come home anytime you want as long as you knock on the right door.

See, I would always forget that I was mad at God because like I said kids forget what they are suppose to and remember only what they see. I remembered being taught that you are not supposed to call your elders by their first name and definitely not your parents, built in respect. I would always ask my teachers that if God was his first name then why were we being taught to be disrespectful by not calling him Dad to begin with. They never would answer me but I figured it out over time with His help.

I was told the same thing as everyone else the difference is I stopped believing adults about everything a long time ago, I just could not unass what they did to me alone. I was told to fear God and believe in Karma and all will be well in life. I have come to the conclusion that this is far from true, just look at the lives people lead who believe this way. I do not believe in fearing someone I am told to trust and I do not trust in someone that I am told to fear. To me that sounds more like an oxymoron taught as a village motto rather then something you say about a family member you are suppose to love.

When I learned that Dad in Heaven is just that, our Dad, I was not so pissed off at the world any more because I had at least one good parent. I also learned that if you believe in Dad and fear Karma then life does not appear so backwards and unknown any more. The more I was cleaning out my Karma the more I realized I was wrong about everything including myself. I crawled up my own bum deep enough to discover that I was getting to the bottom of things through the bottom then I ever was going to through the top. When I finally got to the end I discovered something even greater up there, it was my very own halo and my head popped out the top with it on.

Oh I will not lie to you; it was not gold or even straight for that matter. No, it was bent like mad, tarnished and sits crooked on my head but the fact remains, it is mine and had been all this time. See I told you that there is a greatness that is in all of us but it takes someone else to bring it out. My mum knew that I had a halo and knew that I had it in me to find it with her guidance and since I am as hard headed as I am I knew that I would find it too just for different reasons. I just wanted to find it to prove that I was right all along and instead I found proof that I had been wrong all along. Logic and reality are strange things if you ever start mixing the two.

Logically, when the reality sank in that I was and had always been a good person I realized that I had to stop not caring and start being who I was meant to be all this time…me. I stopped being who I was because someone wanted me to settle for less and I could have been like everyone else and believed them but I choose not to. I then find someone who not only wants to agree with me but also wants me to agree with myself and the first thing I do is go right back to the other side I loath. I will say it again, I am strange but I am at least up front about it.

All of my mates tried to get through to me and I refused to allow it to sink in although I never knew why at first. They all said the same thing in different ways but they were not the ones at the core. I noticed something strange when I was cleaning out my Karma; everyone needed something out of it. I was just going to throw it all away and start over because there was nothing useful in it to me, I was completely finished with it.

When I was going through everything I noticed that my mate would bring up his son, all I could think was, "Oh I forgot I was suppose to be helping you with that." I am good about dropping everything and going to help someone else, (that is not being conceited that is just being truthful and I know there are loads more out there like myself, the problem with this is we tend to stop our lives for others.) The more we talked the more I gave him hoping that he would figure it out for himself. I was also beginning to learn why I snapped at certain people now and not at others. He honestly wanted to know because he wanted answers for his son. Some of the other people in my life only wanted parts of my past to see what they could use against me. What they did not know is once you put meat on the skeletons they no longer bother you, I would just not tell them because down the line they would teach me how they were trying to use it.

When my mind would release memories of what I had been through, I did what I could to hold them at bay because I remembered what my mind went through the first time and now it was my hearts turn to catch up with the rest of us. Everyone that knows me will tell you that I am one of two things, funny or pissed off and sometimes I can be both but now I was learning to have feelings beyond these. I was not pissed about what they had done, I was hurt and angry and I was growing tired of people finding out and telling me I was not entitled to feel any way about the matter. I had been cruelly lied to from the start and now I was being told it was to late too feel bad about the way they treated me. I wanted to smack them but I did promise my mum I would use my head first, to bad that leaves out head butting! Would that not be cool if you could mentally concentrate on knocking someone's thoughts hard enough for them to get the point? When you saw someone walking around and suddenly start rubbing their head you know that they were being put back in their place.

If people as a whole do not understand something then you should stop trying to figure things out, after all the only one it is important to is you correct? If life has taught us anything it is that majority rules and no one person is greater than another. Logically this is what we are told to believe, but in reality people will always change the rules to apply to everyone but themselves. If one person is not greater than another why is there Hall of Fames devoted to an individual's greatness past others? Maybe we should start a Mental Hall of Fame for all those that learn to overcome their own personal pain and grief. To me learning how to overcome your own private pain is more important than a sports score. We could have a Heart Hall of Fame for the ones who overcome a tragic turn of events in their life.

I was more than tired of being told what to feel, think, say and do just because no one else wanted to deal with me as I was coming to be. They all wanted me to cry because they knew how to deal with that but me being beyond pissed off was more than they had bargained for. In addition to them crying meant showing you are weak and that is how they needed me to be in order to completely take over. Why do they get what they want and you are the one left making all the sacrifices? I learned throughout all of this that what was being sacrificed was myself and everything that Dad gave me to be special. I was born funny and love it when I get someone to laugh even if I had to act like I was running into a door. I remembered when I was little making up songs as I went along and singing them like they were top sellers. Now when I look at a mirror all I see is this mean person looking back at me as if to say, "Do something or I will keep looking at you this way for the rest of your life!" Lord knows I did not want that and now I had to keep digging for myself and everything that I wanted to stand for.

I wanted my mum to have the kid I was born to be, not the one they had turned me into and worse yet the one I kept myself the way they wanted me to be. I loved being angry with the villagers, it was the first time that my anger was directed at the correct people. The more I loved being angry the better I had become at it and the more in control I felt over that feeling. I never noticed before how much I had built up inside of me until it all started coming out until there was nothing left. I did this with the next feeling that I had for them; resentment until all of that had disappeared as well.

The thing that was hurting me the most was putting those feelings to memories because it was bringing it all back and I noticed that I was beginning to resort back to the way I felt when I was little, helpless and defenseless. I had come too far in my life to let them win after all this time. Then my mate said something that stopped everything in its tracks for me and gave me a better understanding of how to deal with this. "When the flashbacks start coming pull yourself out and look at it from a third person point of view. You have already been through it once and every time someone asks you to relive the horror you do. You put yourself in that same frame of mind and that is what is doing it to you. Look at it from the sideline about everything this person lived through and how tough they are now. Remember you are stubborn and hard headed for a reason, God are you extremely that way but you are not unreasonable. The worst thing to be in the world is hard headed stubborn and unreasonable. You can look from the sidelines without feeling the impact."

You do not know how good that felt when he said that I was not unreasonable even though everyone was making me feel like I was. "See if you were like everyone else then you would have never gotten this far in life because you would have let everyone push you around and take advantage of you worse then what they already have. You are also smart enough to think for yourself and that alone will piss some people off. You stand up for what you believe in even if you are wrong because you value your thoughts not opinions and you will go 80 miles out of the way to find the answer. That quality alone means that you will not settle for what someone wants to tell you. There is a lot about you that is remarkable but you will never see it because you are too busy getting caught up in other people's feeling about themselves and you cannot figure out their life for them."

Now wait how remarkable can I be when all I have been through is hell? I could not get my mum to understand this either, I tried to cover up the fact that I was damaged goods but now I am being told this makes me a better person. What kind of realistic logic is this? Let me guess they lied yet again, now I want everything they implanted inside of me out because this little by little stuff was killing me. According to my mum, I am not daft, evil or a mistake and that is what my whole life has been about paying for and covering up. You talk about someone feeling completely naked, confused and as helpless as an infant. This is the way villagers like you to feel because they get a fresh start on you again. You are exposed in so many ways but the last thing on my mind was covering up. I just froze because I did not know who I was any more.

I went through this when I was little four or five times when I discovered the truth behind their lies, all the abuse I went through was not enough to destroy me, they had to get me to do it to myself mentally. Everyone has screwed with my head now including myself. What do you do when you find out you are not who you are? You actually feel like you have wasted your life, your mind and your talents however hidden they may be. I would wake up, sit up and think about not being me any more and then go back to sleep, sometimes I would not even bother to sit up. I was drained from thinking, trying to solve others people's dilemmas and learning I am not me any more. Cleaning out my Karma was fun at first but now it was cleaning itself out and all I could do was walk around and wait.

I would hide my depression through either sarcastic humour or helping others. Oddly enough helping someone else made me feel better, then I was told that in itself is being selfish, that you should not feel good about helping someone in need. Why the hell not if that is all you are getting out of it and you did not even ask to feel it? You can only feel good if you ask for something in return even if it is "only" for recognition, now that sounds unreasonable. I learned that every time I liked something and the villagers found out they would find a way to destroy it. If it was a thing they would take it away or if it was a person, they would lie so hard about me that they were believed over me. Even though I never did anything to the person listening to the lie they picked their side over mine.

The more the flashbacks would come the more I learned how to pull myself out and look at it from a different point of view. I learned to look through a different set of eyes at the same thing and I discovered that they do not see the same at all. I had always looked through the eyes that were right in front of me and used my minds eyes if I needed to see past what was there. I also learned to see through the eyes of the one looking back at me; sometimes they were my own in the mirror and oddly enough sometimes they were not. I was actually seeing my life through the eyes of others and it was beyond strange. How could so many people be looking at the same person so differently? How could one person be so many different things to so many "different" people?

The more my mate asked me questions to help him understand his son not letting go of his egg donor the more I looked at my life through the sidelines. What makes these two different things the same? Comparing two different things to come to a conclusion is hard enough, making them completely match gets confusing. To make matters worse everyone had found a way inside of my head and it felt like this time they were trying to close those doors they had so desperately forced open. Why after I had cleaned so much out already? This I found odd above what had already happened and as close as I was to dropping everything to figure that out I did not. You would think that the people you hold close to you feel the same and think the same about you that you do them. The sad truth is they do not and you have to start looking at the people in your life and see how they are looking at you. I needed to talk with my mum but because my life, thoughts and everything else was spinning out of control I did not want to go to her like that. I prefer it when I sound like I am in control of myself when we talk because as I have said before I cannot hide my eyes from her. All my life everyone has always thought that I was crazy but now I feel like I am and that scared me. This was a bad time to go around asking people to help you with your thoughts because I found out that some would help themselves to whatever they needed and used it however they pleased.

I thought that I was having a mental breakdown but what was actually happening was I was mentally breaking everything down to make full repairs. I never would have realized that this has always been in the back of my mind to make repairs had I not have been locked in and learned how to find the light switch. You would be surprised at what all is in there and how it is set up. Yours maybe different but when I was little, I was told that you have a brain, mind, thoughts, an imagination and a conscience be it guilty or otherwise and gave them all separate rooms. I used my imagination to fix the place up and throughout life learned to keep them separated. I always thought that they were different except for the twins named conscience.

Now every time I talked with someone to help me come to a conclusion they would give me things that I needed somewhere else. When you are at your worst not everyone is at their best so please keep that in mind when you open up to someone. I also learned that some people would use the pain you are feeling to keep you pinned in. I finally could not go any further in my mind so my mates took me to see the Counsel of Elders. When your mind has reached conclusions that it does not understand, and the Epiphanies are nowhere to be found, then you can only conclude that you are nuts indeed! Nothing in life made sense any more and now being nuts bothered me because I was calling myself that this time. When they would council me it felt like they were taking all of my mental files and restoring them to their proper order. I loved the fact that they understood what I was feeling, thinking and losing and still managed to make me feel at home and not like you are being judged and then shot. I think that is why we hold everything in, not that they are dark secrets just problems you cannot solve out in the open because of people judging you.

I had a mate that I was close to at the time and we would have deep talks with each other and because I felt safe around her, I would let the things she said sink in and hit without really giving them a second thought. See when I do not like someone I scan every word looking for red flags of screw me later words. She was one of the few people in my life I let get more than arms length close to me. I realized the reason now is because she let me see the real her, look at me I have different feelings because I am human even though people do not treat me like it. When she got depressed and would talk with me, we would share and nothing was one sided. I would tell her how I saw things, how I felt about things and none of it was what she wanted to hear but she understood that it came from my heart. The great thing is that she had the same respect for me and after it was all said and done we were still o.k. Instead of using what we heard to judge each other we used it to better understand each other.

We have always been the strong ones in our own circle and it was strange to see that the mate you felt like matched your strengths needed help too. The sad thing though is that even though we have seen each other through some of the roughest times I did not want even her to see me this pathetic. (I had to draw the line somewhere and this was about the worst place you could draw one because you never know just which side you put yourself on, by the time I looked down it was pretty much too late.) I closed myself off and shut down because it became overwhelming and not in a good way. I get excited when I learned new things and figure stuff out because I earned it. When you learn something new, you should feel excited because it was not something that was just handed to you or something that you just read and memorized. What I was going through now was not something I wanted to learn but in order to have proper balance you need to learn both good and bad so that you will have something to compare it against. I knew all about bad and now it was past time to learn about good, how to find it and the people you can trust to fit inside there.

I learned that everything goes back to what you saw, learned and were taught or not taught as a kid. You look at the adults in your life as role models and someone you admire. If there is nothing to admire then all you can pull in is bad. To a baby, people do not come in a sex, they are just someone they like to get loved on or they are not. They look at what the people are doing in their lives as o.k. because they were taught to. If one parent is being dominated over by the other they will choose which one they are until told differently. If there is a problem in the home and it is not fixed then it will continue to spill out until someone decides they have had enough. No matter how hard it may be at first you have to remember everything was at some point in your life until you got the hang of it correct?

Kids are supposed to have two different parents for a reason, one gives them comfort and nurturing and the other gives them lessons about overcoming the hardships in life and protection while they are learning it. If these simple needs are not met then they will continue to search for them through others. A baby's instinct is to complete what they started no matter how many times they fall or how long it takes them to get there. They need to feel comforted and protected so they can be taught what to look for. Doing this makes them feel worthy of love and being wanted. The desire does not go away just because you do not have one or the other it just keeps building up until the needs get met. (The desire to be loved and wanted also does not go away just because you tell someone to get over it.) This can cause you to enter the real world unbalanced and without a clue as what to hold onto. You learn life at home, and if you are not given that chance, you will always stumble a great deal more in life than others. You may also learn to take fewer steps out until you just stop trying to get up at all or better than nothing you may keep stumbling until you reach the finish line.

I learned the reason I stayed away from my mum was because I was taught to fear and trust the one I came through, I trusted my mum but I did not want to be in fear of her. I had to learn to switch one out for the other and it was hard because I was unbalanced for so long. I was not taught this step in life because I never learned to crawl in real life. I was told that I slid everywhere I wanted to go and I have always spent my life doing just that. Taking a sideways approach to everything in my life and never noticed how much longer it takes me to get where I am going. I feel like I am just now being taught to crawl when everyone else already knows how to walk. (Come to think of it, that might explain why I always bump my head when I go to stand up, my instincts are to just look up and then slide wherever I need to go.) I can stand up somewhat now but somehow still manage to find myself wanting to hit the floor. I learned that even though I do not get knocked down so much I usually get stepped on and sometimes come close to being squashed.

I wanted my mum and that terrified me because this was different and I never wanted to go down this road. I had a weird dream about my mum but it felt good and that made me think about the meaning behind it even more. Everything seemed to be a puzzle piece again but they were fitting together to form a picture I never wanted to look at nor acknowledge. The way I saw it was I had already given up so much of who I was not that this was cutting to the bone. I could not stop thinking about my mum but not enough to call her so she would not worry. One mate would not get off my bum about not checking in and I could not get her to understand either that if I told my mum what all was going on it would make her worry not the other way around. I was still in that mind set that you only check in when things are good so that not only will I not let her down but she will not have to feel disappointed in me. What was so bloody hard to understand about that, and they say I am hard headed and stubborn. I lost count of how many times I have told them that?

Then something happened that would cause all my conclusions to finally come to an Epiphany that would rock my world. I started out on a job site that turned into a family classroom before my eyes and I was learning from a third person point of view. I would hear how she would talk with her children and not down to them. She would make them realize what they did wrong without making them feel bad for having learned the hard way. She held each one close and when they got hurt she picked them up and loved on them, she made everything all better just like that. She even kept the world at bay for them while they fell apart in her arms and she sent them back into the world forgetting all about it. Now that is some kind of super power. I would see and hear all of this through my eyes but in my minds eye I could not stop looking at her legs and thinking about my mum. You had better believe that this confused me something fierce too. The puzzle pieces I find in life are weird but this felt like a piece someone else had been working on and now we traded places just like you do on a real puzzle.

This was becoming increasingly strange even for my mind considering how far I can get it to go out. What was the connection to my Mum and her legs? I kept telling myself that I had lost my mind completely and something deep inside of me kept telling me to keep going and that I was on the right track through strange as it was. The odd thing is I have never been into legs but hers kept making me think on and off the job site. I kept asking myself what legs have to do with mums and this was keeping me up for several nights in a row. Every day we went over to her home to finish up the work and I kept my minds eye on her legs and I am pretty sure I got caught too because I was concentrating on them more than I was my job! Good thing I can think and work at the same time. The more I listened to the way she was talking with her children the closer I was getting to my answers. Oddly enough it finally hit when she walked up the stairs holding her baby. Legs have everything to do with being a real mum and here is how my brain's epiphany reached that conclusion.

A child gets all of its strength and tenderness from the mum and then learns to branch off from there. A mum teaches her child everything in order for them to move on. This includes who to trust, how to trust but most importantly how to be trustworthy. I learned how to look at a real mum through a great set of legs and I could not believe it. They were not weak and far from unstable; they could balance a baby on one and handle the rest of life while standing on the other. They took care of everything and would run to the cry of a loved one in need. You could tell that she would stand her ground too and it did not matter to whom it was against either. I heard that she was talking to her son about not interrupting people when they are talking when an adult tried to interrupt her and she politely put her finger up (no not the middle one) to them and never took

THE PHILOSOPHY OF A THOUGHT


away from her son until she was through making her point. I started laughing my bum off when he told me that because I really did think that was comical and I told him why. "Well did you hear her tell her son that it was rude and right in the middle of it you go and get into trouble for the same thing that she was getting onto him about. Did you hear her say that it was o.k. to interrupt as long as you are an adult?" "No."

"See, if you would have listened to your own mum when she told you that then their mum would not have gotten onto you," and I rolled into laughter. I so needed that laugh because it was heartfelt and it had been a while since someone brought a laugh to me.

The funny thing is when we would clock out from work all we could do was talk about how great it was to get to be around her and her family. Everyone on the crew was missing something in their life and found something in her to take home with them. I kept laughing at the fact that I still could not get her legs out of my head and wobbled on mine when I was around her. All that kept running through my mind was, "I know, I know I am still working on that side of the puzzle board but it does not seem to fit just yet."

I was in charge of that job site but felt like a kid when our paths would cross. This only happens when I respect someone else's authority and by now that was rare. I felt like I was looking at my mum through someone else's window and I was learning first hand how my family works through watching her interact with her own family.

She was teaching me a tremendous amount in such a short period of time without either one of us realizing it. I learned that there are some people in my life that I respect so much that I do not want to let them down or for them to get onto me for any reason. With her I was covering up for a lazy crew that I had hired and was having to apologize to her for covering up for them and lying to her about it. She never lost her temper with me and even thanked me for being honest. When I could not complete the job because I did not have my help any more she said that sometimes you just have to learn when to let things go. Good-night, I have never started something that I could not finish, and this was something that could have and should have been finished. The reason I was feeling so bad with her is she had given us so much and we took it all but nothing was left of equal value in its place. Anytime someone teaches me something that grand I always want to give something back as an extra Thank-you.

Lady Legs is someone that I enjoyed learning from because she made every day interesting and made her home into a beautiful classroom in a matter of speaking. To me life is a never-ending experience and I found another brilliantly gifted teacher who was showing me hands on how a real mum loves her kids, through soft words of love and understanding and firm ones when you need correcting only. Boundaries are not meant to keep you boxed in; they are to give you guidelines so you can learn to keep yourself from getting hurt as you go. I was learning how our mum loves us through her and I found myself growing less scared to go home by the minute. The other shoe had finally dropped and I realized that our mum has the same set of incredible legs only I never noticed them before. She stands her ground and is strong enough to love all of us at the same time. A mum has two strong legs not just one as I had previously thought. A real mum has proper balance in her legs because one is to stand her mental ground on and the other is to stand her ground when it comes to the heart.

When one of her kids got hurt (he head-butted the pavement) she never made it about her, she just loved on him and because she was not panicking he did not either. His world hit bottom for a moment and she put everything right as rain for him and never told him to stop feeling like he did or to stop crying because he did not get hurt that bad. She never dismissed any of her children or the people that worked for and around her for that matter. He did not have to reach out to her; she came running to him and picked him up. She never said, "Well come here," like it was a bother to her life that one of her kids needed her. I realized just then that I had been taught differently by the villagers. The first couple of times I cried out I would get smacked so I learned the hard way to not cry out in any kind of pain or reach out for any other reason. This causes you to have to pick yourself up without being consoled before you go back out into the world. Doing this enough times causes you to grow potatoes on your shoulders not just crisps any more.

I never realized before this job site how much I had missed out on and how much I have been truly lied to. The best and worst part is I realized that I had been hurt so severely that I was actually making my mum the lady who did more than just take in a village disposable baby was being made to pay for a crime that she never committed against me. The weird part is I felt like I had slid up to Lady Legs and she picked me up and taught me how to take my first baby steps towards my mum. I learned what was expected of me as a kid and what I could expect from a proper mum in response. She opened up a whole new world to me and for the first time in my life I liked my head up and my eyes opened. She disciplines just like our mum out of love not controlled fear, you can tell because neither set of kids are scared to be who they are except for me but I am at least learning not to be any more. You can also tell that she knows how all her kids brains and minds work and feeds into their smarts and intelligence and is not jealous of her own creation just like our mum. She works with them and loves them equally and does not pin one up against the other not even for sport or boredom. Her kids learn in different ways and she teaches them according to how their thought process works and not how she wants to force it to work.

What was really cool is when I would talk with her children for a little while, they think the world of their mum and you can tell that it is not because she buys them. They love and think the world of their mum because she has always included them into her life. When I told her little girl that she looks just like her mummy she grinned the same way I do when someone tells me that and so politely said, "Thank-you." She has a son that is incredibly quiet but you can so tell that he has a brilliant mind, they all do even the one that head butted the pavement. See they are all of this already and they are still extremely young so could you imagine how far they are going to go because of her and their dad. If all of us could have started out in life this way Lord knows how far we would be today. We could even have world peace.

Her children are polite, respectful, funny and smart just like the ones they came from. Their mum treated everyone just like she did her kids as equals only she is the one with the authority. I also saw that when she reached out to them they did not pull away because they were not taught to fear their mum. I finally saw the life my mum wanted to give to me all this time and there was nothing to be scared of even if I did something to get into trouble. I finally saw the comparison of a good hearted family vs. bad ones only appearing that way.

I was going to sound great when I rang my mum because of what I just learned and she was going to be so proud of me but life had other plans because that is not what happened by far. Everything I had planned to say to my mum went up in smoke and I was left without a script. The moment I heard my mum's voice I burst into tears without realizing it. She had been there all this time but I never would allow her to pick me up and hold me close to her. I would never let her be a mum to me because I thought that she was not strong enough to hold me because to me she only had one leg at the time. I know now that she has a powerful set of strong legs and always has when it comes to her family. Mums are the strongest link in the chain or should be for that matter and if they are not the kids will not be either.

When I finally saw that my mum was not that evil thing that I came out of I cried out and just like that she was right there and this time I closed my eyes and let her pick me up. I told her everything, all about the bad people and what they did to me and she listened to everything and when I was finished pouring my heart out we talked about the whole thing. I really did feel like I was a baby coming out of my mum's heart just then and learning about life through her love the right way this time. Everything that I was missing in my life she gave to me and I did not want to look anywhere else for the answers. I had everything that I needed right here and it was all for me, I no longer needed to look through the window of my mum's heart because now I was truly in it and I felt her not wanting to ever let me go.

I think that is one of my mum's gifts; having the heaven-sent patience to get through to a hard headed, extremely stubborn person and feeling in your heart that they will come around in time.

She held the world at bay while I opened up to her and kept me safe the whole time inside her heart. She was building my foundation because I was never suppose to but she was proud of the fact that I had made it as strong as I did with what little I had. She could have made me feel worthless and treated me like I was a waste of life but instead she closed the door to that road and took me just the opposite direction. For your mum to say that she is proud of you when you feel your worst in life makes all the difference in the world to the heart of your child.

A mum is the giver of life and logically this should occur at birth but sadly, realistically not all babies are given this gift. Some think they deserve to be called the "M" word because they gave the baby life but then shortly after took it all back teasing them with it. Some never give it at all and leave the baby to learn how to fend for themselves all the while telling the world how great they are at having babies. To me and this is just my thought on the subject matter but being a baby maker is just a sugar coating for an unscrupulous whore who has no intention of ever feeling anything good for what they brought into this world. They care more about what goes in-between their legs then what comes out of it.

When you start out unwanted you miss the first step in life and you have to find your place in order to start out. Feeling unloved and unwanted is not the best way to start out in life but at least it is a start and you can do something with it. See, I think that you get your legs from your mum and to those of us born without legs; you can always use your arms to pull yourself where you need to go until you find yourself a great set. I did and found a wonderful mummy on top of them who did not care where I had come from just that I made it home to her and the rest of the family safely.

The great thing about all of this is that our mum gave me a new set of legs to stand tall on as we were talking. I have always had one big mental foot that I would slam down as needed to keep people from running all over me; the problem with this is it would cause the tender hearted people to go away as well. The other problem is when people would get me through the heart I would fall to pieces because I did not have that leg to stand on and the world could tell. This explains why I fell on my face so hard and so often all of the time. I was the one unbalanced and told the family they could lean on me anytime they needed, no wonder they did not.

The thing about having one heavy foot is once you put it down it is so freaking hard to pick it back up because inside you feel like you are going against yourself. I learned that just because you are heading in one direction does not mean that you cannot change your mind and go about something in a different way.

I had changed my mind about everything pretty much but I had to go to the core to do so. I noticed that scores of people want to change or have changed but do not take the time to find out what they need and want to change about their life. Some think that if you change your surroundings that everything in life will follow and it could. Shortly after their move they fall back into the same habits that lead them right back to that home away from home rut in their life and they cannot understand why or how. Everyone is looking for that quick fix when it took time for your life to get this screwed up in the first place. My life and with it my Karma was screwed up when I was told things that were complex in scale but that did not make them true and instead of just not believing what I was told, I looked as deep as I could to find out the truth behind the lie instead of just trying to figure out how to just reverse it.

The more I went to our mum the more I realized that they are the key to the beginning of your life and you do not have to come through them for this to occur. Your basic needs have to be met other wise you will never be able to feel anything past wanting. To me that is why some people marry a parent more then they do a spouse. They are looking to that person to fill a hunger that has never been met. They look towards their spouse for acceptance instead of balance because they have never been told that they were wanted or loved.

The child should be the core, embraced by the mum and enclosed by the dad but this is rarely the case. More then likely the child is made to feel like a burden instead of being included in both parents' lives because the parents do not include each other in their own lives. Everyone is being taught to live separately and nobody is shown how to be close any more. Everyone is so worried and concerned about what strangers think of them that they never realize what their own families think about them because nobody installed an upgrade in the communications division. When the parents lack verbal skills they pass it on. You can also pass on the reaching out to everyone except to your own family…gene.

Kids are intelligent, especially if you help them get that way and show them how to apply that knowledge. When our mum passes wisdom on she also tells us how she acquired it and what to do with it. She then allows us the freedom to try it out without nit picking that we are not doing it the way she wants; she knows that we have to get a feel for it first. My mum has never told me that I was smart enough to figure it out on my own when I come to her for help because she knows that the reason I am asking for thoughts or another way to look at things is I need them. She knows that smart people are not born that way, they become that way with the help of those around them. Kids like figuring things out for themselves because they get excited and it feels good when they reach the end but still need help and reassurance to meet their goals. They come to you for just that to help them not to give them the answers. The more you stay excited about whatever it is that you are doing the further you will go with it.

If I did not go as far as I did to figure out what was up my own bum I would have never discovered my very own halo and with it learning to feel good about myself and stop letting others make me feel miserable. I would have never learned that Karma has more to do with your thoughts then your actions although one leads rather nicely into the other. I also figured out that when you have a strong flow, be it good or bad other people can see it and use you accordingly because they know how to use their eyes.

People have always had three sets of eyes (four if you include the ones in the back of you head) but very few use theirs and the ones that do can have either good or bad intentions while reading someone else's. What I mean about the eyes are the ones you see life through, second sight and your minds eye. Philosophies come from all three sets looking as one: present, next step and the outcome. How do you think bad people see an easy mark when you are out in public, you may be in your own little world but you're still out in the world! They see the shape your Karma is in as well as your state of mind and figure out how to get you accordingly. Some people are easier to read then others but the hardest one is learning to read yourself.

I never knew that I was an easy mark because I never learned to read bad people; I only learned how to read people in need. Some people use auras to read others, some use the depth in eyes, everyone has their own way of looking at people but I can usually hear the kids living in an adult world because I am one of them. You can tell the people who have gone down the same path as you without uttering a single word. One of my ex-mates saw me with a lady one time that was crying and after everything was over asked me who she was. I told them that I just saw her crying and I went over to her but never asked for her name. Telling me her name was not going to make her feel any better but what freaked me out was their reply, "Well, I would have never went up to a stranger so that they could cry and burden me with their problems. Everyone has problems, get over it and get a life." The bad thing is they never felt remorse when they said it. I went to her first and making someone feel better about themselves should not be looked upon as a burden.

Why were they not willing to reach out to someone in need but never asked for help? Later on when we got back to the group they made it into a big joke and I looked at everyone around me differently just then. These people liked people in need because they made easy prey, only one other person in the group felt like I did and we left together. I learned that moment that first impressions are not everything and what is cool is I learned my mum feels the same way and can do it from three points of view. "IF they are rude to you when you first met them something could have happened out of the ordinary and they are not themselves right now. The second time if they are rude call them on it politely but the third time do not put up with it. The same is true for the other side if they like you right off be cautious. If they push wanting to be in your life right away there is a reason and it is never good. If they get mad because you will not let them into your life stay clear of them. Remember just because someone finds you trustworthy does not mean that they themselves are. They may consider you a mate but that does not mean they will be one to you. The ones who take the time to get to know you, accepts you without implying change one and without digging are the ones you want in your life." The first impressions thing is not what is important; it is the one they leave behind that you should take into full consideration.

I never thought about it like that before but it made perfect sense the more I thought about both sides and the way they look at you. I noticed that the more I cleaned out my Karma the less people I had in my life and this was beginning to be a good thing. I was becoming more selective about who I wanted in my life and I was actually looking at what each one was adding or in most cases taking away from my life. I noticed that when I was doing great everyone came over and some how when they left so did my great feeling. When I was feeling down and the same ones would come over I noticed that I always felt worse instead of better. They felt better when they left because they had emptied out my good Karma, they also knew when to dump theirs into mine because I was to down to notice.

Remember you may not notice the people in the world when you feel good or bad but some may have their eye on you. Some people are so open that the world just moves right in and some are so closed off they do not notice who they enclosed with them. You should learn to have an open mind, not an open heart doing the opposite will cause you to have a bleeding heart that is easy to attack from the inside. Karma is all about keeping bad people out of your life and finding the good ones to replace them with. See you may do good things for bad people but that does not mean that bad people will do good things for you. (You also miss the ones that really are in need of help.) I have helped out the wrong ones before and they tell their friends all about you and you get passed around through your heart. This is how you learn how to put the other foot down.

The way I see it is your mum is suppose to take your trust gate out of your heart when you are born, shows you how to set it up and how to set the filters. You watch the people she allows in her life and how she responds to them be it good or bad. You then learn to add the same people in your life because she sets the example as well as the standards. Our mum has high standards just like the lady with the legs without being snobbish or arrogant because this is wanting only the best for your family. It has nothing to do with material things but the people in their lives and it does not mean that they think they are better then everyone because neither one of them do. You can have all the money in the world to buy you the best of everything but your life can still be a living hell if you surround yourself with the wrong people.

People are the ones who add to your Karma not possessions and your Karma is what makes you rich or poor. Treat people like you have a conscience and your soul will feel forever rich, treat people the opposite and you will feel forever empty inside and out. Nothing will ever be good enough and nothing good will ever be enough to appreciate. Both my mum and Lady legs have an extremely rich soul because they know how to keep their Karma cleaned out so that it does not ruin the family as a whole. If your mum does not get bad people out of her life and keep them out then how are you ever going to learn how and that it can be done? She should be your greatest teacher on earth because the word mum passing from the lips of a child is another name for Dad or God? If you do not have a good mum then find yourself one because you need her for proper balance throughout life. Before I forget, a mum has nothing to do with sex and everything to do with being nurturing. I have seen males take this role and do it just like a mummy hen, so do not get hung up on gender.

I have never bought into that saying that without family you are nothing because in reality you can have a huge family that goes out of their way to make sure that you do not amount to anything no matter how hard you try. I have also never bought into it because there are a lot of people born alone and go further because family is not holding them and making them back down. Logically with the right kind of family you cannot be stopped because everybody is adding to each others strengths not diminishing them. My mum admires other people's strengths and is not jealous of people who can do something better then she can. I can honestly say that I have never seen my mum throw a tit fit of any kind over anything and in turn neither do we because of her example. She taught all of us that you cannot get your way just because you can yell louder and longer then someone else.

After I thought about what she said I figured out how the other leg gets swept out from underneath you. You start out putting your mental foot down by saying no and depending on how firm and strong you are this usually ends the mental persuading. If that foot is not strong enough then they browbeat you with, "Well I will just not take no for an answer." Your response should be, "Oh yes you will because you will not get your way with me and that is the end of it. I said that is the end of it." More then likely after you feel like they have backed you into a corner you respond, "Oh all right," going against your better judgment, picking that foot up and putting it away. You just know that you are going to regret this.

If they cannot find a way past your mental foot be it threatening or by criticizing you severely then they move to the one in your heart because these toes are easier to step on. This works by saying, "Please, I would do it for you if you asked me to. Please, please." You know how it goes. If you put both feet down and they are still coming after you then you had better be prepared to fully stand your ground because they plan on trying to knock you down and hurting you beyond repair if you let them. Your feet are like your parents, they have to support each other and one should not be carrying all the weight. Legs are also your boundaries and without them you will not only be run over, but trampled upon as well. Remember that practice brings about perfection and perfection breeds ill contempt from those who choose not to practice. Practicing however, has nothing to do with you thinking you are perfect so do not be talked out of practicing even after you get it right!

The better you get at something the more you will find those around you going out of their way to not only stop you but to put an end to you wanting more for yourself. When people noticed that I was cleaning out my Karma and the way I was doing it was not only working but was changing my inherent streak of bad luck some were not to happy. The thing about being a kid at heart and an adult is how you view and see the world because your eyes never change, just the way you see through them. Kids let everything roll off their back and look at what is beyond there. Adults let everything get to them and cannot see with their own two eyes what they have right in front of them. The more you clean out your Karma, the more you feel like a kid again because you realize what is important and what is truly a waste of your time.

The funny thing is people are told not to sweat the small stuff but that dynamite comes in small packages and that little things mean a lot. What if you were to put them in order with a few extra words? Here goes: Little things mean a lot and if you do not take care of them they can and will blow up over time. So do not sweat the small things in life just take care of them as they come up and they will not bite you in the bum later on and all at once.

See I think that Karma is all about taking care of regrets and life just changes the scenery and the outside of people's appearance to make you look deeper at your own life and the ones that share in it. Keep in mind that there has always been the saying, "There is more here then what meets the eye." The things that are hidden are what we need to look for the most. You have to learn to use each part of your body and respect the fact that it is not only yours but the only one you have. There will never be a church built any greater then the temple you have inside your own heart so keep that in mind when you invite someone into it. This should be your sacred place so before they are allowed to enter you should double check to see if they are trustworthy enough to see what is inside. If someone does not care enough to keep their own temple clean they sure will not think to be on their best behaviour when it comes to yours. Their thought is: Well if I do not have one then you do not deserve one either.

If Karma is as big as everyone believes and thinks it to be then everyone's should be connected to one another. If that is the case, then I would prefer to keep the bad people as far away from me as possible. Filter them out way down the line and keep your Karma as far away from theirs as you have the drive to achieve.

Let us keep in mind that no matter how clean we keep everything about ourselves we are all going to still screw up because we are all human. Well some of us have been either accused or spotted as an alien from a far off planet but even if that is the case I can tell you that we screw up as well. (Even robots malfunction so they're not perfect either.) How else do you think you are going to learn if you get everything right all the time? Why do you think we have brain farts and bloopers for, so that when we get close to becoming too serious about ourselves this gives us a chance to laugh like we did when we were kids?

Kids are not hung up on themselves and every little thing that happens to them and that is why they can see when someone else is in need. I know this to be true because the more I cleaned up the black hole of memories the more I was seeing other kids in need of help. Kids of all ages and I do mean all ages, if you know how to look into someone's eyes you will find a lost child in need of something basic.

I never realized how many people in life there were just like me, until I realized the fear that had been instilled in me for all those lonely years. I was never scared of the dark, I was taught to be scared of the light and everything that comes with it. Yes, that does include people and everything good that comes with them. I noticed that there are a number of ways to teach this form of fear and it usually is taught at home. If you are not given two legs to stand on the world can stay a frightening place. The worst part is you get accustom to the bad ones knocking your legs out from underneath you because it is usually someone close who has done it to you all your life while claming to love you. When someone good comes along that wants to help it hurts you so deep because the answer hits so close to home that we think the pain is coming from them. Why do the ones that claim to love us not offer the same help with the same no strings attached clause?

The fear of letting go to grab onto something else comes from learning how to walk. Somewhere in the back of your mind all you remember is falling but what is even further from your mind is the fact that you did one day learn to walk on your own two feet. Once you accomplished this you became unstoppable until something new was to be learned. How confusing was the alphabet when you first saw it, I will bet it looked overwhelming at first but look at you now! I guess another way to look at Karma is like a report card that you show to Dad and you have to sign it with your own conscience! Now there is a thought to think long and hard about. Karma is your teacher in life and you not only failed to do your homework but you forgot to get your report card signed and brought back. (The bad thing to ask is how much trouble could you really get into for this?) Now she wants to schedule a meeting with your parents and you wonder why you always feel like you're in trouble. You never learned to ask the right questions and you never paid attention to the answers that were given. You slept in class and were forced to cheat off of someone else's paper who gave you the wrong answers. You were caught because you wrote, "I do not know either." Imagine the look on your parents faces if you were really that honest but we left out the part that we would try harder next time.

This brings up something my mum told me when I knew I was in trouble and stopped checking in. "The longer you wait the worse you are making it on yourself. The faster your punishment is taken the faster it will be all over. " She is correct and right you know, as scared as I was to go home in every sense of the word it cannot compare to the feeling of relief you receive when everything is right in your life again. I guess it is easy to forget that you can start over anytime you would like as soon as you are ready, you just have to find something else worth hanging onto. If something is in your core being then the only thing you will let go of it for is another core for your being.

You have to teach yourself to remember and see things as you did when you were a child. It was about the experience and you knew if you had done this before and not the appearance of what something was suppose to look like. We were not out to expose each others pain but would comfort a mate in need. Experience has to do with feelings, appearance has to do with the eyes and if the hand is truly quicker then the eye you need to learn how to see through your minds eye so you will know if you have already been through this before, or if it is being made to appear as something different. Keep in mind that just because the outer appearance changes does not mean that bad people are not the same inside. When you remember your experiences for what they truly are you will see the road ahead of you from the start before you walk half way down that path.

My Karma was so black that I could only see a bleak light when I would open my eyes, now I am learning that the path I was on is not as hard as the one I am about to take. You see, I learned that the easiest thing in the world to do is see light in total darkness, and walking to it may make you stumble and fall but sooner or later if you want it bad enough you will find a way to get there. The other side is having the ability to see darkness in a room full of light, this is where experience vs. appearance comes into play and Karma is right in the middle watching and taking notes.

Do keep in mind that with every action there should be a reaction unless someone detoured Mum Nature for a while, she always comes back usually unhappy because of the long unnecessary trip. When you clean out your Karma your life can and will change, the moral of the story is will you keep the change going or fall back to the other side out of habit or convenience. Some people find it easier to moan and groan but harder to think of ways to solve their dilemma. Some find the light a delight and forget about going back for any of the others, now they are out for themselves only. These people walk to the other side with a little bit of darkness growing inside of them and learn to feed off of other people's new found light.

There are others who try to make it but they bring all the darkness inside of them hidden and will not let anyone take it from them. The salmon swimmers who want the golden pond learn which ones are which and help them accordingly. See, now you have to learn to look at other people because you cannot be selfish with yourself any more.

Karma teaches us that we have all been hurt before and will get hurt time and again but it is what we choose to do with that pain that keeps it moving on. The life story is not what needs to be shared, it is the way you solved it and how much better you feel for standing up for yourself that needs to be taken in. Think of Karma as your own personal Ying and Yang and now someone has went and shook it all up. All you see is grey and nothing is black and white any more. What use to be clear as night and day now seems like fog and you can no longer see those around you as you once have? If Karma is all about learning from you own experiences and your life builds back up giving you a chance to right a wrong what are you going to do? A great example would be that your whole life you have backed down and now something in your life has built up that gives you a chance to be assertive and stand your ground. Do you take that chance and do something with it or do you pass your chance onto someone else and stay in your rut? I can guarantee that someone will take your chance for you but they will not walk over and ask if you want it handed to you!

Human natures response to you now is, "You had your chance," now you have to wait for the phrase, "Are you willing to take a chance," to come up again. (If it does) If you do not learn how to take the little chances in life the big ones will knock your knees.

When I looked at my own Karma report card, I noticed I had more needs improvement marks then satisfactory marks. I also noticed it has: Shows up for life but does not always participate, needs to learn to be more assertive when it comes to standing up for herself and less aggressive when it comes to the ones that want help. Basically needs to find proper balance so we do not have to keep holding her back, we would like to see her move on. She has the potential but is extremely hard headed even outside of class. Finally learned how to like herself but needs to work on playing well with others and not always herself especially when in class. (Who would have thought that at the time I screwed that up I was almost on to something!)

I did have one excellent mark in the pulling my head out of my own bum department but right under that it read: However needs to learn how to keep it out and not use it for a place to hide. Can you imagine Dad reading this while looking at you, "I am sure you have one of you infamous logical explanations for this?"

The only reply I could realistically have would be, "No Sir, but if you will please send me to my room so that I could think about what I have or have not done and try and come up with one if you let me."

I can picture him looking at my mum saying, "What are we going to do with her?"

The thing about life, logic, Karma and reality is that they do co-exist even if the people in the world have not learned how to yet. If you could ask each one about what their philosophies are I can guarantee whatever they are they would be strong because of what they have all seen apart and together. The great thing to learn from all of them is that no matter how strongly they think or feel about something they do not force the other side to give up something of theirs. They have boundaries and they do not get crossed over unless a strong placement check is required. When you try and force them into something they are not what happens? Do you get your way or does a stronger force put you back in your place? Did it ever occur to you that they could go out together and discuss worldly events and how to solve them? They tell each other how you are not playing fair with all of them and they are being treated like a burden to your life instead of a blessing. Could you just picture them sitting at a round table and it has to be round for equal greatness and separation. Logic looks reality right in the eyes and asks, "How come they never let you out of their sight, not even for a moment? Does it not dawn on them that you need time to yourself just to reflect on what you have just been through?"

"Logic, I know that you want to be there for them too but I am too close to see how to fix things. Life, what is your take on how we could solve this dilemma because it works both ways? There are some lives that I am not a part of and logic is the only thing they think they have but without me they will never feel like anything is right there already in front of them." Life kicks back to reflect on what was just said and thinks about the conclusions they both have come to. Both sides are equally right to feel the way they do and both are correct about the path they both took to think about coming to their conclusions. Life listens to all the thoughts running around and takes them to Dad. "I have two conclusions and all it has caused me to do is think and feel about things and you know me, I am not one to take sides and now my own life is so full on how to solve this I cannot even stop to smell the roses."

"I know, that is the only way I get to smell them too." Dad whispers the answer in Life's ear because He knows that life put forth a valiant effort and sometimes even the greatest of minds can stump themselves.

Life leans back in, "O.K. here is how we are going to solve this. Logic you stand on one side of them and reality you stand on the other."

"Logically that is how we have always stood, even I could see that and I cannot see close up."

"No, both of you want to be that way but you two have always been face to face and without knowing it Karma provokes you two into facing off."

Everyone looks at Karma, "What did you expect me to do. You two are so close and never include me and I was acting out because I was getting left out of the group. Oh sure you let me walk behind you but the only time you two ever include me in anything is when something is about to go wrong. You use me for a scapegoat more than anything else and you kick back like someone else is going to take care of me."

"Oh Karma, we did not know you felt like that."

"Your right, we never give you a second thought, until its time to get out of the way, so that everything comes in your direction. We also apologize to Life for wasting your time about our problem because this changes everything."

Life laughs and replies, "Karma's problem helped come up with the solution kids. See you need a buffer between two conclusions otherwise all you are going to get are sparks and that can only lead to a fire. A fire you never intended to start but before you know what happened it is out of control, now, with each of you standing in between Karma, if they do not stop to smell the flowers, enjoy the wind on their face, start spending time with all of us and start taking care of business, Karma is going to give them a slap on the fanny. If they still insist on doing things the same way, Karma has every right to make those spankings harder every time until they plum up and do what needs to be done. They have to start learning that not everyone is going to take care of things for them and they need to get their hands dirty when bad people try to get over on them other wise they win."

"You know that solves all our problems including the one we never knew life was going through. How did you think of such a brilliant solution that does not hurt anyone's feelings but treats everyone as equals?"

Life leans back and grins real big, "I went and asked Dad for help of course."

They burst into laughter together, "Life, we always forget that you are the comedian out of all of us and solves our problems with laughter being the end result."

"I guess that is the moral behind your solution. If you leave even the smallest of things out you will never get to see the whole picture and the beauty she holds inside of it. The more Karma lets people know that I am here for them the more they will feel how close Dad wants to be to them."

"Life, when did you get to be such a profound thinker?"

"It runs in the family!"

I think that Dad has a great sense of humour and enjoys hearing us laugh. If you do not straighten out your Karma you will never know the true meaning behind what life is all about. The better you feel about yourself the more you have to give to others, the more you give of yourself to others the better you feel about yourself. Karma is all about standing up for good and getting bad people back in their place. You have a chance every day to right a wrong even if it is not yours. If you see someone in need of help and you look the other way that is what will eat on you. The regret that you had the chance to stand tall for someone and yet again by-passed a chance to be a hero in someone's eye. Just because the news cameras are not around does not mean that they do not need help. Moreover, that is the wrong reason to help someone and it's daft.

"Why does God let bad things happen to good people?" I told someone what I thought the answer might be and needless to say they were not grown up enough to handle the answer. I told them that if good people would start learning to stand up for themselves then bad people would not get away with it. Dad does not let bad things happen, people let bad things happen and due to the fact that we all have free will we are free to treat people the way we want to. I am free to treat you as badly as you let me; in turn you have free will to put a stop to it before it gets beyond your control.

Think of Karma as a stand against good or evil, every time you back down from a bully you give their side more power. The thing about bad people is you allow them to become inflated through your fear and Karma gives you a chance to take it back. How do you think that ordinary people such as us become stronger or weaker over time? We either stand or we lay down, plain and simple. Karma is about answering the call of duty in your own back yard and not many respond to give her aid. Karma needs our help when it comes to bad people and not everyone knows this fact.

If something is going on that you do not agree with then say something right then and there. Learn to take a chance not only with yourself but with your life as well. We all go through trials that are assigned to make us stronger, smarter, more patience or what ever your need might be but you have to go through it first before it is rightfully yours. If you pray for strength something will happen

74

in your life that at the end will give you the strength you seek. You do not think that Dad is going to give you a big sword to yield before you practice the basics with a stick do you? If you ask for patience does something not happen that tries the ones you already have and when you pass do you not feel like you have more?

Karma goes back and tells life what you are lacking and brings things full circle until you get it right. I am mentally stronger then when I first started out in life because I past my trials. The more you pass the harder your next test is going to be because you are improving. Did I pass each one the first time, well no, half the time I did not even know that I was being tested or I failed to show up for the finals but once I started seeing life in a whole new light I wanted to study harder. The more we study the further we can move on.

Before now it used to get under my skin when people would tell me how incredibly hard my life is and ask why I was not making it easier on myself by just giving in once in a while. First off if you give in once the other side will come to expect it, second you do it once and it forms a habit until it just becomes convenient. I know that I have a hard life but I would not have it any other way because that would mean that I would have to give up the strength I rightfully earned. I could not get them to understand that vital part, I already earned it. I learned that some were jealous because I was stronger than them but they failed to see just how I became that way. I guess they thought that I could just hand it over or stop because they did not like the fact that I was something that they were not but could be if they wanted to earn it too.

People like that only dwell on what you have and not what they are. They could have the same strengths as I do but they do not want to go through the trials to acquire it. Dad is not going to hand you the reward before you start because you know that some people would never start. An example would be: "If you clean your room you can have a cookie."

"If you give me the cookie now I will clean my room later." What happens when you give them the reward first? They feel like they do not have to do anything after that. Do you really think that Dad does not know how minds work, please He is the one that programmed them in the first place. People will always try and get away with what they can and it is up to us to set them straight. Now that does not mean to go around telling people how to live their lives but stop letting them get away with things that you know they should not be getting away with.

The saying that Dad helps those that help themselves is also a vital one to remember. Do you like working with people who sit on their bum asking for this and that and not lifting finger one to help? Well, if you feel that way do you not think that He feels the same? I know that I have had my fill of lazy people not pulling their own weight and I have not had to put up with it since the world began, you know that it has to get on His nerves. Dad wants you to be strong and a fighter because that is the only way you will stand up to evil as it appears. When I hear people say, "Why is God doing this to me," I always wondered why they never thought they might have brought it upon themselves or that there might be another force involved.

We teach kids all about good vs. evil but somehow when we turn into adults evil does not exist any more. Could it be that maybe it just blends in better and you refuse to see things for what they really are? I was always taught that there was good and bad all around us and since I do not live in a bubble I still believe this to be true. Do we blame God because it is easier than blaming the real culprit involved? We tend to do that as a society, blame the victims and go after them with a vengeance when their only crime was not being able to defend themselves. The criminal does not have to justify their actions but we make innocent people feel like they have done nothing right in their lives leading up to this tragic event. We go after them until they just want to die, while the criminal gets to sit back and smirk. Should it not be the other way around and the victim in the end gets to sit back and do the smirking because justice was served?

Do you not think that Dad and Karma feel the same way? They get blamed for things that they have nothing to do with, it is the people not doing their part that could put a stop to half of what is going on. I mean remember in Kindergarten when one person would do something to get into trouble and the whole class would have to put their heads down when they did nothing wrong? When are we going to get tired of being forced to put our heads down and start standing together to make that one person pay? I have allowed people to do this to me and I learned that in the end the person I was angry with the most was myself. This would not have gone on if I would have stepped up regardless of whether or not someone was behind me or not. I forget that Dad is right there if I would learn to ask for help, after all it would not end up costing me my soul.

If we all did our part to help each other then we could feel just how strong our side is and how much stronger it can become. We have to stop waiting for the others to stand up for us because we will never feel stronger for it. When I go to my mum for help even though I listen to the advice and wisdom it does not truly sink in until after it is applied. Keep in mind that just because you were taught one thing does not mean you cannot teach yourself something different.

Being true to yourself also means being true to your mind. If you go back and fix what was wrong when it was beyond your control then you will notice your present for what it is and you will have a better control of which direction your future goes.

You will remember the road for what it is and fix the mistakes you made going down this one the first time, you will also notice that doing this causes you to come to the end of the road more quickly. With every experience life brings at least two things: One a better understanding of yourself and what you are willing to go through. Second the knowledge that things like this do go on and sometimes remembering what you have already been through puts you steps ahead that you have earned. Life is a staged classroom and there are tests to see if you are qualified to move on or if you are like me and get held back a lot due to the fact that you are hard headed. Life use to frustrate me until I realized that there was something here that I was supposed to learn if I would just catch on. I will admit that life would be a tad easier if elders were appreciated for their wisdom so that more of it could be passed on.

I agree with our mum, I would prefer to learn from other people's mistakes then have to make so many on my own before I can apply what I have learned. Could you imagine being this hard headed and having to rely on learning from your mistakes only? I would still be thinking that my head was free from my bum instead of realizing when it really is.

What makes me laugh about life the most is the way people look at each other, not so much for who they are but more so for whom they are not. Then they become appalled when it comes back around on them. This is when I realized that Karma can also come back on you because of something you said. Remember when I said I would go around making verbal fun of people for having something up their bum and then look how Karma came back on me. Had me all twisted inside of myself so that I would learn not to judge others. I have been told that time and time again and I guess I could not take a hint and had to learn the hard way. Did I learn my lesson; I can only say that I sure hope so because living your life through your bum is really hard on those around you.

Karma is more then just a word or a simple phrase and since I have been blessed with getting to be a part of my mum's I learned I do not want to go back to the way things were before. This is a whole new world to me and now I have a hand to hold onto when I go to explore. If I become scared somewhere in life's journey I have a source where reassurance is over abundant and someone who started out loving me more then I loved myself. I may have started out questioning her every step of the way because of what I had been through but even as stubborn as I am I learned that there comes a point when you need to stop because its hurting them. Do not put them on trial and make them justify why they want to open their heart to you. The thing about Karma is that the payback is not always bad, if you have been good to the wrong people sometimes a person will cross your path that has enough generosity that they will bring you into their circle.

I finally figured out that even though I may screw up a tremendous amount I still must have done something right to have a mum as great as her include me into such a generously loving family. This makes life worthwhile to me because I never had it before. The meaning of life is simple once you stop to figure it out. The deeper meaning of life is the one that becomes more complex because now you have to figure out what to do with all of this?

Mate, I did it. I wish that you could have been there because I know that you would have appreciated it.

Have you ever starting farting and it just kept going and going one right after another until that one that was suppose to be just like the rest of them was more than slightly different? You realized that you did more than fart your trousers and if you were all alone that would be just something that you could cover up without anyone being the wiser, but this happened in front of people and you know that it happened so there is no need to bother checking what your facial expression already shows. You do not dare walk away in fear that something may fall and you know if it did that you can not say, "Now how did that get there," or "Where did that come from?" Nothing you say could make it less embarrassing! The only thing you can think about at that moment is, "Did enough of it come out to be noticeable?" *Keep this in mind when I tell you what happened!*

I was talking to one of my mates when the unthinkable happened. You never hear about it happening to someone else, so how could it happen to you? Do you remember that brain fart you and I had at the same time? Well, I had another brain fart and no matter how hard I tried I could not stop having brain farts and it just kept getting funnier and funnier until I thought that I was going to have another one and I even squeezed so that I could get it to come out but this one was greatly different!!! Mate, I had one of those farts that are really wet and squishy only this was mentally. That's right, I mentally shit all over my own brain. I do not know how it happened I just remember the look on my face like, "who has to be the one who cleans that up?" Then I began to wonder; did enough of it squirt out that someone can tell? How do you go about checking

79

and what do you wipe your hands on? She kept asking me if I was o.k. and part of me wanted to ask her if she had any water so that I could clean myself up, but I just rubbed the top of my head and told her no. Then when she was not looking I smelt my hand the first chance I got, I already knew what I was going to wipe my hand on.

So having water on the brain and being a shit head go hand in hand.

I guess that's the moral of this story. If you decide to play Russian Fart Roulette be it with your bum or with your mind, be prepared that not all of them are going to be dry and you could just very well ending up shitting yourself in front of people. This is a true story, I wish I were kidding!!

# Chapter Three
# What to Do with All of This!

Believe it or not, the shoe can be placed on the other foot; I have met some parents in my lifetime that have really bad kids.

I was working at an in-store bakery one time and I looked up and noticed a woman walking towards me but something made me put everything down and really look at her. My line is, "How can I help you today," but instead I asked her, "Are you o.k.?"

She shot me a look and replied, "I would tell you if you really cared."

I looked at her firmly and said, "I would not have asked if I did not care," and she could tell by my eyes that I meant it.

She told me that she was on her way to commit suicide but something made her stop at this store and come inside. When she noticed that I did not react to her killing herself she went on and told me the reasons she felt that low. She had loved and raised her kids the best way she could and now they want nothing to do with her. Well, that is unless they need something from her then they will include her. She told me how they do nothing but break her heart every chance they get and disrespect her just as much. She told me everything and at the end said, "I really do not know why I came in here," she wanted to turn and walk away when I looked at her differently just then.

"Well, my lady, I am not going to tell you that I do not know what to tell you because the whole time you were talking I was trying to figure out how to help you with this." I will never forget the look in her face for as long as I live.

"As far as taking your life, I know how that feeling can become overwhelming. Sometimes when life knocks the wind out of me I think about doing the same thing. I will picture doing the whole thing in my head and then I will let out a big sigh. The reason for the sigh is I know that with my bad luck I will somehow screw up and instead of killing myself I just maim myself severely and put myself worse off then before I tried that," and I started laughing. "Now as far as your family goes, screw them," she had a surprised look on her face when I said that. "I mean it, my lady, I know that people will tell you to keep them in your life but you know what? I have been on my own for a long time now and I am doing so much better without them. They do nothing but cut you down and make you feel bad about yourself and what have you, so why do you need them? Now I am not saying that you have to sever ties with yours like I did, but just them cut them for a time and go on with your life. Do not put your life on hold waiting for them to come to you make them catch up to you. If they straighten out, keep them, if not lose them."

We talked for a long while after that but before she left I told her that I was glad that she came in. I never stopped thinking about her and always hoped that she was doing better than that night. There was no way to find her because I never asked for her name. There was something about her that just stuck with me. I was still at the same job and thinking about her when I looked up and noticed a gorgeous lady walking towards me. I am talking breath taking and when she walked in every eye was on her. She never looked around to see if anybody was watching her but they were. She just had this confidence about her that poured out and radiated through every part of her. I smiled great big when she walked up to me because I was going to get to wait on her.

She looked at me so sweetly and said, "I do not know if you remember me or not," all I could think is if I had ever met you before I would defiantly remember. She bends down and whispers in my ear, "I am the one that wanted to commit suicide." I looked up at her and my brain became scrambled but she and you look, my eyes grew huge and my mouth hit the floor. I wanted to ask her so much or just try and open my mouth to get anything to come out but all I could think of was, "You, you, you." Years and years later I finally finished my thought, "Look gorgeous." This lady felt great about herself and you could tell that it was not at the expense of anyone else.

What that Lady did with her life is remarkable and it showed. This had nothing to do with her outside appearance because she did not have a face lift or anything along those lines. The woman I first saw looked so little compared to the tall Lady who walked in that second time. I remember two different people because they did not look the same. I would have never in a million years believed they were the same people if someone had just shown me a picture and said, "See this is her and yes she is still alive." I knew she was telling me the truth when she whispered that in my ear because nobody else was around when we were talking the first time.

I never have stopped thinking about her and I learned that there is no reason to. Thinking about her makes me feel good, not about me, but about her and what she went through to do all of that for herself. When my thoughts would get me a little down I think about her and use her for my inspiration. I figured that she hung in there and never let me down the least I could do is hang in there for her as well.

All we did was talk that day, no more no less but the impact of that path crossing is something that I hold extremely dear to me even to this day. I never thought for a moment, "I am glad that my advise worked out for you, I did that, I, I" it had nothing to do with me and everything to do with her. She did it all by herself and did such an exquisite job of it all. I think that is why she had this unbelievable glow all around her because she did it. She never gave up and you could tell the moment that she walked into the room that this was a lady who had come all the way and was here to stand tall. There was not a drop of conceit in her body but yet she radiated beauty. The only way to describe a true before and after is she felt like hell before and she is living proof that there is a bright light if you want it bad enough. She is also proof that you can do it alone if you need to.

The sweet thing about our paths crossing is she helped me to hang in there without even knowing how she changed my life as well. There were a couple of times that I felt the same way she did that night and did not have anyone to talk to but I would remember her and hang tough. When I finally broke from the hell my life had become I too found my glow only it was not inside of me like it was with her, mine was inside my mum's family. The ones I have spent my life looking for.

See, there are two types of light sources and both her and our mum are the same types. They are the flame themselves and the ones who show us the way when we become lost. They make us feel warm and safe and that life is worth living even if it does not feel like that at the time. They have the ability to relight our pilot light when it somehow gets blown out. She just needed to find some pilot lights is all and apparently she did, I needed to find a flame and have.

See, there are the ones like my siblings and myself who are more like lanterns if you will. We carry the source with us everywhere we go, most people do not have either one to work off of so they just die out from the inside with nothing to pass on or get things passed down to them. The cool thing about being a lantern is you get to pass your light onto someone else when they need it more then you because you know that your source is strong enough to relight yours again. Sharing your light actually makes it stronger not weaker surprisingly enough. We all have to go through our own trials but we know that we do not have to go through them completely alone.

The great thing about both lives is that you can find what you are looking for if you are willing to break from all that you have been led to believe. Sometimes you can give birth to bad kids; it happens and has nothing to do with your character. Sometimes you can be born to the wrong people it just happens the important thing to keep in mind is that your strong enough to break free. Look at everything that you have been through and you made it through that. You do not have to keep bad people in your life no matter what they try to convince you of. If it is not good for the family then its not good. You should be able to turn your back on family because you know they have yours without a doubt. If you feel like you cannot stand like that with them then something is wrong. The only way to solve this is to fix the problems not just go over them.

I have told a couple of people basically the same thing as I told her but it fit their situation but all I received from them is, "Well, they're my whatever, and I love them." Feelings that are one sided, stay that way and being disrespected for any reason should not be tolerated especially by people in your own blood line. You should learn to take your own feelings into consideration instead of the ones hurting you all the time. I am straight forward when I say they will never take yours into consideration. My mum has made certain allowances for us as we adjust but she does not make excuses for any of us, there is no reason to. If we step out of line we know that we are going to be punished for it and we do the full time. There is no getting off for good behaviour or because we yelled long enough to get on her nerves. She sticks to her guns and that should be commended because she keeps her word which in turn shows us how to keep ours.

I have seen people ground their kids and the next day let them off, that sure showed them who was in charge. I have seen kids throw fits and scream, "I hate you," then it dawns on them that they need money for something so they take it back just long enough for you to hand over the cash. There is a difference between being loved unconditionally and being used repeatedly. I had a mate

84

that has a kid who has learned how to hold her mum hostage without there being an actual gun involved. She knows not only how to break and use her mums heart but when and how deep. She looks at her daughter and you can see a source of love wanting to flow. Her daughter looks at her mum and sees a never ending source of cash flow.

The sad thing is there is a source of wasted love just waiting to break loose and it may never get a chance to. See I learned that you cannot get rid of feelings you can only redirect them. I followed my own advice and now have a mum who wants my love and does not want to kick me when I am down.

I have told people the same thing and you can tell the ones who were strong enough to go the distance because their lives are happier. No it is not easy letting go of something that we have held onto for a long time but maybe that is all there is to growing up is letting go of our security blanket for our part of the quilt. I did not even have enough thread for a needles worth but my mum never cared, she had enough blanket to include me. Now when you have been left out in the cold for as long as some of us have been, you can either let it be a pride thing. "No thanks I do not need your charity I can freeze my bum off all alone because I have learned not to need anybody." When you get knocked in the teeth enough, that tends to be your response. The best thing to do is look closely at the blanket, and see how it was made. Hers was thick and you could just tell that it would be so warm and fun.

I was terrified but I learned how to overcome my fears because nothing was going to stop me from getting under this blanket. Believe it or not I even had someone threaten me with my own life. I had a choice, I could either keep the rag that they gave me (and kept tearing up as my life went along) and they would over look this. The other would be to keep my Family and them loose me. This was not the time to be truthful and that is why I said that I do not believe that Dad minds us telling the now enemy a fib to keep yourself safe. Now inside my head I was thinking, "Pick the people who have been cruel and mean every time I see them or pick the family who called me one of their own and does not hurt me? What kind of daft moron are you?" The problem is they were not just daft but dangerous and that is a bad combination all in itself.

Some people can be reasoned with and some will never listen to a word of reasoning so you have to be careful and use your head especially if they have you by the heart. They may not come directly after you but someone you love so be careful in dealing with someone you want to break loose from. The important thing to remember is keep your head and your wits will stay with you for the most part. The thing that scared me the most was not being threatened but the thought of losing my Family. The hell that these people and people like them have put me through is nothing compared to losing a family of people who love you not just ones pretending to.

If it feels good then why not hold onto it and incorporate it into your life. We can all feel miserable and bad because that is the way life is set up so there is no contest in that. The point to life is, are you strong enough to want more than this? Life is like a game of red rover, you trade back and forth until you have the strongest chain there is correct? Then why would you not want that same chain for your family? I know that we have all heard that you are only as strong as your weakest link but if people would learn to explore deeper they would discover that there is more to this saying. If you have a weak link in your chain, fix it or get rid of it.

I remember one of my teachers telling us that our chain is our armour and if we know ahead of time that there is a problem and we do not take care of it where do you think that arrow is going to go? Right to the weak point every time, after every battle you have to fix the damage before you go out again. Learn how they damaged your armour and make it that much stronger for the next battle. Keep in mind that just because you are beaten does not mean you are defeated by any means. Learn not only from your mistakes but from your opponents as well this way you will have double the knowledge and half as many scars.

She is also the one who taught us the deeper meaning behind teaching someone how to fish. Anyone can teach you the basics of learning how to feed yourself, but what happens if your fishing pole breaks? What happens if someone steals it? Do you give up and say, "Well that is that time to call it a day," or do you learn how to make your own so that it fits only you? Life, people is going to do what it can to try and break you and you have to learn how to be unbreakable. You can either be a blade of grass bending and being pushed in which ever direction the wind is the strongest but do keep in mind that grass is only allowed to get so tall before someone decides to mow over it. Grass may be pretty to the eye but it does not get much of a view besides people's feet.

You can be a tall tree looking down on everyone around you but do keep in mind that even through your big and appear mighty someone will always have the urge to want to cut you down and other people to back them. Now when you are a kid you picture both these versions and try and figure out the best one to be, the grass who gets cut down all the time or the tree that only gets cut once? When I looked at her she could tell that I was trying to decide and I remembered that she just smiled at me great big and went on to say. "Now the best thing to me to be is your very own mountain, you can go through a mountain but you will never completely destroy it. The wind can come at you like a tornado but you stand firm and hold on tight because this is not the first whirlwind that has come your way and it will not be the last."

The funny thing is I had also heard the saying, "I am making a mountain out of a molehill," so I put the two together. Anytime I stood my ground I would always think to myself, "I am a molehill turning into a mountain, I am a molehill turning into a mountain." Keeping that picture in mind I would look at those around me and I noticed that there were more people who were blades of grass but had it in them to be mountains. There were a great deal of trees that should have been cut down long ago because they were not mighty just dead inside and was killing off all life around them.

Anytime she would talk about life like that I would hang onto her every word and she knew this. I would daydream in her class sometimes but not when it came to things like this. The other students would daydream when she would talk about life and strangely enough she taught us differently. Being smart with books was not going to be my thing and she never minded because she knew that I paid attention when it really mattered. She would also give me extra assignments to make up for my daydreaming. I would have to write down what it was that I was daydreaming about and believe it or not she would read it and we would go over it. When your favourite teacher says, "You amaze me sometimes with the way you see things." I never questioned if that was meant as a compliment or not to me it was like receiving a trophy.

If you do not like your life then look at it from a different point of view and see if things can be fixed by being firm or if you need to just cut loose from the whole thing. Sometimes you are better off floating by in a dingy until another ship comes along. The worst thing to do is stay on a boat where total mutiny has been called on you. Wisdom is knowing which one you are on and addressing your actions accordingly. I learned that sometimes I was better off alone then surrounding myself with people who wanted to use me but hid it under needing help.

I know that I have been given a great deal of grief about the way I go about living my life but that is the thing it is my life. The more I realized this the more I was able to regain control over it and take it away from everyone else. When I put all feelings aside about everyone in my life and put them back through the trust gate my mum had fixed for me I noticed red flags went off everywhere. When I looked back on when I met these same people it was always the same, when I was at my lowest. I let them in thinking they were mates but they turned out to be little devils in disguise. When I severed the tie with all of them the grief I was receiving also was severed.

Sometimes the source of constant pain is coming from the one you open up to the most. If someone is hurting you then trade them in either for someone better or for no pain at all. Now I am not saying that loved ones will not from time to time be a pain in your bum, I am talking about the ones who do nothing but go out of their way to hurt you. I realized that aside from the Family our mum fit me into I only trusted three other people. I gave them the feelings I had for them back, threw out the rest and never give the other ones any thought. The way I look at it is the more I think about them the less I think about the ones that truly matter.

I used to think: Well if it was their loss then why do I feel it? I have since had a complete change of thought and realized that what I was feeling was not the loss of them it was losing the drain they had on me. When you learn to change your way of thinking you can change your mind about anything. The thing is though you have to change your mind and keep it that way. I use to get depressed beyond normal means and since I cleaned out my Karma and with it my life I no longer even come close to that feeling of despair any more.

Now when something happens I think about how to take care of it and I do. The only time I feel is when it comes to the ones I love as it should be. If I do not trust someone then there is no reason to have any feelings of any kind for them. I keep my heart at home and only bring my head out into the world as it should be. The less people know how to get to you the less they can get to you. You have to learn how to close your heart off to the world and keep yourself open to the ones who love you. Even though you may need and want someone to care about you if you do not care about yourself you will only continue the cycle.

You have the capacity to rewrite the wrongs inside your mind if you will learn how to drive that far out. You can take people along the way or drop them off as you go but fix what you need and learn to move on. If you were told something that you know is not true then figure out what the truth is and keep that with you instead. Ignorance never settles a question but the truth does and the longing to find it needs to come from you. You are the only one who can stop yourself and give up because you know how to get rid of the people in your life that try and do that to you. You also know how to refuel if you will and who to go to for supplies.

There is nothing that you cannot do if you will learn how not only to make up your mind but to set it straight. Your mind is like a kid and will try to convince you to back down in your own way of thinking but that is when you have to stay the strongest. The key to remember or to keep in mind is that it is yours and you need to learn how to control it. There are going to be times that it wants to panic and you have to stop it and calm it down. There are going to be times that it wants to stop and you have to have it in you to make it go on. Learn how to control your mind first and then you will learn how to adjust your thoughts as you go. The more you do this the easier it will become and soon it will just become second nature to have positive thoughts.

Your mind will teach you when someone is trying to distract you because they are trying to deceive you. Your mind will teach you how to look beyond what is in front of you and see the hidden depths of life. Your mind will decipher more quickly between the problem and the solution and learn to set its own sights on how to obtain it. You will also learn how to see other people as clearly as you see who you are so you will know beyond the shadow of a doubt if you want them near you or not. You have to basically loose control of your mind in order to see how much you need to control it so that it does not do that any more without your permission.

How you ever noticed that some people faced with a crises know exactly how to handle the situation before it gets out of control while everyone around them are freaking out? Did it ever occur to you that all it may be is something as simple as a mind set. You may have control over your mind under normal circumstances but when do you need it the most? You have to be able to keep yourself coherent so that you can keep yourself calm because everyone knows that bad things can happen before your blink of an eye has finished. The more you have control of your mind the more you will listen to it when it tells you that there is something more here. If you do not listen to yourself then your instincts will never be as strong as they could be. Have you ever had a gut instinct and you did not go with it? Then you wonder why something gnaws at you, it's you telling you that you are going to be sorry for not listening to your own built in warning system.

I learned that it was not my mind that was lying to me, how could it tell me the truth when it was not told the truth? What was bothering it was the fact that it had known that it was lied to but needed me to realize it before any changes could be made. When something is weighing heavily on your mind there is a reason for it and it will not rest until it has what it needs to go on. The same thing when someone enters your mind to such a degree that you cannot stop thinking about them. Your brain tells you what your top priority is, and knows which buttons to push to try to get you to listen. We were all taught to listen to authority but there comes a time when you need to listen to your own authority. What do you think that inner voice is used for?

The reason why anything bothers you be it your past or present is somewhere there was misinformation given to you and you went as far as you could with what you had. Maybe that is all there is to growing up is learning when to listen to yourself over someone you know is wrong. Growing up is learning to take that part of you that was always being dismissed and allowing it to be a part of you once again. I learned how to be whole because of my mum and now I am not looking past myself for that inner peace any more. I am not looking for something to make me feel complete because I received the help and guidance that I needed to fix what I could not see.

You have to learn what was beyond your control go back and fix it because now it is in your means to control it. You have already gone through it and now that you are in charge of yourself put a stop to it. The more doors you open and clean out mentally or in your heart the more you will go through in life. You do not have to tolerate being talked down to by anybody including yourself. If you do not like who you are then you have to fix it from the inside out. There are going to be times when you will have to do something that may not be pleasant but that does not mean that it does not have to be taken care of.

You have to rehabilitate yourself because you are the only one who knows what is truly bothering you. The thing to keep in mind is how much pain you went through so you will learn to appreciate the ones who do not put you through that and keep them in your life. Remember that it is your life and you are the one at the helm so figure out what you need in order to stay your course.

Learn to feel good about yourself even if you need the help of someone else to give you that little push. Your outside appearance only covers you it has nothing to do with what is inside of you. The more you uncover the brighter your light becomes and you will come to realize that you had more depth inside of you than you gave yourself credit for. You should also learn that you have more then just your body going for you, you should have a mind, heart, thoughts, feelings, a spirit and a soul amongst others things. If you have a tie of any kind constantly making you feel bad about yourself it always will. The same holds true for the other side, if they always make you feel good about yourself they always will. Your life is in your hands more then you know but you have to find or ask for the strength to break a tie that you know is bad.

Some people do not want to hurt someone else's feelings so they put up with it but the thing is they need to care about their own feelings more. What would you do if Dad asked you, "How was your life?" You then proceed to tell Him as you watch a picture of your life from start to finish and then the life you were meant to have playing in the back ground. "All you had to do was go against the grain and take a chance. Get a hold of yourself instead of allowing everyone else to put a hold on you. Look," He pauses your life, "Right there you could have said something that would have made all the difference in the world to your life but you stood down and what could have been a chance turned into a regret. Look at all the opportunities you had to say what was on your mind and you never took a stand for yourself. Do you realize that I did these things to help you but you would not take them to help yourself? I was trying to make your life easier but you would not learn how to use the tools that I first gave to you."

He gave us thoughts to use not to dismiss and the same goes for you. Could it be that the reason that you do not know why you are here is because you will not leave the safety of all that you were taught to branch out? You are supposed to be more then what you were told, you just have to want it enough for it to become a desire. I would rather tell Dad that I screwed up because my head was up my bum then because I let someone else run my life into the ground. You have to learn how to keep yourself safe from all harm even if its coming from inside of you.

Being grown up means doing what needs to be done even if its not considered popular. People would rather blame everyone else first before they look at themselves. I learned to watch what I wonder about because life will let you see it from the side that you are questioning. The thing about guilt is you have to learn if it belongs to you or not. I was made to feel guilty for being born until I realized that I should have never been the one to hold onto it. Being born was out of my control but what I choose to do with their mistake is in my control. Some of the best things in life come from mistakes and I decided that that is what I wanted to be, something good that comes out of something bad.

No matter what you have been through the end result is the same how did you and only you handle it. Some people may not be held accountable for their actions here but they will come their judgment day. The thing to keep in mind is, will you be one of the ones that hold their head up high, because you are not being led around by a collar, rather than someone who feels the need to hang their head so low they step on it. There is a huge difference between being conceited and being proud of who you are. There is also a difference between being arrogant and feeling good about yourself.

Remember that you will always have people around you that want you to feel as low as you can and knock everything that you do down but only you can let that stop you. The harder someone knocks me the more I know that I am onto something and it makes me want to keep going. They all may laugh at you now but guess who gets the heart felt chuckle in the end? You may have to let go of someone that you care for in order for you to get on with your life but maybe that is what needs to happen in order for them to grow up too. I do not care how many people go against me or try and put me down because my reply is always the same. "Your opinion of me neither makes me nor breaks me, the one that matters the most is the one I have of myself." I learned that the best way to stop the ones taking pot shots at you is to start taking shots at them. Believe it or not the stronger you are the less you will need to take because yours does more damage.

The old wives tale of, "Just ignore them and they will get bored and go away," wrong, they just receive more opportunities for getting to do what they want and they know this. Ignoring something does not put a stop to it and it sure does not make the problem any better. You can turn your back to someone getting raped but that does not stop the action from continuing on or the effects from coming afterwards.

You have to stop letting it be someone else's problem and get involved and you have to start with your own life. I learned how to become involved in my own life and learned not only that I had a lot of screwed up things but that I did not like some of the people involved in my life. The reason I stayed miserable around certain people is because they themselves were miserable people. They did not want to solve their problems they just wanted you to feel miserable for them so that they would not have to. I learned that this is indeed an easy transfer if you are not careful.

Why in the world do you think that there are so many people in the world? Some feel so they will have more people to use and make fun of but the truth is we all have something that we can pass on to each other if not, then you did something wrong. You can pass on a kind word, a smile, a hug to someone in need of one but you have to pass things on in order for something to be passed onto you. The ones who hoard are the ones who will never give anything back and are always owed something. Nobody owes me a good life, I owe it to myself to want more and I owe it to Dad to get it done in the time He has allotted for me. See I learned that some people wait for a near death experience to change their ways but because it is not sincere they fall back into the same habits as before. When you realize that every day is a near-death experience you change and stick to it. There may come a time when you forget to wake up because you forgot to breath.

I do not want to live in a life full of misery and the thing is I am not going to. I know that I have it in me to go as far as I can and even though it does take time I am heading off in the right direction. I told my mate the last time I saw her that some people start off with a bright past but end up with a dark future and some started out with a dark past but end up with a bright future and that I knew which one I was. I could actually say that now because I realized why I was getting knocked in the head so much all of a sudden. I had to realize who I was in order to have a future because without this knowledge there was to be no future of any kind for me.

I had to realize that just because I went through what I did does not mean that I am a bad person. I also realized that I am a fighter by true nature not a quitter. I have been around people who give up at the first sign of trouble or just because something was not going their way. I have also been around people who did not know when to stop (I stayed in with them) but I also learned that these people can be just as bad sometimes. The ones that are in my life now have taught me when to keep going and when to stop and just let it go.

When I was threatened I took it as far as was needed then I let it go because I realized what was more important for my life. The difference between being brave and being daft is not letting go when your supposed to, all that needs to be done is proving you will stand up for yourself but it does not have to get out of hand. If they had any honour inside of them then we could have settled it respectfully but when you feel the need to be disrespectful then you know that they have no honour. See I honour my mum, dad and family because I respect them tremendously and would never do anything to break that respect. Putting myself in a situation that may cause my life to end is showing my loved ones total disrespect for their feelings.

I wanted a real family and I have one but it does not stop there, I have to put into the soup bowl as well. My family feeds me through love and support and if I do not give back then I would have caused my own family to starve. The more they give to me the more I am able to do something with my life and give back to them. Do I want to give back to them out of obligation? No. I want to give back out of inspiration.

When you are given a chance to change direction with your life, why would you want to take it down the same destructive path? If you feel the need to cry and you still hold it in what do you think is going to happen? If you feel the need to stand up and you back down the same rules apply. School does not end just because you left the classroom. You have to learn from your mistakes and from those around you if you want to get anywhere in life. I know that there are some people who will never own up to their mistakes and that is their problem not yours.

The thing to keep in mind is that not only do you need to learn to stand up for yourself but you need to learn to stand taller when you make a mistake. The reason being is that they will always come after you harder when you screw up so if your head is held high before they get there it will take a great deal of wind out of their sails. The easiest thing in the world to do is laugh and point at someone who has fallen. The hardest thing to do is be the person who worked so hard and now has to justify being human.

I use to hear, "Did you hear what so and so did?" I no longer hear it any more because my reply is always the same, "This is your business because?" You should be just as proud of your mistakes as you are your accomplishments because you need both in order to achieve anything? The ones who do not make any mistakes are usually not doing anything at all except for waiting in the shadows to take your credit or to point the finger. People make it easy to go after someone who has gone the distance to make something out of themselves instead of the ones who have made life harder on the rest of us. I was told when I was little one time that you cannot change the world until you change yourself. I do not like being around people who gossip because I know that I am not safe from it when I leave. I have come to learn that there are just certain people I am not going to like, and that is o.k. If they do not want to listen to reason I am free to leave and that is just what I do.

There is a difference between talking badly about someone and trying to get answers to solve your dilemma. I have matured enough to know when someone is gossiping and when someone needs an answer. People will always expose their true nature around people they think are not a threat. You have to listen for key phrases that can be altered. "I did this to," is one that should be taken as a dead give away to stay clear from at all cost. I even knew someone who used their schooling to manipulate everyone they came across because people's lives were a game to them. The destruction did not matter nor did the aftermath, all they cared about was that they got to do it and that they got away with it, for now.

There are people in the world that will go out of their way to go after you simply because you like yourself and they do not. All you have to do is stop being likeable and they will change their minds about you. What do you get out of it, being less than who you are to fit in with people who do not care about themselves much less you. For some people that is the only reason they need to dislike you, the fact that you like yourself. The question you need to ask yourself is why you want to be a part of a group that will go out of its way to make you feel like you are less? Do you not think that you deserve better for yourself and those you love? If you do not then figure what is stopping you and fix it.

I figured out that mine was not the abuse but what was said that I needed to fix. I also learned that I can go toe to toe with someone no matter what their size but that if my feelings got hurt during the scrap I went down. I learned to solve this problem by not allowing anyone I do not trust to get close enough to know how my feelings work. I no longer allow my enemies and friends close to me because I grew tired of not only them hurting me but keeping me away from the ones I love. Anyone can help guide you along the way but you are the one that needs to put a stop to it and change the way you think and with it the way you feel.

Yes, I have a warm and loving family now but that does not mean they are there to use or dump on. When you are a part of something that is bigger then you, you have to do your part so that the family stays strong. I have been around people that use their mum and family for every little thing. They put such a hurt on the family that nobody says a word, they once again just deal with it. When do you draw the line, just right before they break you or right after? I mean I think that my mum is a number of wonderful things but in reality she is human and can only do and take so much. I do not want to make her life harder or put her in any misery and I cannot understand the kids that do that to their parents when they were given good ones from the start?

When you do not have something you do not appreciate someone else being wasteful of a great source. The thing is though the ones that have done without are grateful for just a little something and the ones who have never missed out never realize what they have even after its gone. I think that if you cut ties and force them to pick themselves up they will because they have no choice. How are they ever going to learn how to walk out in the real world if they do not learn how to pick themselves up? Some of the toughest and smartest kids come from either broken homes or no home because they learned how to survive through their own private war. No matter what life throws their way they fight to get through it. Some kids have had it so good that when a simple problem arises they fall to pieces over what turns out to be nothing. They have never had to face consequences; much less a crises, and to make it worse they do not know how to listen to reason. If you ever listen to people they all have the same complaint but it's what you do not hear, how they took care of it.

You also hear people say, "My first thought is that I was going to die," why;

it's your life why would you not want to fight for it. I may have gotten low enough in the past to want to end it all but when I needed that fight inside of me it was there. You have to not only have the will to live but you have to know where to find it when you need it the most. When something happens tell yourself, "I need to find a way out of this," and do it, after all, the easiest thing in the world to do is give up. Remember that just because a war is not published does not mean there is not a personal one being fought. Learn how to win instead of remembering how to give up.

Find the people who make you feel stronger and figure out how to disregard the rest. Life can be an incredible journey through not only your thoughts but your heart and eyes as well. We have it in us to let go of whatever is hurting us, the problem is having the courage to see it through. The unknown seems terrifying instead of a chance to grow into something new. We are taught to believe that the life we are born into is the life that we have to lead and there are many that know this is a lie. All it takes is for someone to believe in us and allow it to sink in so that we may come to believe in ourselves. We have all gone down a hard road but not all of us want off if you can believe that. Some think that if they stay they can change the person who is truly cruel.

The saying that there is good in everyone if you just dig hard enough is not true. There are some people who are nasty to the core and always will be but yet they are the ones who never get discredited. The ones who were never trying to hurt anyone are hunted down like animals because all you have to do is point the finger and everyone will turn and look. The problem is because kids blend into adults or grownups and have been told so much we cannot figure out if we are good or bad kids any more. There are no defined examples anymore and very few that want to set any. All I had been around were villagers and had I not have found the courage to go at it alone then I would have never known what a good family looked like or how to be a part of one.

They have hard times but it is the way they go through it that makes all the difference in the world. They open up their minds and hearts when needed and express through love not fear. You may not come from a strong family but that does not mean that there is not one out there for you. We all want to be loved and wanted and just because we did not start out that way does not mean that all is lost. We cross different paths each and every day and if we cannot find what we are looking for today there is always the hope of tomorrow. (Look how long it has taken me, some of that is due to being stubborn.)

To be honest I gave up completely as far as being a part of a family and kept myself busy so I would not notice. The thing is that just because you act like something is not bothering you does not make it any less painful, nor does it mean it does not show. Did it hurt growing up the way some of us have, yes, and I know that what does not kill you makes you stronger but even strong people need to find comfort in order to move on. We have to start learning how to reach out to ourselves in order to learn how to reach others. When I finally got through to myself I learned why I could just walk away from them and fought so hard to stay with my Family. I never cared about them in the first place, it was not taught so I never learned it.

The hardest thing to get over or recover from is feelings. I told my mate who has the son that before he found out that his egg donor was like she was he had feelings for her. The hardest thing to recover from, is knowing that the one you came out of has no feelings for you. People think that just because you get older you outgrow certain things like feelings and you do not. You can bury them all you like but sooner or later they do expose themselves.

They can even hide and spill out in other forms but they are there waiting to be released. His son has a big heart and you know that has to break it when he finds out late in life what her true nature is and to just stop feeling. It is bad enough when you find out a friend or mate has betrayed you but for it to be one of your own or worse the one you came through. She holds onto him through controlled fear and because she hides behind that word, she has a free ticket to torment him. He is not the one that has a hold of her she has a hold of him from behind. A child is supposed to be able to confide in their parents and vice versa but when that link is broken for any reason the family will always suffer. The reason being is that if there is no form of family, there will never be any boundaries much less guidelines. How could there be when it is the family members crossing the line? When you hurt one of your own and you show no remorse then they should not have to put up with you in their life for whatever reason.

Society rules are that you have to live life like they always have since time began but how can we do that and develop into better human beings if we do not find the need to change? The wanting to give your kids a better life should be at the heart of things not what you can put in their hands. I have seen more spoiled brats coming from poor homes then wealthy ones. Why because the parents do not want to enforce the law and say no. Big deal the kid throws a fit, what did it end up costing you? Not a dime, what did it cost them, some lung power. Why should you feel guilty because you cannot afford something or be made to feel guilty just so that you will buy something that they will not appreciate?

Guilt is a wonderful thing because you cannot see it but people have stumbled into the fact that it can be used. The odd thing is it can also be instilled to such a degree that you do not even notice that its there. His son stays out of the guilt being placed on him and that is being used to control him. The Lady who came in left because she had nothing to feel guilty about and therefore could not be controlled by her offspring. I left because I would not be controlled but carried the guilt of leaving the few I loved behind. People have a tendency to make you feel guilty for having survived going through hell and we as individuals have to stop allowing them to make us feel bad.

You should not feel guilty if you want to better yourself after all what do you think this life is for? People all want to improve the world but they loose sight that the world is made up of individual people who have all gone through life differently. Their mind is just that and all you can really do is change yourself so that you can be an example to someone near. You have heard the expression that it is easier to give advice than to follow it, the reason being is that in order to follow your own advice you would have to get up off your bum. Most people have no problem in the world telling others how to run their life because secretly theirs is falling apart and they do not want anyone to know.

People, when are we going to learn that we are all human no matter how super we can be at times? We all have our limits but we need to learn when to say enough is enough in all aspects of our lives, enough with feeling bad, enough with being made to feel lower, enough with people posing as loved ones hurting us from the inside. You have to figure out if the guilt is truly yours or belongs to someone else. The kid from that talk show is holding onto guilt that does not belong to her, it's not her fault that she was born. The sad part is her egg donor never allows her to forget the feeling of being a mistake.

I was told, "You need me, and I do not need you." The funny thing was I did not need them and that is how they broke their own tie. I was always better off without them; they were just hoping that guilt would be enough to hold me in my place. When I looked at the lady on TV all I could see was this little kid being made fun of by her egg donor and having to defend herself from someone who has grown into this huge monster? Have we stopped teaching compassion for others because none was shown to us? To me that would be all the more reason to want to give it to someone who needs it now because we know that is what we needed.

When kids go through something traumatic then they need to talk until they feel better otherwise they grow older and have less people to talk to who are even less understanding. I noticed that when some people want you to open up to them all they are after is the story behind the pain; they have no intention of helping you find relief.

Some things are going to be beyond your control for a while but that does not mean that you cannot plan ahead. Why do you have to stay with someone because everyone else does? "I just do not see how you can just cut ties with someone, have you no heart?" Does it not sink in that I have heart and that I am tired of it being used as someone's toilet paper? The ones who have never been down that road miss the big picture because they refuse to open their eyes, afraid someone might yell boo I guess. I have told kids who have a family of their own to cut ties and they all argue the same thing, "I cannot, they gave birth to me." You can tell the ones who only want to gripe about their life because they will argue with you the whole time you are giving them another way to fix their problem.

The true definition of insanity is repeating the same thing over and over again expecting different results. If you do not change anything about your habits then how in the world do you expect anything to change outside of them? You tried holding onto the ones that hurt you hoping they will see for themselves how bad they are getting to you and the truth is they do. They feed off of your hurt and they do not want to loose their source. The truth of the matter is they need you to do little improvements so they will constantly have something to needle you about. You cannot needle them because truth is they do not do anything but get onto you and ride your coat tails. What are you going to do tell them to improve on the way they jump you?

The logical thing to do is stop what you have been doing and see if something else will not work. You have been going through drastic measures to hold yourself together, why not go through drastic measures to straighten everything out? You have to and you cannot expect anyone else to be on board with you until after it is all said and done. It was a drastic move to cut ties with all that you have known or have been told and to venture out past normal means but how many of us are the better for it? Yes it is unknown and scary at first but do not turn that into fear. Being scared of something is not a bad thing people, it just means that you are unsure and what is wrong with that? Fear in itself is nothing more than a smoke screen made to appear bigger than what it really is so learn to look beyond that. Also the thing to keep in mind is that when you become scared, nervous or just plain unsure that is just your instincts trying to tell you that now is the time to focus and most of all be strong.

Learn that there are people out there who will love you just as you are and will help you to grow into who you what to be. You do not have to stay with individuals who break you every time that you start to feel good about yourself. If we all can learn how to walk by ourselves then surly we can remember how we did it, alone. I love the old way of thinking that if it is not good for the family then it needs to be cut loose. What happened to that style of family? Did modern technology replace everything including how we think?

There are very few families that are close any more and if you really look at the ones in the group then no wonder. You should want a pure blood family and the generation after that should learn how to clean it out even more. Love is the tie that can either break a family or make a family depending on how it is used. If there is no love then everything becomes fragile and bitter where only resentment can grow. Love that is used to heal wounds no matter how wide or deep will learn to thrive no matter what the outside conditions bring. Keep in mind that there is a difference between birth and blood family. Anyone can come from a birth family but blood family stays tight, also birth family will trade you for money because to them money is thicker then blood.

Families that love give you time, people who act like they love you will give you a time limit to do it their way. See, when I ask my family for help I will also allow them to adjust me along the way. If I ask someone for help and they tell me that I am smart enough to learn it on my own then no one is allowed to adjust me because I gave them a chance to be a part of it from the beginning. I will always ask for help when I need it but if they do not want to help then I see no reason to allow them to criticize me in any way. I am the type who likes it as I go not all at once.

I have never been one to tell people how to live their own life but I will always be there if someone needs me to listen to them, at the same time I do not appreciate people putting their two cents worth in when I did not ask them for it. There is a huge difference between advice and critiquing, one is asked for the other is given by force. The funny thing is that people who go around critiquing people's lives do not like it when someone does it to them. They tell you to stop because it hurts their feelings, well what do you think that it does to the ones they do it to? Some people feel that they can do unto others but you had better not do the same thing to them, what a load.

If you do it onto them I can guarantee that they will stop because they are getting a taste for how it feels. You have to do it more then once because you know they have. If they truly repent for being a whole ass you will know because they truly do feel bad, they just did not know any better. More then likely though you will have the snot nose adults that tell you they learned their lesson and as soon as your back is turned then they are at it again. I have had people tell me to stay out of it because it was not my business or my fight. I reply, "When you go after someone who cannot or will not defend themselves for what ever reason then that makes it my fight because I like a good fight. To me a good fight is two people wanting to go after it not just one picking on the weaker ones because no one wants to stop you." Known truth I always have liked knocking bullies on their bum but now thanks to my mum I have learned how to go after people using words instead of my fists or head. (I am one who always liked to head butt first.) That is funny; I was always using my head just not the way she had intended for me to! All I can say for myself is, "I am still learning but I am getting it too!"

The thing I love most about some of the people I have learned from is that they were never pompous in their teaching because they knew I would never be arrogant when I finally caught on. Any time I have ever learned something and I show someone else or they ask me about it I always tell them who taught me. I like giving credit where credit is due because without these people I would have never gotten this far in life. I would have held onto the grudge and hate instead of learning to do other things with my mind like explore or to think. Remember it really is hard to think straight when all you can see is red.

I remember being taught that you could be anything that you wanted to be so due to my lack of height I picked a giraffe. Imagine the look on my face when I was informed that I could not be that, "But you just said that I could be anything I wanted to be and well, I want to be a giraffe when I grow up." That is when the statement: "Within reason," was soon instilled in me. O.K. let us compromise, "I will be anything I want without being unreasonable there!" I became a little of everything and the ones I liked more I went back to. All the other kids around me picked one thing and some even stuck with it but not myself. I never wanted to be one thing and I have learned throughout life that I am not. To me you limit yourself when you go around being taught that all you can ever be is just one simple thing and nothing more.

I can be funny, smart, shy, a pain on my good days in the bum on my worst I reach for the neck. I can be goofy, daft or whatever I want to be. I have met people that all they were is what they did for a living and nothing outside of that because they had a reputation to uphold or they had standing. Prestige if not handled correctly can end up costing you your very soul and anything else you hold dear. I am all for self-esteem and self-worth so long as you are using it to better yourself and not make someone feel like they should live under your boot.

I have been to a lot of different places in my life and to my surprise people are really the same wherever you go, (they just talk differently.) They all have the same basic needs and struggles, the same villagers and the same hardships. The only difference that ever showed is in the places where they had very little, they seemed to be closer. Every day was a struggle and it never showed because they had each other. They never pined over what they did not have but took care of what they did have and never looked back. Some people will never know that luxury because they are to busy reminding others of what they are not. I learned that I have never looked down at anyone until now and that is because they deserve to be looked down on. I am not talking about sinners just evil people who want to choke the life out of everyone and everything that crosses their path.

I have been around people that the first thing they do is apologize for what they have as well as for what they do not and I always point out to them that as long as it was not ill-gotten gain then no worries. Remember: I once griped about not having any shoes until I met a man who had no feet? I told my teacher, "Well maybe if I had some shoes I could go and help him find his feet." I was never quite sure what I meant by that but my actions were smarter than my brain sometimes.

I have always tried to be grateful for the little things in life and try to show my gratitude by adding onto and giving back. I learned through watching other people what I did and did not want to be in life. I did not want to be a snot-nosed, wet behind the ears, young whipper-snapper and at the time I only had this type around me. Now it is easy to say that I will not be like this or that but there does come a time when you have to change that for something. I soon learned to admire what little there was and just add it all together. This would also help in my being whatever I wanted to be because I really do not believe that you should limit yourself to only one thing.

I know that people want to try and convince you that you should stick to one thing and do it well. The thing with that is look at all the possibilities that you leave behind or that leaves you behind, not only that the more you learn the more you will notice just how incredible all knowledge blends in with one another. You could learn something way over here and years later tie it in with something way over there. The only real limit you have besides the human race is yourself, learn to challenge yourself in ways you never dreamed possible then you will become unstoppable.

If you give up and become like them you will notice that you will need to find someone to feed off of and to me the worst thing in the world to be is a bottom feeder. The sad thing about life is that you can be easily tempted to the other side after all it is easier to be a jerk to everyone that you meet instead of just to the ones that deserve it. Bottom feeders designed life so that it gives them a free ride because they know they're too lazy to be a salamander and go against the tide.

There is a saying in Euripides that says: The wisest follow their own direction. How many of us started out on the wise path and then somehow along the road were bullied someway into becoming just like everyone else? Oh, you know my hand went up more then once but the thing is I no longer want to raise my hand on that one any more. I know that we have all been taught in some form or fashion that to be singled out is wrong and will make you feel like you are being put on display. How many of us believed this while watching a single individual receive a trophy once again? What kind of logic can come from being told two different rules or just when they can apply? What happened to being in a class by yourself and learning how to break the mould? What has happened to us as individuals? Have we become so comfortable in a group that we are willing to give up our unique identity and become whatever the group wants? What happens if you are not told the true identity of the group until after it is too late? Now what are you going to do, find another group so that you can learn the same hard lesson as before?

I would rather be wrong on my own then to be highly mistaken in a large group. We have no more leaders to speak of and we sure as hell will not have any if we do not start learning how to produce them starting with ourselves. There are people who are natural born leaders with the highest of instincts and these are usually the ones who are made to stay at the bottom of the rung. I know, if they are natural born leaders how do they manage to stay at the bottom. Elementary, no one is willing to back them up when they walk through the firing line. How many of you have ever been in this situation, "We have banded together and want some changes." They intimidate the rest by just looking at them and reply, "Do all of you feel this way?" Everyone either looks around or at their shoes; "No, no they did this alone," the ones who are still standing are then threatened with their jobs.

More often then not people in power who abuse it are no more then inflated bullies who can be taken down more than one peg at a time. Like I told my mate's son when he was faced with an adult bully who was hurting his mum, "All you have to do is start knocking holes in their defense, they do not have to be very big but you have to start doing it. Once you start do not let up and they will fall." Anybody else or I should say any adult would have cowered, argued and gave a million reasons why it could not be done. I am so proud of him for not only wanting to protect his mum like that but for being brave and finding the courage to go in alone. He knew he had all of us to protect him but we were nowhere near him in a sense, but in his mind he knew we were all there.

I have seen people in military power panic over less of a threat and completely freak out but this little guy kept his head through the whole thing. You have to realize that kids know when something is wrong because they get a feeling and listen to it. The hardest thing about being a kid is getting adults to listen to you because the grownups are nowhere to be found. Adults dismiss everything because it would take effort to do anything else. I have had more then one kid come up to me and say, "If I tell you something, you would believe me?"

"Yes I would." They have such a hard time because they know something is wrong and have no idea of how to fix it. They deal with some pretty big issues and if you would ever stop to listen and hear them they do give things a tremendous amount of thought to what life has surrounded them with. They try to figure out how to help bigger people because the bigger people just do not have the time to deal with it right now. Talk about an unselfish act of kindness and what do they get for all their troubles, half the time they get yelled at. The other half of the time they are being told that they are to young to understand what is going on when the truth of the matter is the person explaining it is the one without a clue.

When a "normal" kid starts acting out instead of yelling and carrying on why not sit down and listen to them. This does not mean to drill them with questions because all you do is confuse an already confusing situation. You would really be surprised at not only what is on their mind but just how deep their concern for a situation taking place really is. Start giving them some credit now and you will not have to wait for a piece of plastic to come through the mail for them to feel worth something. You can tell when something is weighing heavily on a little ones mind but the thing is you need to let them talk and not stop them at every single thing. I had a kid tell me that every time she tried to talk with her dad she would just start to get something out and he would hear just enough to fly into a rampage. She goes on to say that had he have waited and heard the whole thing he would have realized that he was no where near the topic she was trying to talk with him about.

The funny thing is he flew off the handle again when he found out that she had talked to me about her problems. I was trying to explain when I found myself in the same situation she was talking about but I did something she would not. I told him where he could go and then proceeded to treat him like he did his daughter. Believe it or not it was not until then that he saw both sides. He wanted to be there for her but instead of listening all he ever did was react to what was being said. You would think that teaching someone a lesson would entail that you would have learned it at some point too but no that is not always the case especially with me.

I will admit that I have better patience listening to kids than adults in crises because you know which one wants to find a solution and which one will not listen to a word you say. I have told adults, "Have you tried it this way," and give them what ever solution that fits their needs and all they want to say is, "No, no that will never work. You are just not listening to what I am telling you." Later on you either find out that everyone has told them the same thing or they followed your advice, it worked and instead of being thankful they try and pull a fast one. "I was already going to do that anyway so you had nothing to do with it." These people are wind bags who later turn into tit bags and no they will never change. They are also the ones who can never think of anything but after the solution is presented to them now have thought of everything. These are also the type of people who will hire someone for a job and stand there throwing tit fit after tit fit because they do not know how to do it and you are not doing it their way. All I can say is that if you are one of these people either let them do the job you paid them to do or better yet do it your damn self and quit paying people just to ride them. (These people should have learned how to play with themselves so that they would have learned how to please themselves and not rely on others!)

Adults are so busy keeping up with the Joneses and trying to put their blame on others that they do not see the big picture and try hard as hell to convince kids that they do not see it either. Kids know in their heart that it all has to do with good and evil, what they do not know and need to be shown is which one is which, kind of hard when the ones raising them do not know what to look for either. I had a parent yank their kid up and holler, "What have I told you about talking to strangers," and the kid so sweetly replied, "But there is no one stranger than her!" I could not stop laughing because they were on two different pages and you could tell that from their facial expressions. The kid knew I was not a danger to them and I would always show them cool stuff to do and nothing that would get them into trouble.

The bad thing is the parent thought that everything was a danger and missed the big one right in her own family. The reason the little one was hanging out at my place was she did not like staying alone with her uncle and for good reason. To make things worse her kid came straight out and told her this and was informed that she had her facts mixed up and her brother would not do anything like that. You know it is one thing to dismiss someone else's kid but to do that to your own because you do not want to face something? What about what that kid has to face knowing they did tell someone they thought they could trust. When they informed me what was going on the first thing I told them was not to be scared nor worried and to tell me everything that was said to them (that way I could counter it before it had a chance to sink in and effect them.) Kids have to be rehabilitated otherwise they stay victims of not only sexual predators but they stay in the predators main stream network.

I turned it into a game so it would be less traumatic on her and during our talk she asked me why I believe her when nobody else would and I answered her honestly, "Because I was not believed either. I was told that I had better be grateful that I had a roof over my head because I could always be put out on the street." (The bad thing was they knew I wanted to live out on the street so that I could be away from them.) She asked me what I did and I told her, "That was the moment I learned to hate and that is something that I do not want you to feel so you and I are going to fix this together."

I told her how I went about things and what I did wrong and known truth she came up with some ideas that rocked, I wish she was a grownup when I was a kid! We carried our plan of action out, made four copies of the proof and gave one to her then parent. I say then because when I saw the look in her face I knew from My own experience her egg donor knew all along and not only did nothing about it but put her kid in that situation every chance she got. She yanked her kid from me because she knew I posed a threat only it was not a sinister one and she could feel it. I was not the first person her kid told this to, I was just the first one who would not only listen but helped make a plan of action come to life. Kids are all for whatever help they can receive but that is the thing, nobody wants to really help them. Throwing money to some organization to clear your conscience is not solving the problem because you do not want to actually get involved. Do you for one unselfish moment think that a kid or baby wants to be the one involved?

We teach them as babies that if they reach out they are going to get their hand smacked and told "no" so what the hell are they suppose to think or even do for that matter? "Oh it just breaks my heart to think of someone doing that to an innocent child," and that is all the effort they are going to put forth. Well they are not innocent any more now are they and the longer you close your eyes to this the more their innocence is being raped from their soul. The worst are the ones who get confided in by the child and instead of being on the phone to authorities they are on the phone gossiping about the matter and now everybody whispers while that child is forced to keep silent while silently screaming in their own version of hell. Yes, throwing money to an organization that claims to benefit from this cause therefore making it someone else's problem will make it all freaking better. The bigger question is why would you want to give money to a group that benefits from this kind of evil anyway? The child should be the only one to benefit and money is not going to make the memory go away.

You know as often as I have worked with kids and learned that they have a better mentality than adults I found that they are easier to rehabilitate and get over the worst things imaginable with the greatest of ease. All you have to do is logically hear how they are hurting and realistically help them to solve the problem. I remember hearing a song about hell when I was little and it being for children, and if you stop to think about it, it is because, adults cannot not handle the heat. Adults will belly ache and throw tit fits over the daftest things and fall apart when the wind changes direction, they should take a page from their kids' books before they rip it out. Oddly enough they are always the ones in the kitchen though barking out orders that they themselves would not follow. I have been all the way through more then one kind of hell and I learned something cool. I do not have anywhere near the ill contempt for the people in the world as some adults who have not been through a forth of what a lot of us have been through.

I think that saying, "What does not kill you makes you stronger," has a hidden deeper meaning that has just been uncovered. If we go through this and come out stronger for it then what does that say about the people who stand on the outside of hell? They convince others that they are the weaker ones but when the truth is finally exposed look who it turned out to be all along! The ones who have been through hell and have come back brought something with them that is worth more than gold. They brought wisdom, understanding and more importantly courage that it can be done. No wonder the weaker ones want us to hand everything to them on a silver platter, they know they cannot come out on the other side because they give up before they enter the door. They need us to go the distance for them and to tell them what all we have been through so that when they tell the story they can replace us with themselves.

I may have a tough life but it amazes me how many people find my life to be most interesting. Why, because people like me should have ended it a long time ago, after all, they do try and convince us that there is nothing in life worth living for. In a strange way they are correct, life lives itself and does not need or want us to live it for them; that is respectable. However the side that cannot be seen is the one that I am after and the ones like me live for. Finding things in life worth fighting for and learning that sometimes it may be ourselves.

There are some of us who have a built in fight or flight response and that is what gets us through to the other side. There are some who spend their time reading or watching someone else's life while theirs just watches them and wonders why they will not be a part of their own. There are also ones who give up at the slightest breeze and because they can tell it is going to be hard they do not want to do it. There are no rewards without efforts and seeing it through to the end. The reward to me is feeling good about yourself and knowing that you can hold your head up high because you have gone the distance. (It does not matter how long it took you to finish, just that you went past the finish line.) Why would you not want to feel good about that or let someone who sat on the side line take that away from you?

They want what you feel because they see how good it looks on you. Have you ever noticed that when you feel on top of the world everybody wants to be around you and a part of what you have? They see in your eyes that you have something great and they look all around you to see what you have but they miss what is really there. The glow that you feel has nothing to do with your surroundings because that has not changed, it comes from the inside. The thing to keep in mind is that if you give every thing that you are to everyone that wants a part of you they will not give it back and you could very well find yourself torn to pieces. I learned the hard way to stop letting people take whatever they wanted from me because all they were doing was making me less then what I earned the right to be. They wanted to take away my courage and turn me into a coward like one of them. They wanted to take away my fight so that I would not have the flight ability and would have to stay and put up with them. They wanted to take away my understanding of the situation at hand so that I could stay easily confused and had no choice but to believe what they told me was for my own good. They wanted to take away my dignity so that all I would feel is ashamed of what I had been through.

They wanted it all and I allowed them to take it because I thought that they needed it more but I learned that without all of what I am I am only half of what I could be. Everything that they took from me made me who I am so I learned how to get it all back. After all since I had already been through everything all I had to do was remember what I earned from it and re-instill it. I also learned that since these things are what everyone was after I need to protect them even more. I also learned that I am only half my size without them. (It is kind of difficult to hold your head up without having the courage to do so and the dignity to back it up.)

We do not have to feel ashamed because we learned from bad people. I would rather learn from bad people than be one of them! I learned that evil or bad people take without replacing and good people replace without taking. Good people enjoy being around someone who feels great about themselves because they know they earn the right to feel like that. Bad people dislike being around anyone who feels good because they also know they earned it and do not like the fact that you feel better then they do. They also do not like learning anything new especially from someone younger than them. This makes sense since they will not pass anything on nothing will get passed onto them.

The thing about trials and tribulations is that its character building and that is why people try to assassinate someone else's character because they know it took time to build it. See it is not enough that they went through hell to earn it now they have to be punished and be put through hell to inform the world how they acquired it. They see something that is greater than them even by a degree and instead of appreciating it for what it is at that moment they become threatened and begin to break it down. They only feel the need to destroy it so that all that is left is them feeling good about taking something down that they felt was more than them. Some of the greatest wonderments in life come in a complex state and should remain that way because they earned it over time. Mystery leads to wonderment and if we take all the mystery out of life then there is nothing left to wonder about. You would have no choice but for your mind to come to a complete stand still which makes your life follow suite. Life does not pass you by it just withers and waits for the silver cord to be cut so that it can come back again, this time to hopefully someone that will live life to the fullest. You do not have to jump from anything or face death on a daily basis for you to feel alive. Learning how to be completely yourself makes life worth living because you find out your own capabilities by exploring the great unknown, life and your part in it.

I may go through what seems like constant hell but look at what I get to keep when I make it to the exit, thicker skin, a broader mind and a smaller opening to my heart which is my blood line to life. I actually feel sympathetic for the people who refuse to be tried and tested because they never approach the starting line. "No, no someone might belittle me and if you go ahead that is what I will do to you." Believe it or not that is the one time they do keep their word and actually build upon it! I have seen parents do it to their kids thinking that they are building strong power houses but all they are doing is building hollow shells of what could have been a human being.

Words of encouragement are the keys to crossing not only the finish line but staying and encouraging the one behind you that they are almost there too. They do not have to cross the same way you do in order to receive help from you. I think that the more different people's lives are the more we can learn and have to pass on to others. We as people have become hoarders when there is greater reward in sharing. Have you ever noticed that the better you feel the more you can accomplish? You do not have to give of yourself or give up any of yourself but give of your talents, your wisdom and understanding. Give from your hands but let it come from your heart so that no string no matter the size can attach itself to it. Giving from hand to hand will eventually choke the life out of you due to the enormous amount of string used to bait you in, its an entanglement that you are not meant to get out of.

The same rule applies to someone you are learning from, if they teach from the heart their hand will reward you with a pat on the back and "I am so proud of you, I knew you could do it." If they teach from the hand the other one will smack you and say, "So you think because you got it that you're better than me now." These people do not want you to improve in any way because in their mind that makes you better than them and they need to be the centre of attention even when there is nothing to see. They become jealous over not only your strengths but oddly enough over your weakness because they know they amount to something too.

We have inside ourselves at least five levels of natural strength and they can all be powerful alone but when combined they become one. Look at nature, you have wind, water, earth and fire and since we are part of nature it only makes sense that its in our nature to have this as well. "That put the fire back into them, and it took the wind right out of their sails, they're down to earth and you're in hot water now." If we learn to explore all of these elements inside of us and learn how to enhance them imagine what the combined powers would have on our spirit. The wisdom our souls could pass into and through life. The reason advice is harder to follow is it is uncharted territory and wisdom is based upon more then one persons experiences.

I go to my mum when I need wisdom and I will ask my mates for advice, then I can always go back to my mum and ask her for wisdom about the advice! The funny thing is, there is no wisdom to be found in criticism and wise people do not criticize because they know you cannot learn from it. You always hear, "A wise person once told me." Who do you think writes fortune cookies and who wants criticism at the end of a good meal? One gives you something to think about, the other gives you something to work on. Did you ever wonder why fortune cookies come with your meal as a family? It used to be the place where wisdom was passed on and listened to, why because when youngsters are feeding their body you can feed their mind. The dinner table is the best place because since they cannot talk with their mouth full they have no choice but to listen to everything before they ask questions. Nowadays it is hard to have family talks when nobody eats at the table any more.

I know, some people wait until Thanksgiving to come together as a family but look at how they act at the dinner table. They act like arch enemies forced to break bread and be giving when they are not even thankful. Since they never earned wisdom to pass on they however did learn how to pass down criticism like it's a family recipe. To them it may very well be a way to keep the lid on the box and to keep you from ever thinking that there is an outside to it. You would think that people would want their loved ones to feel good about themselves so that everyone's life improves but not everyone looks at it like that.

I guess that is one of the great things I love about my family, when we get down someone is there to comfort us until we can pull ourselves together and nothing is ours, it belongs to us. We learn how to turn our greatest weakness into someone else's greatest strength and some how down the line it gets returned. See if you let society do your thinking for you Lord knows what you will get in return or what you could be missing out on, if your family communicates thoughts you know your return will come in the form of improvements. There is not a single member of my family who has ever tore me down,(and they had every opportunity to do so but never took it,) they accepted me from the start and helped me when I wanted to make improvements. Out of everything that I have come to them with the only thing they make me hold onto is being the far from normal one in the family. I think that with everything they have helped me with that is a pretty reasonable request.

The thing that I have noticed about my family is that they do not expect anything, there are no expectations put on us except to be a good kid, the rest is up to us. The thing with setting bars is that if someone else sets them for you more then likely you are going to knock yourself out with it because you do not know where they placed it. They can also move it down just right before you get there so that you do end up flat on your backside and them standing over you looking down.

I have actually had people do that to me, tell me that I can make it and when I believe that I can they pull the rug right out from underneath me and then try to beat me with it. The thing to keep in mind is when they go to rolling up that rug as long as you're not in it you can always duck and leave. This is where wisdom and courage meet with you. Wisdom will give you the courage to see it through to the end; courage will also give you the wisdom to see that something will never come to an end so just leave well enough alone and learn that you are brave enough to walk away. Being brave is not always about the charge, sometimes there is more wisdom to be found in the knowing when to retreat.

I learned that I was brave enough to stand my ground when my life became threatened but not nearly as daft as they would have liked me to be so that I would have ended it. Today may be a good day to die but I do not feel like dying today so I think I will fight to go on living. I may lie down at times but it is not to die, it's so that I can gather my thoughts up to think about them and not have to worry about someone sneaking up on me from behind. The earth has my back covered and you could not ask for greater protection. It goes back to the elements inside of us that we are learning to enhance. All of them can be used to destroy or build depending on who they are inside of. Fire can be used to warm a family, to give them light in darkness and can be used to gather loved ones around when the world threatens them with the outside cold. Fire can also be used against someone who threatens to bring harm to the family, you can see the flame burning inside their eyes to stand down and stay clear. The enemy can also use your own fire against you causing you to burn the ones you love with the same fire meant to keep them close.

Water can come in many forms but tears come to mind first. Crying a river of tears is not always a bad thing because they can come from laughter not always from pain. I also learned that if I had not cried the river of tears from pain I would have never flowed into the other side where my tears now come strictly from heart felt laughter because my family is nuts. Water can cleanse or drown depending on how you want your tears to flow. If you drink water you can laugh so hard that you pee yourself or you can pee yourself out of fear or you can just feel like you have been peed on. Water can make things grow or if held in to long can one day burst and destroy everything in its path.

Earth is being solid as a rock while moulding with your family. I get a kick sometimes thinking of my family like an active volcano, we are a huge mountain with hot molten liquid earth bubbling inside and then when we erupt we pour down the mountain together. Instead of being less because we slid down the mountain we actually made it harder and therefore stronger to the outside elements. Now please do not think that the only time you can erupt is when you are hot headed because you can also erupt out of excitement, encouragement and even brain storms. My brainstorm is that I am a mole hill that finally gets to be part of a grand mountain and I love the view because I am with all of them.

If you put everything together you have the courage to know when to fire up, the bravery to throw water on a set fire, the wisdom when to let things cool down and blow over and the strength to move other mountains out of your path to success without completely destroying them. There are times when you will be forced to completely destroy someone because that is the only proof they will accept that they have built their foundation strictly on a fault line and nothing more. They find faults with everything you do and they will always cross that line. When this occurs and you find the need to stay and help them to pick up the pieces you had better pay attention to see if they are helping because if they are not then while you are building for them they are knocking yours down for their own supplies. More than likely, if they are that lazy they will just take over your spot of king of the mountain and lie to everyone and say that you surrendered it to them.

If someone forces me to completely go after them I am not one to look back and see if they need help rebuilding. The way I see it is maybe they will learn not to knock someone down just because they are different either in someway or in everyway. I also do not look back because they have a way of making you feel guilty for something that they brought on themselves. The way I see it is maybe if they were humble they would not have become so inflated and maybe if they were not so inflated they would not have taken such a hard tumble to learn how to be humble. Ha Ha.

I try to stay humble because I have learned that it is easier to fall on your bum and recover then falling from such egotistical heights. Besides that my mum will not allow me to get on a high horse, she only allows me get on a pony; (it's a safety thing.) I used to get on high horses all the time before my mum because I never saw the danger in it. Did you know that you can rear up, loose control and trample on innocent people just because something spooked the horse you rode in on or the one that rode you in? Good thing my family knows how to tame wild horses without breaking their spirits or their backs. I also love the fact that they corralled me so I would learn what it is like to feel secure when I am surrounded.

I came to my mum with wisdom that I had heard but never earned because I never had role models that applied anything and they stayed clear from everything that could be considered knowledge. I was missing a generation link in my chain and my family supplied it. I had a great deal of answers to life's questions but could not figure out when to apply it. I learned all about life listening to my elders, I learned how to live life staying a kid at heart and now thanks to the dedication of my family I am learning how to grow through all that I have been taught and appreciate what I have learned through others.

When you screw with the generations you screw with the cycle of all of life and not just your own. When you do not allow kids to be kids and force them into adulthood before their childhood you are making them jump into a generation they are not ready to be a part of. When you force people to remain children especially in the work place you are screwing with a generation. How are they supposed to show their kids strength when they are coming in from work broken down all the time? How are they supposed to pass down that hard work pays off when someone else is reaping their rewards? To kids, well to good kids their parents are a human form of God and to see your God being forced to be treated as less then a peasant is more then any kid should have to witness. My mum is humble she does not need someone to break her and yet when you look around a great deal of parents are having their spirits broke.

I know that some people do this because it makes people easier to ride and some kids never outgrow the piggyback rides their parents use to give them and later find out how to turn them into horses and making them work like Clydesdales too. I guess some parents never learned when to tell their kid to get down and that it's enough for right now. I do not use my family to ride and none of them ride me, instead we prefer to walk with each other. The way the walk through life should go is Mum and Dad are out front arms around each other setting a loving example, all of us kids are walking behind them messing with each other, laughing and carrying on like normal kids do even with an oddball in the group. Behind us should be our elders looking ahead and saying, "Remember when ours use to do that very same thing?" They never say, "Oh what it would be like to be young again," because they are a part of the youth, that is why it is in front of them and not behind them. They are not walking away from it they are walking towards it and keeping a watchful eye on their generations. The parents are out in front to show the younger generation how to not only live life but how to enjoy it and take it all in. To fill your lungs with such fresh air that you can taste it and exhale from the pleasures and not out of contempt.

The problem is families are no longer separated into generations and they are even being mixed. When you screw with Mum Nature she does go back and tell Father Time you know and when he gets mad all hell will eventually break loose giving you an opportunity to fix things and make them right. All hell broke loose for me because someone else screwed up my generation gap and made Father Time pull back into moments what should have been fond memories. The thing is when the opportunity presented itself to right a wrong I jumped at it. I may have jumped inside of myself then up and down and probably back at least once but eventually I did land on it.

I missed the generation that was supposed to set the example so that I would have a better understanding of how to apply the wisdom. I missed my parents. Kids are having babies and instead of growing up they stay children themselves and now you have two generations living off of one. We have totally dismissed the cycle of life and are doing things the way we want, big mistake with some things. Where are the defined lines between babies, kids at heart and elders? Now I am not saying that everyone cannot live under the same roof because with the cost of living sky rocketing and wages fixed so that you cannot even get by more and more are moving back home. The thing to keep in mind is that even though you move back home you still have to manage your responsibilities. You have to give the generation ahead of you time to reflect and they cannot because they're still busting hump.

I know that I would not have picked up on half of what I did if my elders were working odd hours at a job that would not respect them. I am not saying that all they should do is sit around, no because none of the ones I grew up with did. They were always into something but it was something that they loved and enjoyed doing. They had worked hard at a young age and had even been through wars but now was the time to enjoy the payment. I always respected and admired my elders but I never knew why so much. Now I know because they are no longer referred to that any more and I think that is a title that they have rightfully earned and should be allowed to keep. When I was growing up you never saw someone inexperienced being put into a place of authority, now everywhere you look you have the younger generation bossing their elders around and being beyond disrespectful to them. Companies were not handed over to the kids unless they knew how to run it and now all they know how to do is run it into the ground. They treat their co-workers like replaceable machine parts and all they receive for their thirty-year service to the company is an I.O.U. because they spent your 401k on their SUV, they did not think that you would make it this far.

You have children babysitting the cookie jar and the money is no longer finding its way in. Since they have never learned how to face consequences they more then likely have never had to work for anything either. I remember when you were grateful and now when you ask someone what that means they just look at you. These babies do not like to be told no either and when you do somehow they find a way around you and still get what they want. I cannot tell you how many times I have heard one of my mates tell me all about how badly her child treats her and I keep thinking the same thing. Then put your foot down because a kid will never play their parent and if they still refuse to straighten up show them the door. Maybe if they have to struggle for a roof over their head they will learn how to plum up before it even gets that far.

I have never seen kids have to struggle any more and to me that is going to get them killed in the long run. They have everything so good that they loose sight of what is really important, somebody is working really hard and it sure is not them. No wonder everyone is walking around like everyone else, nobody has defined character any more. I guess they must have heard that someone broke the mould and that was that, no more try harder next time. The thing about trying harder next time is that you have to at least put in the effort and popping out babies does not take any effort.

I am amazed at how many people just want to have babies and have someone else take care of them. It does not matter the burden as long as they get what they want and then they wonder why they are more than unhappy. "I just do not want to be alone," so you would rather be miserable. There is more to life then what meets the eye but we all have to start putting forth the effort to ever begin. Even though the people in the world have made everything disposable that does not mean that everything is. Families are suppose to be found in the home and close colleagues are suppose to be found in the work place and now it is the other way around.

We have begun to treat people like disposable commodities instead of appreciating the service they supply you with. This brings me to the daftest thing I have ever heard in my lifetime, "The customer is the most important person there is and that means they are always right." Oh Lord what a load, first off it says in the good book that to error is human so therefore even though they are a customer they can still be incorrect. If you do not believe me then take it up with Dad because it's His rule not mine, I was just stating the obvious. Second the people working for you are the most important people because they not only help run things they are the ones taking care of business. They are the ones who put in the long hours and give up time with their families and if it was not for the employees you would not have a business. Think about it do you really think that you can trust a customer to wait on themselves and still be honest enough to pay?

If you treat the people busting their backside for you well then they will in turn treat the customer well. I had a boss tyrant lip off one day, "Yeah, good help is sure hard to find," and they all looked at me and laughed.

I responded, "Do you know what is even harder to find then that? A decent employer!" Then I was the only one laughing but I sure made up for the rest of them. I keep having to remind people that they are only renting my services they do not own me. The sad thing is that if you look around we are being treated just like the Egyptians, building on some man made power trip. What happened to keeping one day for rest? If you ask me man has gotten way to out of control and the only way to correct this is by putting the parents back in charge. The parents are supposed to be running things not a sibling even if it is a big brother. They are going to try and get away with everything they can and torment those he is suppose to watch and protect until he hears the parents drive up.

He was a big bad bully up until then, now he cowers and threatens, "You had better not tell if you know what is good for you." If you know what is good for you then you will because that is the only way they will ever be stopped, is if someone stops them.

The cool thing about our Dad is that He already knows so we do not have to worry about them being believed over us. I know that people here give me a tremendous amount of grief over cutting ties with evil villagers but when my day is called I can stand proudly with my head held up and say, "Dad they were being mean to me and I did not want to play with them any more so I left." They are the ones who are going to have to atone for their actions and the great thing is they cannot lie or get it thrown out on a technicality. I learned that man teaches one thing and that Dad teaches something else and since it is my soul I think that I will listen to Dad over man any day of the week.

Dad teaches us that if we Honour our parents they in turn will have Honourable kids. I knew in my soul that I was not going to turn out Honourable if I stayed and the only way I was going to find Honourable parents was on the other side of hell. The cool thing about coming out on the other side is there they were but because I came out burnt they gave me time to heal. My mum knew that I was not going to just get over it but that with time, understanding and more patience than the world could hold I would eventually heal from it all and that included my heart.

I think that my mum has always had a place in Heaven but Thanks to her she helped me to find mine right beside her, dad and the highly other weird ones she calls her kids. I am the one who gets pointed at but please, you fit in with your own kind and if I can be called a "Scientific Experiment" (they just were not to sure if I had run a muck or a stray) then you know they are too. The great thing is I love having a family that loves having me. I know that I am with the right ones because my mum has the same authority over me that Dad in Heaven does. My mates freaked out when they found out that I could be deflated if someone said, "Do you want me to tell your mum?"

I would love to take some of these kids who disrespect their parents and put them in the village I came out of and tell them right before I walked off, "You think you have bad parents because they will not give you everything you want? You are about to see the evil side of bad parents." The same with parents who do not appreciate that they have good kids, trade them out for some truly evil little scoundrels. The more pain you have been put through the more you will truly appreciate those who do not treat you like that. I guess that is why I tend to drive my family a little up the wall sometimes because I know what my life was like before they came into it and what it is like today. Dad is not the one who screwed up, I just landed in the wrong village and misplaced my compass. The odd thing is the more I look back over my life the more I realize that I would have never made it this far in life had I not have challenged God. I never declared war on Him ever, but I did dare Him to challenge me and no matter how many times I fell I was going to get to that finish line. The people may have done all those things to me but He was doing it through them to see if He could break me. I was three at the time so what did I know, I just knew that He was bigger then me and I was trying to look tough and brave in front of Him.

Anytime I felt like giving up I could feel someone tapping me on the shoulder and it would put the fire back into me. "Oh that is right, we were racing." When I crossed the end I did not want to pick my head up because I thought that I had beaten God to the finish line and that is not what I meant to do. The funny thing is Dad was never racing me but He was there the whole time waiting at the finish line because He knew I was going to cross. It was not until this chapter of my life closed that I finally realized who I had been racing against, it was the villagers and they were hot on my heels too let me tell you. They made a grab for me while I made a dive and now that I have crossed they can no longer reach for me any more. The best thing is I received two rewards for the same race, I got to stop feeling in my heart that I was not one of Dad's kids and Dad gave me a real mum and I am one of her very own.

The thing is I may have been hard headed but I am not hard hearted and I just got tired of being hurt. Now that I have a family who gives me not only a sense of direction but a sense of purpose my life has taken on a whole new meaning. The wisdom I have accumulated over the years is starting to come together and the world looks brighter every day. I have problems but I no longer get depressed about them because my thoughts will no longer allow me to go down that dark road any more.

I think things through and I call my mum which always puts me back on track. The right mum can make everything right as rain and make you feel so good for being born. I realize that I am not a mistake, they made the mistake of not treating me correctly and that is why I let them go and now thanks to my family I no longer have hard feelings because I am not there any more and cannot be brought back to that place even mentally any more. It may have taken me a great deal of my life to get where I am going but I sure like the fact that I am going to get there with the help of my family. I have never complained about what I went through I just thought that it was normal, now I know that it is the people in it. Bad things happen to good people so that they can build a spine out of one Heaven of a backbone.

We have screwed with things long enough and now it is time to fix them without the attitude, "I did not break it," or "That is not my job." You never know if you can fix something that someone else broke if you do not try. Who knows one of your hidden talents may be compassion. We need everyone's help including the elders.

Dear World,

I know that I am just a drop in a vast ocean but I learned that drops do make ripples if even just for a moment. I learned that it is what you do in that moment that means the entire world.

I also learned on my journey that the meaning of life has two answers but the first is the same for everyone. The meaning of life is indeed happiness but what throws people off is the second part they do not know what makes them truly happy. For each and everyone it is different as well as it should be.

I learned that in order for "To thy own self be true" you need to learn how and what makes you true to yourself and not what someone has led you to believe is a part of you. I learned that I am strong in life but that I can be soft hearted when it comes to the ones I love. I have enjoyed that lesson most of all.

I also learned that people will always be themselves even if they do not know what that may be. Some people crave the challenge to swim up stream but lack the ambition to follow it through because someone might disagree with their choice on how they live their life.

I also learned that others pay the price for leaving the safety of the herd so to speak. Although others may want to follow, the mere thought of going against them leaves you out in the cold. The past of every great being started out going against what everyone else believed so hold fast to your dreams no matter what the fad of the time may bring.

I also learned that we as a whole have lost our way out of intolerance and instead have learned to thrive off of it. We have groups dedicated to cause problems for others instead of allowing each to be their own. We also have groups that cause problems for the ones causing problems but none that really puts a stop to anything. I know because this has been going on since time began as you can very well attest to.

I learned that in our own way we are still held in bondage, be it to a thought or to a minimum wage boss so that we can just get by. All of us want to be free but we just do not want to be another drop in the sea, I guess some want the ocean view while others prefer being on a lake. The point being to all of this goes back to the number one plan. You really cannot please everyone all of the time, even two people with the same view will disagree on how they both arrived at the same conclusion.

I learned that behind every great love and every act of war started with a thought. A thought can bring you greatness or destruction. I think that I will stick with being who I am and just add to it. If someone comes along that needs something that I have inside of me you know in my heart that I will share. I learned the hard way to share with only the ones who also want greatness because they too will share and the others well, let them fend for themselves for a change, maybe than they will learn.

I learned that inside of me is a monster that I can use when I am scared or to freak the bad people out. I have control over it now since I took it out of the closet and let it sleep at the foot of the bed. We imagine the evil ones with little tutus on their heads before we say our prayers and go to rest what is left of our minds. You should try it sometime because now you know there is no reason to fear them.

I learned that anyone outside of yourself is from a different planet so why not make contact like we have been talking about doing for years. If we learn to make contact with those alien to us in our own backyard surly it will get around to other alien towns.

I learned that a thought can be admired or undesired depending on who comes up with it. A nasty person in power can come up with an undesirable thought that will some how be admired. A person who came up with a thought on how to take the undesired person out of power will some how never be admired.

I just wanted you to know that even though I am just a drop in the sea added to the rest, I plan on making a big splash so get ready for us. Who knows maybe someone will want to jump in with me, or at least send me a raft. I keep thinking that hope will someday bring courage but for right now I feel like when Mosses parted the waters I was the only drop left at sea. I am content so far because I learned how to turn fear into eternal hope and now its time to appreciate what I have learned before I go to applying it.

Respectfully,

A little ripple for now

# Chapter Four
# The Elders

I remember a long time ago when cereal came with a prize at the bottom of the box and if you were smart you flipped the box upside down to make the prize appeared on the top. There was something else that appeared at the top, but you did not have to flip it upside down to retrieve it. In the good old days they were called The Elders and they never had to demand respect, it was just properly instilled that they were given the top honour of holding the highest office of respect. They were not only listened to, they were sought-after and every word was considered part of the golden rule. They were wise because they could see the future in those wondrous eyes looking back at them. When you could not understand your parents you could always go to the elders so that they could explain them and the same applied for the parents. They could turn to their elders when they were driven as high up the wall as they could go from their kids.

You could find The Elders in one of two places, their own home or in one of their offsprings' homes. The Elders took their rightful place and everything just seemed to be more peaceful, more content. There were no "elderly" homes because there was no need for them, there was no question about them staying with a family member. This was of course when family took care of family, now the only thing they want to take care of is helping themselves to whatever they want. The worst part is when you hear someone say, "Well they're spending my inheritance." The sad thing is steps are taken in this matter but not like they should be. Steps are taken to ensure that very little of that money is spent on the people who earned it instead of those who do not deserve a dime of it. Why these people are not being corrected and told, "That is not your inheritance, that is their nest egg that they need to live on because you are being too selfish now to help anyone when they need it." I have seen more people cry over what they did not get then over the person who went home for good. Do they not realize that they will never come out to play again, never be on centre stage? All they care about is what they left behind and it makes me wonder if humans will ever draw the line to enough is enough.

When are they going to realize that they have a precious, natural resource that if not appreciated will wither away? You wonder why the world and all the people in it are screwed up, because the young ones are not being taught to respect themselves, their parents or much less their elders. The grandparents should not have to discipline the little ones, they should visit that way. Everyone walks around like a know it all except for the ones that really do and they are being made to feel ignorant and therefore ignored. I myself would have never gotten through half of what I did had I have not listened intensely to the elders stories of war, hardship, depression and how to ration but not make it feel like you are.

I remember being the only kid allowed to sit with the elders (after they caught me listening to them) because they knew I wanted to learn. What better way than through the ones who taught from experience, I was taught things through word of mouth because each generation added on to it. Sometimes I would hear the same story more then once but I never said a word. I figured that it was important enough to have made a great impact on their lives, all I had to do was listen, and they had to live it. What was just a moment ago and could be summed up in a story lasted months and sometimes even years before relief was felt. I looked at these elders not as fragile but as the most courageous and toughest people in the world and could not figure out why they were not written about in the history books?

There was not a single time that I would go to them with a problem that they did not have an answer for me right after I was finished explaining things. I grew up adoring my elders because they to me are what legends are made of. The thing is even when I was younger I knew that being an Elder was an Honour because not everyone made it this far. Some went back home before they stopped being childish and became a kid at heart. That is one thing my

Grandfather passed on to me and something I will never allow anyone to take from me. He taught me that the only way to live was being a mature kid at heart and for the short time that I knew him he was. He is the one who taught me the most and when I tell someone some of the things he taught me all I ever receive is, "I cannot believe your Grandfather would teach you something like that." The funny thing is right after they say that they automatically become someone I will stay clear from. Why, because my Grandfather was the only one I ever trusted and he taught me how to be just like him, a fighter no matter what the circumstances are or whom is involved. He was also the one who taught me that I was only born my gender but that did not make me who I am.

"Limiting yourself because you were born a sex is daft and when you start there it will never end. Then you begin to stop yourself because of your age, height or (lack there of) and before you know it you have made yourself weak for no other reason except that you set your mind wrong from the start." I had someone try to drill it into my head that I was a girl and even went so far as to try and change my mannerisms and how I wore my hair when I worked but like I said when they go to telling me that they are correct over my Grandfather it is only a matter of time before I cut and leave. These people only wanted to get close enough to do one of two things, change me into a little doll that you pulled out to play dress up with or destroy me when I would not let them change me. They wanted me to turn me into a girl so that I could feel helpless and then when the world was done taking their turns on me they could later on turn me into feeling like a victim instead of someone who survives hell. Nice considering they said they wanted to help me get through all of this. "Males are no tougher then females, its just that some people are just tougher then others." That is how all the elders saw one another as people not as their gender.

I loved the fact that my Grandfather turned me into a tough see it through to the end even when everything looks bleak toy soldier. "Being tough takes mental discipline and is a state of mind nothing less." I was also taught by him how to take up for myself and fully defend myself if need be. He taught me how to not only survive but how to keep my head, not panic and get out alive. Why in Dads name would you want someone to give up that part of themselves just so they can be like everyone else and cry over spilt milk? I can tell you why, because when you take away that fight or flight and you take that courage of toughness from them they become easier to control and make for wonderful targets. Now they are so scared of everything that you can manipulate them to even greater extremes. If I did not have my Elders to turn to at such a young age I know that I would not be alive today to find my loved ones.

I learned from them that there is a time to use your wits, a time for mental and spiritual strength but that you should never drop your faith even in the darkest of night. I learned that there are people who can and will turn on you because your faith is stronger then theirs ever will be. The sweet thing is that is one thing that I kept learning from each and every Elder I have ever come across, they're not losing faith no matter what the cost. My Grandfather said that was one thing he wanted to make sure I had completely before he went home was that I knew beyond the shadow of a doubt what it meant to have faith and mental strength. He would ask me if I had to see something to know that it was there and just because I saw something did not mean that it was not staged or made to appear just how I was suppose to see it. My Elders were impressed with the fact that my mouth never opened until the end of their discussions and that was to ask questions that pertained to the subject at hand. I was always amazed at how in-depth the subjects could go and at how passionately the subjects were talked about and felt. The meetings would all end the same, with everyone laughing and wishing each other well.

Elders were turned to, not turned away, they had dignity and rights, now all they have is the right to is relinquish their belongings to ungrateful leeches and if they are lucky they can go home with a drop of their dignity still in tact but do not count on it. I cannot and do not want to count how many times I have heard supposed loved ones saying, "Well I had to find a home to put them in because they just cannot take care of themselves any more."(But leave out the fact that their parents allowed them to move back home when they could not take care of themselves.) If you can afford a home then you should be able to afford them moving in with you after all did they feel put out when you could not take care of yourself? The bigger thing to me is when we were helpless babies they did not put us in a home because we could not feed ourselves or change our own nappies when life happens back there so why do we do it to them? I know it might inconvenience us.

I do believe that everyone in the family took care of the little one because they could not take care of themselves, after all is that not what real family means? The taking care of one another and looking after them, especially when they have earned the honour of being taken care of, I think that is one of the saddest things in the world besides abuse and that is treating our Elders like a bloody burden.

We have gotten so accustomed to having everything disposable and wasting to such an alarming rate that no one sees or cares that some of the greatest philosophies comes from the minds of our Elders. We have learned to dope them up enough to take everything from them and then throw them away. If they cannot make enough to extort from then who needs them, they are a drain to everything. Now how ignorant do we really want to stay? If it was not for our Elders being wise, tough survivors how many of us would be here today? None you daft bum and this is how we show our gratitude to the people who gave us the wisdom of the world?

How many generations are we going to breed of daft, ungrateful, everything belongs to me right now, I do not have to do anything especially take responsibility for my own actions babies? How daft can you be, do you not think that you might turn into one of these same people you are making fun of if you live that long? We have a generation of people who do not remember, a generation of people who do not know and still another one of please do not forget. The do not remember ones forget what it was like to be a kid and how you were always being pushed aside for something more important and yelled at for every little thing that you did by adults who were more daft than you. The ones who do not know any better are being ignored by the ones who do and are basically being told either you will pick it up sometime or just do it my way so that we can get along. The other group is please do not forget that I am still breathing and I have more to offer while I am alive then can ever be found in a will after I leave.

Each and every generation is being taught to separate from the one ahead of its time and from the one they're just slightly ahead of. The known truth is that each generation feeds off and into the other one and because this is not happening they are all dying off in alarming numbers. We have one group that is dying while made to feel alone, one that is killing themselves because they have to do everything alone and we have the ones that are spiritually dying on the inside. Why when we have so many people in the world could it have ever gotten this out of control? We went from getting along with our neighbours and looking after one another before a disaster struck to everyone not only looking after themselves but more then likely shagging someone to get ahead or what we want.

You have more people holding their head up then ever before but not for the right reasons. You have been given so much and instead of doing something with it you toss it aside waiting for something more or better to come your way. What happens if that was the last of it and now there is nothing left? Do you really have to wait for that to occur before you pull your head out of your bum? Let us say for dramatic effect that all The Elders were gone, they all went back home at once. Who in the world do you think you are going to turn to when you need wisdom, kids? Heavens no, because we figured that if you were daft enough to think that sending all the Elders away was a brilliant idea you would be to daft to reason with from here on out.

That is just as daft as sending the younger ones away until they "learn to grow up." Now how are they supposed to do that if there are no elders to show them how or parents to filter through? Each generation should in itself be a buffer and when you pull one out you will always have uncontrollable friction. While the grown ups and adults earned the kids were suppose to learn from their elders and in turn the elders could teach the old ways of Honour, Loyalty, Respect and Morals of both self and family values. It was designed so that no matter what the crisis was you always had someone in the family to turn to in your time of need. The elders would remind us that while we can learn from other people's mistakes we have to make our own if we are going to grow into civilized human beings. I never minded not getting something correct in front of them because they would always tell me the same thing, "You are still learning so give yourself time to understand."

I also remember my Grandfather teaching me something and I was becoming more and more frustrated by the moment because I just could not get it. He asked me, "Are you even trying."

Without sounding like I was yelling I said "Yes I am."

He just rolls with laughter while I just look at him and says, "Well no wonder you cannot get it, stop trying." I know that I had the facial expression of what all over my face when he looked at me and explained, "You have to give yourself time to get it first before you venture out and try it on your own. Once you get it then you can try and do it but first you have to get it down, understand."

I just kind of nodded yes while trying not to look so unbelievably confused. He could tell that I was working it over in my head but that I had not yet grasped the concept. "So should I just learn to be confused before I actually try and figure out that I am confused or that something is confusing to me or should I get the hang of being confused first before I know that I am actually confused?"

He smiled great big and replied, "Yes, now you have the hang of it."

I think that was just easier then trying to figure out what in the world I had just said. He was always sweet like that.

I learned from them that it does work if you just hang back and observe, them mimic until you get the hang of it and then try it for yourself. I would always hear all of them say the same thing, "Those young ones always rush into things before they even know what they are doing. Who knows, one of these days they might just learn how to open their eyes." Now I do not know how you were when you were little but I would always picture everything that was said, explained or talked about. I was also the type of kid who believed what I saw in cartoons so when I hid behind a pole I knew that no one could see me. I remember one time I had fallen and I hid behind a pole to cry and right in the middle of being upset I heard one of the elders ask me if I was alright. I stopped crying just like that and asked them, "How did you know I was here?" Lord love them because you could tell that they did their best not to burst into laughter, they forgot which kid I was up until that moment and I forgot about being hurt and went on.

They looked at me and told me that a bird told them how to find me and I was satisfied with that. I loved the fact that the elders played with me no matter how far out my mind would go. They never pushed me aside to watch TV and they had patience in their teachings. My elders are also the ones who taught me that if a teacher rolls their eyes in the back of the head they will not have any more pupils. (Yes my elders rolled their eyes a great deal when they were trying to teach me but that was o.k. because when their eyes came back around I was still right there being their pupil!) My Grandfather was also the one who taught me about laughter, humour and using what was around you to be funny. He said that anybody can be mean, vindictive, cruel and spiteful but that very few people make others laugh whole heartedly without hurting someone's feelings.

Anytime one of the elders would teach me something I would start to notice it in life. There were more mean people in the world full of malice than there were who could make someone laugh. I looked the word up when I was little after someone spelled it for me and it basically says to do an act of harm to someone without having a reasonable cause. I gather in some people's eyes being jealous of someone gives them reasonable cause to be malicious. I watched all of the elders but mainly my Grandfather because he could make everyone laugh until they were laughing through tears and holding their sides.

I learned how to explore life through other people's thoughts and I soon found out that they can go all over the place. I loved listening to the elders because they would talk in-depth about life and holding your head up even if you have to grab yourself by your own hair to do so. These were some of the toughest people in the world and because of that no one challenged them for their place as head of their family. When there was a serious problem they would all gather and even though there were a lot of heads of families in the room they agreed on a solution. They're the ones who taught me that it is not just one persons idea that is the answer to everyone's problem but a combination of everyone's different thoughts to come up with a grand idea that solves matters in the end.

Nowadays you can very seldom get someone to agree with themselves much less a roomful of people. All you get any more is one person using everyone else's ideas to stay in control, then uses that control to extend into people's thoughts. The elders that I knew had been through too much to be scammed or pushed over in any way. I heard some of them talk about having started out with so many kids but because of the way they treated them or acted towards them they were no longer a part of the family in any way. These people enjoyed life because they had learned to filter out the bad people throughout their lives even if it was one of their own and had surrounded themselves only with those who truly cared. They did not care if the world agreed with them, the fact is it was their life and they had fought to live it. They deserved to be happy and carefree and for the most part they truly were.

I watched as they worked together and helped each other out when they would become stuck. I also watched how they would screw up and instead of becoming mad or making the other feel small it was all good to them. I watched what would upset them and what they would let go; after all since they were in real battle they would know the difference between the two. I saw nothing to be ashamed of when it came to the elders and it truly amazes me how many people treat them like they are the plague itself. They lock them away from the world and basically make them keep to themselves. Elders do not need to pass on wisdom to other elders; they need to pass it onto the younger ones so that they have a better chance of maturing the right way.

The Elders of my time have since passed and in their place are people called elderly and for some unknown reason they do not hold the same power. They are treated as though they are feeble in the mind, body and soul. Their independence is chipped away until they too are treated like babies who should be put in time out. The sad thing is I find it hard to talk to the elderly because half of them do not know where they are due to all the medication they are being put on. No wonder they cannot pass on wisdom, they are to busy being occupied with trying to figure out what pills go with what meals.

All of my elders took pills too but they were all natural and never cost them their savings to live another day, I believe they called them something like vitamins and herbs. None of them were fragile because they were not made to be that way. With all the drugs being pumped into them, now they could break in the breeze. They were never meant to be elderly and due to that role they are being forced into their being disassembled piece by piece. We have to start turning the elderly back into the Elders and put them back in charge, they have more then earned it and sooner or later if you are one of the few lucky ones you could someday reign from there too but not until you have put in your time. Big brother should not be in charge of anyone but themselves and I do believe if you look they are doing just that. Big brother should not be the head of the family for any reason, the Elders are.

It really does break my heart to watch these great people being broken down and being treated like the only thing they are good for is an inheritance. I over heard an elderly person say, "I plan to die broke that way the ungrateful bastards I spawned will have no choice but to mourn over me because there will not be anything left to pine over." They had given their family everything, was always there and now they were being thrown away because in the families eyes they had become used up. Well whose fault is that, both if you ask me? One for doing nothing but using them, and the other side for not stopping it sooner. I learned though that if you take away their power, what choice do they have. I guess that may be why the elders of my time got rid of them before that stage came up in their life. Nobody fought over anything because everyone knew how they had acquired whatever they had received. Through someone's passing. Memories were exchanged instead of dirty looks and you wanted them back in your life not what they owned and left behind.

The Elders never tried to kill themselves to fill their house full of meaningless possessions; they fought to stay alive and together. They had lost their homes, their place, family members and what could be touched with the hand but they never lost the ones who had survived. I never heard the elders gripe over what they never had or moan and groan over what they had lost over the years. They just talked about it as being a part of life and learning how to start over using just the basics. They never dwelled over the horrors they had become a witness to and they never surrounded themselves with reminders of the horrors. "Learning from your past does not mean that you have to keep everything right in front of you."

Sometimes what I learned from the elders went way over my head at the time but I never let go of any of their teachings. I figured sooner or later I would understand what they were trying to instill would sink in when I needed it to and it does when I am not being hard headed.

I think that could be why I never let the horrors I had witnessed bother me and why so many people were determined to try and force them to. I was taught early on how to have the mind set of an elder and I used what they had taught me to keep from getting backed down. I had wisdom in my backbone; the only problem was I could not always get it to my head in time before I would react. Wisdom without applied knowledge can leave you kicking yourself in the bum, (not a good thing to do if your head is up there too. Could cause yourself a tremendous amount of brain damage.) I have done that so many times trying to figure out just what the elders were talking about.

I did however learn that the philosophies with the deepest meanings come from the complex Epiphanies of thoughtful elders. They have learned throughout their life how to have greater understanding of the world they are a part of. They also know that even though they are wise beyond your years, once you get it you will learn how to build onto it. They want you to be able to reach far beyond them but have the ability to also come back and do the same for others. I learned how not to be stingy or greedy from watching all of them, the only thing I never noticed is who they were being generous to. Sometimes you can be to close to the picture to see what is really going on even if you are catching on. They shared with those they loved and left the rest out in the cold, they never let anyone close enough to the family to hurt them. When someone would try and weasel their way in everyone stuck together as one and kept them out after all they were protecting the same heart.

Any more if someone has a problem with somebody else they all side with the person causing the problem and turn on the ones they have known forever. What in the world has happened to loyalty, I guess it eloped with common sense! Loyalty without the elders to properly teach how to instill it has become a commodity that applies to the top bidder alone. The sad thing is that if later on down the line if the first bid can be out done even by just a dollar the person who just swore their loyalty to you is now handing you over on a silver platter along with everything you just told them. My Grandfather would always tell me, "Soulless people have loyalty for sell, Honourable people hold their loyalty inside their soul so be careful who you swear your loyalties to. The wrong one could sell your soul without you being the wiser."

I learned the hard way in life how true this piece of wisdom really is and why it is the most important one to apply. I have been placed in situations where I was informed, "But I told them that you would do it because I know how you are." The worst thing in the world you could do to yourself is feel obligated to someone who has forced you into a situation where they swore you would keep your word instead of swearing theirs. I have gotten into more verbal fights over, "I do not care what they told you, I did not say it so therefore I am not going to be held to something that I did not agree to in the first place. If you have a problem, take it up with the person who started this." I learned how to do that from the elders. They would not let someone get up on them because they were the closest ones at the time. Instead they made them take it up with whom ever they had the grievance with. To them that was taking care of business and not pawning it off on someone else just to get it out of their system. They took care of business and did not allow it to take care of them. They had a strong work ethic and it applied to the home and family as well. They enjoyed strong people and if you were not one then they would help you with that or anything else that you needed because they enjoyed people becoming more than who they were.

Elders were not just the spice of life they gave life spice and enjoyed everything that went with it. They were not out to control the family or have them do their bidding, they just knew that a family out of control will do anyone's bidding. The Elders were even honest enough to say when they did not understand something instead of acting superior to a little one. I love my Grandfather because when I would ask him something far beyond the norm he would say, "I do not know but let's go find out together." When he would work on something and I would come in to watch he would always move so that I could fit in. He is the one who taught me that work is your signature and says the world about you. "Be the best you can be at anything you do even if you have to shovel dung for a living that way you become an asset and not a burden. See if you become an asset you have a little pull because you earned it and if you need something changed or fixed you can use your pull to have a say. If they do not want to hear what you are asking them to fix then let the burden fall on them. You did the best that you could but for people who appreciate burdens, not assets. Since you are an asset and not a burden you should leave because they will never appreciate you and you need to find someone who will." Believe it or not he is also the one who taught me when to give a two weeks notice and when not to. "If it is on you for example your moving or something then by all means put one in because you are leaving on good terms. However if they are treating you disrespectfully and will not correct the problem you do not owe them anything except for what you have already given them, your best. Why would you be respectful enough to give someone a two weeks notice when they would not give you the same respect of telling you that they are going to fire you in two weeks? Remember little one it all boils down to respect on both sides and not just with work but with everything in life."

I would notice that more and more with him, if he did not respect you he did not have anything to do with you and that was that. He would not allow anyone to talk him into changing his mind either. "Oh but you do not know them like I do, they're…" and he would always stop them right there. "If I get a bad feeling off of someone I will not stay around to figure out why I do not like them because it will end up costing me somehow. They do not fool me because even evil people can fake a smile or a good heart when they are after something and they know how to mix truth in with lies to get their bidding done." The thing is my Grandfather was always correct about people and he said that the secret was learning from not only your own experiences but from what you have seen others go through as well. He knew that some people did not have a drop of good anywhere in them and that you were being feasted upon while you were fooled or fooled yourself into looking. He also knew that some people act badly just because they do not know they have good inside of them. There were people who possessed both but only used the good to lure others in and used the bad part of them to keep them there. He is also the one who said, "Sometimes you can hurt someone who is so soft hearted that they never come back."

I think that is how he was but because of what all he had went through he could not be like that any more. I remember looking into his eyes as he was talking and this was the only time I had ever seen him long for something. He was always good but he could no longer be as soft hearted as was in his nature to be and I knew that he missed that part of himself. He could not afford to be soft hearted any more and not just because of the war but because he was in the same village I was in. Two prisoners of war and we stuck together and through him he taught me how to escape and to be the one who does not come back. In return I showed him that I was more than willing to learn everything he could teach me and that I would put everything that he taught me to good use and make it in life because of him. We had our own code and nobody else was allowed to be a part of what we had.

He taught me how to be stealthy and make things into games, this way when the impact of what happens hits, you will not be there to feel it directly because it is all over. When the little girl talked to me I did the same thing my Grandfather did for me, made it easier to go through mentally. If my Grandfather would have come right out and said, "You are surrounded by evil people who want nothing more then to destroy you in every sense of the word and that is why the elders and I are teaching you this," how well do you think that would have set with me? I would have concentrated on that instead of finding a way out, plus that would have over whelmed me to the point where I would still be there because it would have seemed impossible to get out. He made living in those surroundings fun and when he left so did I.

The greatest thing I learned from my Elders is how not to make a bad situation worse and how to see what is beyond me. To use your life experiences to help someone else through something that they cannot understand. They were not hung up on themselves, I was the one hung up on them and for good reason, they were life to me and all that it entails. They had been through it all the good, bad, ugly, the beauty and everything else in between and lived to tell about it. No, these people were far from elderly and would not allow anyone to treat them as such. If they needed help they asked for it but it was because they needed extra help outside of what they were already putting in. Now when helped is asked for they have to give up everything before it will be given. The only way to best describe that is cruel and usual punishment because they have gotten this far without being broken. That is something my elders could not figure out, why we feel the need to break things just because we do not understand them. I myself cannot understand why we have to break someone in order to want supposed better understanding of them. If you break something that you know nothing about you run the risk of destroying it forever or do we already know this and that is why we do it? The thing about breaking people is you may not like the way they break or they may not break the way you want them to.

Look around you, we have kids destroying each other, we have adults doing the same and the only ones not really doing any harm are the elderly and they are receiving the blunt of the trauma, why because everyone else is. Kids have been given powers that were not meant for them to have much less harness to the degree that they have. You have some kids wanting to do good in the community, but how many stop to visit the elderly; after all they are the ones who would love to help make an impact on people's lives if given the chance? What if all it took was for us to include them in our lives for them to become elders again? If that is all it takes and we still do not do it then what does that say about the human race? To me that is being self destructive and something that we cannot afford to be at anytime in our short lives. They say that a thousand years is a day in Heaven yet some of us do not make it out of bed to come to breakfast and we are trying to cut our lives shorter why? To have total control over something that we were never meant to own in the first place. I heard an elder say that we do not inherit the earth that we are simply borrowing it and since that is the case look at what we have done to it.

Earth is a big place yet we still find the need to ostracize (my mum's favourite word,) anybody and everybody at will or when anything gives us the chance. Why do we feel the need to become superior to anything when we ourselves are a mere dot in the full connection? Did we get that way somehow through playing connect the dots when we were younger, we all want to be that big starting dot because somehow we find it demeaning to be anything less? If that is the case then why are we trying to fit in some click of little dots following everything that becomes a fad? What if the elders and elderly all got together and started acting like the younger generation, going around vandalizing everything that did not belong to them just because someone else worked really hard for it? How much could you look up to someone who did just that and went beyond without repercussion? Elders teach us whom to look up to and all we have done for them is take away human contact.

All of us need some kind of human contact and this is especially true for our elders. Why because the world becomes even more lonely because you have lost more loved ones than people a third of your age. When you're young you are surrounded by all kinds of people but the only time people want to surround the elders is after they have gone home. We wait until it's too late to do anything about it and all that is left is helping ourselves to their belongings.

Elders created their own path and handed down what they could for the next generation to hopefully build on. Nothing was handed to them and yet they are more appreciative of the little things in life then the ones two steps below them who are given everything. I was always taught that if you want something work for it yourself because you will take better care of it. (Is that why we destroy everything in our surroundings because we did not work for it?) I saved up one time for something that I have wanted for a long time and by the time I had enough money they jacked up the price. I figured that this was a way of telling me that I was better off without it and to just keep the money saved. I learned how not to use credit cards through my elders because they never had any and it was a hot new fad.

I asked my Grandfather what they were and why he would not have one. He said that they were a means to an end, meaning that if you get caught up in all of that then it can put an end to you because there is no way out that anyone knows of. Moreover he was already who he was going to be so he did not feel the need to buy anything just to make a false statement about who he was not. "When I need something the Man upstairs helps me out," and he is correct. We went through hard times but always came out of it because he knew how to survive and apply. He said that before he went through anything hard he would always apply for help first from The Man upstairs and he would have to survive so that he could receive it. He shared his experiences with me and how he felt about The Man upstairs. He told me that he never said his prayers, he would just talk to Him throughout the day anytime he felt the need and so did the rest of the elders.

He taught me a tremendous amount about The Man upstairs and not just things found in the Bible either. He taught me that sometimes when you ask for something it might not come until everything is all over because this is when you need it the most. You may ask for strength at the beginning but you do not receive it until the end because you had just enough to make it through on your own now, you need the strength you applied for in order to move on and here it is. I asked him if he ever asked for anything because of me, he smiled when he said, "Yes, all the time but I always ask for the same thing, the ability to keep up with your mind when it wonders off. Your brain goes so fast sometimes that even the speed of light is stopping to scratch its head to ask did you see where little ones thoughts wondered off to because I lost them." Neither one of us could stop laughing especially when he does his facial expressions.

He was an Elder who was not afraid of anything or anyone and taught me everything he could so that one day I could be the same. The cool thing is that everything he taught me a lifetime ago, my mum is showing me how to apply now so that it is not just floating knowledge not doing anyone including myself any good. My Grandfather went home a lifetime ago before my mum took me into her family but I know that if they could have met he would have told her, "Apply mainly for patience because you are going to need a tremendous amount with this one. You might want to apply for courage too so that you can go the distance with little one because she can go way out there but has no sense of direction to find her way back to tell you what she found." I am glad that my mum found out on her own though just how weird and strange I can be but just like my Grandfather she can go way out there with me. (Known truth, I love it when my mum and I go on weird mental journeys together and neither one of us is steering the ship, you would be surprised at what you can come up with together.)

When my Grandfather went home I lost the only leg I wanted to stand on and with it all the teaching the elders had wanted me to instill in myself. When I did that and I will be perfectly honest it would cost me everything each and every time. They do not teach us because they have nothing better to do or because they want to see us throw everything away at the drop of a hat. They teach us to better ourselves and that means you are suppose to get better not stay the same. They never wasted their time blaming others for life happening to them, they just learned how to deal with it as it came along. They also taught me that sometimes it can be someone else's fault and not yours but that you had to be smart enough to know which one is which. If the mistake is not yours then let the one who made it apologize, if they will not they are never going to own up to any of theirs. If the mistake applies to you apologize. Do not say you're sorry for two reasons one that leaves the door open for a jerk to reply, "I know you're sorry now apologize." Second the more you say your sorry the more you will begin to believe that you are until after awhile you are no longer apologizing for what happened but you actually feel like if you were not born this would never have happened.

They also taught me that if you are not ready to accept someone's then be honest but polite enough to say so, when they apologize and you accept it then you can no longer bring it up again, not even as an example. Doing this causes a grudge on both sides because this was something that you both should have gotten over the minute, "I apologize, I accept," was said. The thing to keep in mind too is that if you tell someone that you are not ready and they throw a fit then they never really meant to apologize sincerely anyway so you are better off staying clear of them in the future. Do not allow yourself to get hung up on technicalities that do not matter or loose valuable information that could give you insight because you want to hold a grudge. Some things are better left unsaid but know when to speak your mind.

All of the Elders had a different way of looking at things due to how they went through life but they all had the same thing in common. None of them had a single regret; they said that life had given them too many opportunities to keep making the same mistake over and again. Life was not about going down the same path but learning how to walk through many different ones so that you can see more, how not to be so stuck in your ways that you miss out on a chance to grow and experience something beyond your wildest imagination or dreams.

They also held fast to it is darkest before the dawn and that most people give up right before it is all over and it causes them to have to start all over when they did not have to. You may feel like everything is overwhelming but that can be a feeling that if put to good use can work out in your favour. Hanging in there means going past your normal means and digging as deep as you have to in order to make it through. If you do not put yourself out there sometimes you will never come back with anything to work on, even if it is just some thoughts to work through.

You have to work on having thicker skin if for no other reason than for your own safety. You have to learn what to let in and get close and what to stay clear from. If you are not exposed to anything, everything will shock you which can weigh on your nerves heavily. If you are exposed to things in moderation then you will learn how to make up your own mind as to what you think about the matter at hand. You can gather up other people's thoughts to help you out but in the end you need to figure out what you think and how you feel. Learning to trust your own instincts makes them stronger and more reliable then what someone wants to lead you to believe. My Grandfather always said, "There is a reason that The Man upstairs gave us our own built in alarm warning system and mind, it's so that we will use them." If he had a feeling about something he never strayed from it and would not be talked out of it, all the Elders were like that.

They were all different from one another but that gave you variety and spice for your life. They never tried to change one another and actually thrived off of each others differences. They accepted people as they were and appreciated the things that set them apart from the rest. They knew beyond the shadow of a doubt that no two people are alike or ever will be for that matter. They thrived off their own differences and never let anyone hold them back because of it. What do we thrive off of now besides hurting people who are different? They may have started off being herded into a group but they did not end up being someone they could not stomach. Some of the elderly I talk with now do not like who they have been forced to become, fragile beings having to be dependant on everyone because so many things have been taken away from them. The main thing being their dignity and self-worth, after all without these things what are any of us? The great thing is they started out in life just the same as we all did and they have more than built upon it. We want to achieve what they have in life but we need them to show us how to get there in order to appreciate it.

We dope up our kids; we dope up elderly why, so they will not see us making the biggest mistakes of our lives? To me that is the daftest reason in the world. I do not care how perfect you think that you are, all of us make mistakes. Now there are some choices we make that others may feel like is a mistake but you have to learn the difference between the two.

There will be times when we have to make a hard choice and stick by our decision but that does not make it a mistake no matter how hard someone tries to convince us otherwise. The thing to keep in mind is that you do have final say so in the matter and you need to keep that in the front of your mind not in the back of it. If we spend half as much time invested in ourselves as we do in changing others this world would be a much different place. The parents would be running the home; the kids would know their place and the elders would be there to keep friction to a minimum. Right now you have elderly being put in homes, kids running all over the place and parents are having to put off with dealing with the friction because minimum is now considered a wage that is suppose to take care of an entire family.

I know that some people are under the impression that reaching a certain age makes you an Elder but these people missed something that I have said earlier. Age is a number and you need to get off of that merry go round because it leads to nowhere. I have had people try and get on me with, "You need to respect your Elders," because I will not do something that they want. That is just it, I do respect my Elders to the degree that they deserve but just because you made it to a certain point in life does not automatically make you an elder, it makes you an old fool. What, do you think that evil villagers magically turn into something less sinister just because they reach a certain stage in life? To believe this makes you foolish and this is one area that I am not about to be fooled in because I was taught by the best. We have all been told many things but there does come a point and time in your life where you have to start putting things together. Think of life like a puzzle, it is in pieces, some of them are turned to where you cannot see them and you go through the box finding what? All the border pieces first, why to have something to build onto? You would think but no. Boundaries, after all how many of those pieces are going to work outside that frame? Now how fast do you think that puzzle is going to look like a picture if you do not start applying those pieces to where they go? We have more patience putting a table puzzle together then we do putting the one life has given to us.

If this puzzle is ever going to come together we need to learn that we need all of the pieces not just the ones we think will fit. Kids are going through the box grabbing, "I want this one and I need that one," they are hording pieces. The elders are being picked through like they do not matter and the parents are not getting to enjoy anything. Kids may want to play house but that does not mean that they should be running the one they live in. Parents should not be elders because they themselves need someone to turn to and elders should not be turned into kids.

My Elders were larger then life not inflated oversized monsters. They never nit picked and I heard them say time and time again, "Well what do you expect, they are kids, give them time to learn and explore." They gave to us the benefit of the doubt and without them what do we have? A world full of corporations that thinks perfection comes in human forms. We have to be perfect and not make a single mistake because we work for them. I would hear the Elders and listen to the elderly and it all boils down to the way we treat them. The Elders never had to undertake sexual harassment as part of doing their job and since the elderly are not being allowed out of the work force to enjoy their lives they have to be sexually harassed for a little bit of insurance? To me when you have to pull your trousers down and put something between your legs just to keep your job that is sexual harassment even if they sugar coat it by calling it a drug test. To do this to our Elders should be immoral but to have the ability to do that to whomever we please anytime that we feel like it and for what? Did the corporations somehow acquire that god like feeling from the doctors and now they feel like they need to know what only your doctor should know. We drug test people trying to make a living but do not make it mandatory to test prisoners making a killing for doing nothing. Instead of testing them for drugs why not test them to see if they have stupidity that would be detrimental to the company?

We make it mandatory to have insurance on automobiles but not on people, we give hard core criminals the best medical care there is but when it come to the Elders lets hook them on pills that they cannot afford. I guess that is one thing that nobody feels any more shame, humanity and the difference between right and wrong. I do not need the big brothers of the world to parent me and neither does any one else. I need my parents to guide and get onto me and the Elders to enforce it not an inflated sibling. The Elders wisdom is not being passed down and without it everything is going to get worse. We tell kids to listen to this person and to listen to that person but those people always change, the circle of Elders never does for a long time. Everyone is in such a hurry to grow up that they run past life and then when they look again instead of flowing into it they try to avoid it.

The elderly are becoming hollow shells because we do nothing but use them and discard them when we cannot take from them any longer. There was nothing hollow or shallow about the Elders and they went home with full Honours and with all their dignity still intact. Now we send them home like they failed with their head tucked way inside their bum. Why did we go from respecting The Elders to loathing the elderly, because we fear what we will one day become or is it because some of us know that we will never get there? Do we just want to wipe them off the face of the earth so they will not remind us how they lived life gracefully and all we are doing is running after things that we do not need? They got it right and all of us have missed the boat? The smart thing to do would be to build a raft or something but no, we prefer to stand in our groups of sexual intellectuals (you know starts with an f and ends in know it alls, I laughed when one of my mates put it that way,) and blame everyone instead of solving the problem. Elders need us to move on and we need them if we are ever going to get anywhere.

The Elders knew that we needed time to catch on to something, to let something hit home or to be able to grieve. They filled their time with memories both creating them and reminiscing and we fill ours with the latest gadgets and miss out on creating anything worth remembering. I learned about the hardships life can put you through and the torment as well but what I learned most from my Elders is that everything can be over come as long as you have faith in the Man upstairs, yourself and never quit before the dawn has a chance to break. I knew that when something became increasingly difficult it was because it was nearing the end and it would always make me smile. I knew then that I had made it more then half way through and the darkest before the dawn was about to come true. They survived everything they had went through and smiled because of it not despite it and were happy to have one another.

Nothing makes any of us happy any more or at least not for very long. I love enjoying the finer things in life just as much as anyone else but I learned from the best just what the finer things in life are. The Elders all knew that a hug given when really needed, will make you feel like a million dollars, a room full of laughter cannot be placed on any mantel and heartfelt love and devotion always carries on and gets you through the darkness. The hard times come and go but the ones who love you will always be there even if we choose not to look at or acknowledge them.

I miss my Elders because they taught me how to laugh and made sure that no matter what I did not grow up bitter. To my Grandfather it was better to be pissed off at the world and let it out then to hold it all in until it becomes a sensor on your tongue. Having a bitter taste from life on your tongue leaves a bad taste in your mouth. They would all tell me that everything is connected; you can distance yourself from it but that nothing in life gets left out. (Good thing they are not around to see how the Elders are being treated now, I guarantee there would be a tremendous amount of ears being grabbed and an equal numbers of bums being smacked.)

They knew the meaning behind the spare the rod spoil the child thing. They knew that discipline was a part of love and showed that you did not want to see them hurt. Allowing a child to do what ever they want and get away with everything shows that you do not care enough to give them a safety net. If I was getting a little too full of myself my Grandfather would set me straight and not to where I felt broken but enough to know that I did wrong. My world would fall apart if he got onto me because he liked laughing and I did something that did not make him laugh. I looked up to my Elders because they included me in life as they knew it. They did not allow anyone to pull them in a direction that they did not want to go and would not be told what to do by someone that was still a baby.

When they said no there was no getting around it or using other family members to coerce them into changing their mind. They had been around long enough to know better or to see clear when you were frantic. They had already lived that stage in life and knew that some things were not as they appear and that you were too close to see it. They never reacted to what was said because they had been in strange things too and knew that this was just your road on the way though life.

They knew that achievements no matter how big or small are all worth celebrating and it makes you want to achieve more. They had all achieved a great many things on their journey but the fact remains is that they got to the top and never looked down on anyone once they got there. They sat there and explained how sweet it was to go through the hardship and joys and this view was their reward. Now we side line them and think that reaching the top means that you get to boss everyone around and be as tyrannical as you can be but that is not what they were about and because you are trying to jump ahead of them you will always miss it. They were not about controlling and bossing everyone around, they were about leadership and guiding and wanting everyone to do their best. Now you have people making sure that your best is never good enough but try harder for less time and again.

When the elders retired they had a pension, now the only thing they are given is a kick in the teeth and a view of the curb. We make everyone the same so that there is nothing to thrive off of and no reason to want to better yourself from the person ahead of you. Different people and people who are different can create new ideas and allowing people to be themselves makes this happen, not building a corporate robot where everyone looks alike. When the elders where at the helm, everything ran smoother, the ones now do not know how to release their grip. They need to learn how to have a firm foundation not a firm grip and none of them want to grasp this concept.

Family businesses were run by elders who included everyone in their success and now we have childish corporations that include you up until the sharing of the reward. We have learned to separate ourselves from anything remotely human and have somehow become part of an unknown machine. The human spirit is dying off and instead of stopping it we are running towards it. Life is being taught that it is suppose to make us miserable as we go on and that is not the case. Elders worked for family owned business and enjoyed life after they left the work force. Corporations are sucking the life out of people so that by the time they leave there is no life left in them to enjoy. Somewhere along the line a wire became crossed and now what is being learned is pure greed, everything for a dollar.

"I have this much so that makes me better then you."

"Oh yeah, well I can take that much away from someone who has earned it so that makes me better then you because I did not have to earn it." What a vicious cycle to create in a world of greed. We act like knowledge is worth not a red cent but where would we be without it? Right where we are today. Nothing is being passed down and the only thing we are teaching our kids is how to fill in a bubble and think like everyone wants you to while somehow still managing to getting them to believe their being an individual.

Instead of the elders being demanding, it is the kids demanding things they do not have a right to. The kids should be asking if they can have this or that and the elderly need to start demanding the respect the elders have already earned. Somehow through the temper tantrums the kids somehow found themselves in charge of ruling a world they do not understand while the rest of us are made to sit idly by because they have made us helpless. Kids or even childish people are under the impression that they can do it all by themselves and no longer need grownup supervision. If that is the case what are we going to do, sit back until they screw everything up beyond repair? Do you not think that alone is daft? We have gone from one extreme to the other and now it is time to start finding the fine line. It is one thing to stand back and allow someone to get a feel for things while they are trying it out for themselves; however it is another to stand back while knowing that someone is going to get severely hurt and do nothing to stop it. When a child reaches for a stove that is turned on do you give a warning, "Be careful because that is hot and you can get hurt," and then make sure that you keep your eyes open for the hidden danger. Most people would but there are those who wait for that child to burn themselves and then say something clever like, "Did you get hurt?" Really, how much wisdom can be found in stupidity or sarcasm, yet this is all the young ones have to pass on. If they pass on what little wisdom they have without fully understanding it first what will they have left besides a smart mouth full of nonsense?

The cycle of life has drastically been changed and we need to start changing it back because we are rapidly killing ourselves off from the inside out. We think that outside appearance is everything. I was taught by my elders that the wrapping has nothing to do with what is inside and that sometimes the pretty to the eye wrapping is used to cover up one trashy gift. "Oh they are so good to look at that I just want them." Now that you have them and unwrapped what was on the inside how good do they still look to you now? We somehow think that if it catches the eye it cannot be all that bad right! Just because someone or something catches our eye does not mean that it is worth holding onto. Did it ever occur to you that they might have used that glitter to sucker you in because they know you only fish in shallow waters? A good rule to keep in mind: If they make you laugh keep them if they make you cry throw them back.

The elders knew all about depth and it was not handed to them, it came from years of fishing in shallow waters, catching the same thing all the time and wondering why. If you want people in your life with depth you have to get off the shore. The more you are willing to brave the sea, the more you will realize how much depth there is to you because you know that shallow people cannot make it out this far. It has nothing to do with them and everything to do with you. There are always going to be shallow people swimming all around you if you stay in their waters so why not leave. Do you stay because shallow people are easier to read or are you scared to unlock the depths found within yourself because you know that it would cause you to want to leave what you have known all your life?

Elders knew that just because something was familiar did not make it good for you. A beating may become familiar after a while but that does not make it good for you now does it? What happened to breeding courage instead of ill contempt for those who changed what was at first glance beyond their control? When the elders saw you doing something better than them they were proud because you did not just learn something but you found a way to improve it and make it yours. My Elders are the ones who taught me how to paint a house old school and how to fix things. (Old school meaning old world style craftsmanship.)

Now all that is being taught is how to sabotage someone that worked harder or just plain wanted it more than you. "Stop working so hard because you are making me look bad." You can tell just by looking at them that it never crossed their mind that their laziness is what is indeed making them look bad. The bad thing is the ones doing a better job either learn how to stop doing a good job or they are made to do it all. My Grandfather told me that he grew tired of his boss making him do everything when there was a full shop of people capable of doing the same thing. "You are the only one who will do it," "No you are too lazy to make them pull their own weight and think that I am the mule who is going to carry it all. You either be a boss and make the people you are paying do their job or I will find another boss who will." My Grandfather said that the worse thing in the world to do at that time is threaten your only good employee which is what his boss did. My Grandfather was always one to keep his word so he left. I could not stop laughing when he told me how his boss came over and it was all, "Please come back, I did not realize how much you did for my company until after you left. I will give you this and that if you just come back." His response, "First off no to the coming back part and here is why. I have been working for you for how many years and you are just now realizing what all I have done for you. To me that is a slap in the face, second I asked you to help get this weight off of my back and distribute it evenly and you refused. The thing that gets me the most is I would have changed my mind had you have come over to apologize instead of insulting me with a bribe." (Just in case you have not noticed he is the one who taught me that a company needs good people in order to stay in business and that bad people can take a good business down.)

The elders all knew that doing a good job had nothing to do with what was in your system but rather what was in your heart. "If you hire daft and lazy people then do not be surprised if you have no fresh ideas coming forth and no work is getting done." They knew all about drugs having gone through the sixties and surprisingly the elders all said the same thing, "If you were daft before you smoked that joint then do not blame it on the joint for you being daft." Now what gets me is if they know this then how come everyone does not know this. If you hire people who do not want to give an honest day's work for an honest day's pay then whose problem is that and why are you making it every ones except for the one that hired them? If they are giving you an honest day's work and doing their job why would you want to humiliate them by forcing them to pee in a cup instead of paying them an honest day's wage?

I heard an elderly person just come unglued after they went through a tedious job interview and was then asked to go down and be tested for drugs. "I am the one who showed up for this interview not my urine. I am the one who filled out the job application not my urine. Does my urine tell you that I am smart, am a self starter and work hard for everything that I have? No." I was out in the waiting room filling out my application and giggling the whole time as she continued. "Why do you think they call it my urine and the good Lord gave it to me? If it was so valuable or said anything about my character, do you really think that He would just let us piss it away! My job skills or lack of them is all that should be needed in order to decide if I am qualified for the job. If I start giving you my urine now for something I am barely going to get by on then Lord knows what you will start taking from me later on for the same nowhere job." With that she threw open the office door and walked out.

He followed her to the door with this stunned look on his face and I was laughing so much that I knew I was not going to get the job. He looked at me all hateful and said, "What do you think is so unbelievably funny!"

I replied, "Her telling you off," and I took my application with me and followed her outside. "You know its humiliating enough not to be able to retire at my stage in life but to have to pee upon command is going beyond public humiliation. I would not be taking all this medication that I cannot afford if I could pee when I needed to. For an employer to have that much power that your personal life is made public. No, I do not think that they should have a right to my medical history and that is all there is to it."

We sat down at a park bench and I just listened to her, "Some companies go beyond testing for drugs, they test for things that will keep you off the medical insurance. They told my girlfriend that they could not put her on their insurance because she had a pre-existing condition. When she had asked them what they were talking about they came right out and told her, "It's because you have cancer." She never knew and to be told heartlessly by someone who has no intention of hiring you. Needless to say it devastated her and I lost my girlfriend of fifty two years. My husband lost his job because the corporation tested him for drugs and found the steroids our family doctor put him on. He tried to explain and even gave permission to call and verify with our doctor but they would not have it. They fired him four months before he was suppose to retire, now neither one of us can afford the medications we need and if I do not find a job soon we are going to loose our house too."

I know, if having a job was so important to her then she should have peed in the cup right? Her husband thought that the job was important enough to do it and look what it cost him. These were proud elders at one time and now they were being reduced because of a urine sample that should have been nobody's business but their doctors. She said that when her husband went to work the day after his test all his co-workers were making jokes about them finding steroids before he was ever called into their office. Now how did they find out before him and is that not suppose to be confidential, it is with your doctor! I guess that is the difference, your doctor takes an oath to keep it between the two of you and your employer swears they will use their finding to destroy your life if they can.

It was not enough to have the government tell you how to run your lives in your own home, now we have our employers putting their nose in an area it does not belong. Both the elders and the elderly have more than shown that they know how to run their own lives and have more than proven that they can. We are the ones who should be listening to them, not telling them what they are allowed to do. I am not an elder by any means but I am sick of watching them be degraded by spoiled childish brats. These people cannot run their own lives but yet they are putting themselves in charge of everyone else except themselves. I mean company policy should only apply to the company and should not extend into people's private lives. "You cannot have a glass of wine with dinner because the corporation does not like their hired hands to have alcohol in their system." Should that not apply to while on company time and how many big wigs have a scotch or two at lunch and come back to work after they ate?

I asked an employer one time why they felt the need to test for alcohol when it was legal. They replied, "We are a perfect family here and drinking alcohol even if its away from here effects all of us, after all we are all one." (If my elders were here I could ask them what the difference between a cult and a corporation was because I cannot find one.) I firmly believe that there is a great perfection about my family but to think that they are perfect or ever will be is just plain nuts. For an employer to think that you are their family and to treat you the way that they do is ludicrous but to say that you have to remain blemish free is not only arrogant but ignorant as well. My mum will tell you that even though we maybe a family, a family is still made up of individuals who will sin until their last breath. Try as they might not to they are still going to. (I think she called it something like human nature or some kind of foreign word like that.) I might want perfection in whatever I am doing but I will never find it in myself and nobody else is going to either because it is not there so stop being perverted and quit looking.

What was the difference between the way the elders had started off in the work force and the way it is now, the atmosphere. You could relax and be who you were and have an accident here and there because it just happens. Now you have employers belittling employees to the point where they clock in pre scolded and scared to be human. "You have to do it this way or I will threaten you with your meagre wage job." They give you all these safety rules to follow that they themselves have no intention of obeying and make a federal case out of you being human. They work you past your means and consider it safe. I was coming down a ladder one time and I had my back to it and I actually had a boss run over there and tell me to go back to the top and come down the right way, now what the hell! I thought that I was at work not at school and should I not come down the ladder the way I feel the most comfortable?

I stayed right where I was on that ladder when we got into it because it forced him to have to look up to me instead of down, it took all his inflated power away. "If you want to play with puppets on a string then stop hiring people. As long as I am getting the job done it should not matter how I do it, the important thing is its getting done and correctly I might add. The only reason you came over here was not for safety reasons but you think by reprimanding me in front of everyone it will make you look bigger and give you more power. You are just proving to the crew that I was correct about you being an ignorant controlling horse's bum all along." I then proceeded to get off the ladder the same way I started. Now you know that he was not about to be shown up in front of a crew he caused to gather around.

He climbs up that ladder, gets to the top and yells, "You will climb up and down the ladder like this. Do I make myself clear little girl?"

He was not even a third of the way down when it fell backwards trapping him underneath it. He fell pretty fast and landed twice as hard. I walked over to him and asked, "Now is it clear little boy why I climb down differently than the way I went up you controlling moron. Now is falling off a ladder the safest thing to do?" I then went to the foremen who had witnessed everything and asked to either be transferred or I was just going to leave because I cannot do my job with someone on my bum wanting everything their way while standing there doing nothing. I am very honoured to say that I was not transferred nor did I have to leave. The bloke underneath the ladder is the one who lost his job. The first safety rule of any job should be: Do not piss off your employees because they are the ones doing all the work, they work better when they are happier and this makes them more productive. Life gave me the same situation that my Grandfather was given and I learned from him just how to take care of it. (I am not as verbally nice as he is when it comes to having my fill but now I have my mum to help me work on that!) I also learned at that moment that everything he had taught me about proper work ethic had indeed made me an asset and we got rid of the ass, I mean burden.

Why do I respect my elders and think so highly of them, look at what their teachings help me to become. Most adults teach you just enough to become an ass but the elders teach us how to become assets in not only work but in our home life. They laughed when we did not quite understand what was meant or implied but never belittled us for it. I was playing outside in the pouring rain (like I still do) when one of the neighbours yells, "Do you not have enough sense to come in out of the rain?" The first thing I did was check my pockets for coins and replied, "No, I did not know I had to have any money." You could hear my Grandfather laughing all the way down the block. He knew when I was being a smart brain and when I was just simply in another field playing.

I guess that is one of the reasons that I miss the elders of my time because they knew the difference between more than one thing. I was never reprimanded for the things that would come out of my mouth; instead I was corrected and told what would have been a more appropriate response. I asked my elders what the difference was and they said that one is used to point you out as the error and the other one is used to take the errors out of something. Now days nobody explains anything any more or if they do it is to people who already know what is going on? Why not share what little knowledge you do have with the ones who know even less? What are we scared of, that they might figure out something that we have been stumped on for years and show us up? If we start teaching like the elders did then there would be no reason to feel shown up or instill the need for one-up-man-ship now would there?

Because there has been a forcing in the changing of the guard there is now a fog of arrogance and it is getting worse. "Let me show you the correct way of doing that," is all you ever hear any more. What does it mean, basically because I am from this country or was born in this manner that makes me better then you and I know everything. People, just because someone has their own style of doing things does not mean that they are doing it incorrectly and just because they are not doing it your way does not make them wrong. Why do you not watch them and see if you can pick up something or would that indeed prove that you do not know everything! All of my elders were from different parts of the world and they were never disrespectful to each other because they were from a different nationality and with it had different styles of doing things. I would hear the elders exchange ideas and all you would ever hear is, "So that is how you were taught to do it? How interesting, I would have never thought to do it like that." Now that is all anyone needs in order for them to come after you, all you have to do is be different.

Is that how we consider a diverse melting pot to be? Some place where they boil you alive until you let go of everything that you once were to be the same as everyone else? I for one am a proud half breed and both my nationalities are equal to the ones that I am not and the other way around as well. (Now that I am a part of my family's nationality I am also part nut part fruit.) I have been a great number of places and if I see something in a culture that I admire I will incorporate within myself and I was taught that there is nothing wrong with that. We are suppose to be diverse people and way to many of us have been stuck on that being just one thing for far to long and it is time to enjoy the other rides in the park. Besides that just because you are on the ride of, "I am always right because I said so," does not mean that you are.

Elders were not about doing it their way; it was all about showing you more then one way of trying different things. If you could not catch on one way then there were plenty of others ways to catch on to the same thing. Now all you get is maybe one try at something and, "Well, there are plenty of other things to try." Why do we feel the need to throw in the towel because we cannot get something the first couple of times? Is it because we see other people struggling and we do not want that too happen to ourselves or is it just easier to give up and just say, "Well I thought about trying but it just looked to hard." We have somehow been taught to resent those who go further in life then we do and to simply make fun of them because they are doing something that we are not. We have become so self indulgent in the tearing down of something or someone that we do not understand and somehow this has become socially acceptable. We somehow feel justified when we destroy a life or a family just because we can. I do not believe that the elders of our time had this in mind when they survived their hardships and lived through wars. I do not believe that they wanted to give us more so that we could turn into greedy, arrogate, self righteous over indulgers who found a new game called: Who can we go after next until they break?

We have disconnected ourselves from anything remotely human and use modern technology to keep that distance between us. "It is all fun and games until someone gets hurt." As long as it is someone else being hurt we never bat an eye but when we are the ones who get hurt then oh put the world on hold because we are the ones who suffered an injustice and someone is going to pay. (Usually someone innocent but as long as it is not us personally then who cares.) We use technology to spread rumours as fast as lighting, to keep gossip at an all time high and to keep tragic events in the public eye. If we had to write all of this by hand I wonder how much of that gossip would now be worth mentioning.

As long as it devastates that is all we care about, as long as we can keep you hurting then lets not stop until we have dug at someone so hard that they take their own life why because it is news worthy. Then after they take their own life lets splatter it all over the headlines until we stop making money off of it. We sensationalize the ones who murder and give them their lifetime worth of fame but not a word is mentioned about the life that was taken. Why is that, because we can make more money off the person who created the horrific act then we can off of the dead victims? Nice world that we live in when the only time you can receive justice is when you are the one who committed the crime and somehow the victim gets turned into the culprit. We had innocent until proven guilty when the elders were in charge and now because we have dethroned them all we have is, "I apologize but you cannot afford your innocence's." Elders made the criminal pay with their lives if need be and the victim received justice which turned them into survivors and made them want to hold their head up high.

We had elders who were so thick skinned that petty things did not bother them and now you have to be politically correct or you might just hurt someone's thin anorexic feelings. I apologize, if you want to remain a baby all of your life that is your business but do not make the rest of the world lie down and die with you. Putting a name or a label on something just to make it more palatable shows just how ignorant we are making ourselves. How many of us have heard our elders say, "You cannot please everyone all the time so why try." Why have we gone to such great lengths to pacify those who want to stay weak minded and then go to the extremes that we do to attack those who have a strong will and spirit? Simple, weak minded people are easier to control and manipulate because all you have to do is convince them that you did something great for them and they will not think to question it.

Our elders taught us that if we wanted to go far in life we needed a good education correct? Now we are teaching them that education will get you nowhere but if you are good at some kind of sport you can write your own ticket and do what ever you want as long as you win that trophy for the case. We took everything that they handed to us like it somehow always belonged to us and have left nothing in return. The elders fought in wars over the violation of human rights and now we only fight in wars that will bring more oil and do not care whose human rights are violated as long as we get want we want.

I do not believe that the elders fought for freedom just so that later on we can go after the weaker ones and make them pay through their nose. They fought for civil liberties and now you have governments selling their own peoples out to the highest bidder and you have no say in the matter because they did it behind closed doors and therefore behind your back so you will not be the wiser. They fight to be the super power because they want to be the only one in charge but this is somehow suppose to be different then want Hitler and Lucifer were after and the corporations are leading up to becoming. I thought that we already had a super power (DAD) or do we choose to forget that until something disastrous happens or we need someone to pin it on?

We tell kids that they are not allowed to pray because that might take away from their faith in the school system but do you really think that you are conceited enough to stop them? All of the elders will tell you that you may take prayer out of school but you cannot stop kids from praying in school, just ask any kid who did not study for a test the night before! We tell them that they cannot pray when they feel the need but tell the nation as a whole when they can come together and bow their heads to pray as one. Excuse me but if a nation can pray together as one because a tragic event occurred then what is stopping the world from praying together as one before a tragedy happens! Does it really bloody well matter that much how you want to pray or is it more important that you know there is a higher power above you and it is not the government?

The elders did not preach one thing, teach another and then do whatever the hell they wanted or could get away with. They taught by being the example and left the rest up to you. If you complied you were rewarded and if you had to be reprimanded you lost your reward. They were brought up that way and look at how they turned out, hard working people who took care of each other so much so that they could leave an "inheritance" instead of debt. We sure are showing them by breaking all the rules and landing where we did. The sad thing is I think we are trading debt for faith. That could explain why: "In God We Trust" is on the back of money and not on the front because a nation that follows the rules will never be in debt and neither will the people who live in it.

My elders left me with some questions that I still cannot figure out. When you pay off your home note, why are you still paying for it until the day you stop breathing? If you cannot pay your bills they can take everything that you have until the debt has been satisfied? However if you live in a white house you can become trillions of dollars in debt and nobody blinks an eye. How come the white house has not been repossessed due to financial debt? I am not a mathematician by any means but I thought that a trillion dollars was more than hundreds of dollars at least?

See if the government would run things like the elders had set it up then they would know that you have to work for the money that you earned and that keeping the home fires burning was far more important then burning the midnight oil for a soulless corporation choking the life out of your family. This is not rocket science it is just common sense, if you lead by example the rest will follow. If you preach one thing and do another do not be surprised if no one wants to listen, follow or believe you any more.

We teach kids at a young age that fighting never solves anything but that war is the only way to bring about peace. Do we even know what an oxymoron is any more (pointedly foolish) or do we not pay attention to what we are teaching? "Do as I say not as I do" is a village saying and have we not yet learned that they make for lousy teachers! Freedom is not free because there is too much money to be made from it, if peace were more profitable nations would not be going hungry. I guess it makes bigger headlines to announce how many people have died killing someone else then how many kids we fed in our own backyard. We prefer to spend money killing people for oil then we would making sure that our kids have something to eat every night. We cut funding for education because nothing is being taught any more except for, "This is the proper way to fill in this circle," and it does not take a lot of money to teach that kind of nonsense, and the elders fought for this!

We allow criminals to further their education, even give them free housing and how many square meals a day do they get? I remember a number of times where I went to bed hungry and the only crime I had committed was not being able to afford food because I needed a roof over my head more. I once heard that it takes a hundred thousand dollars a year to support one person in prison yet I have to work ten years to make that much, now that should be a crime. We yell and scream over sweat shops and how they are working long hours and not being paid a living wage but if you sugar coat it by calling it a minimum wage job it makes it somehow different and therefore o.k.? I cannot find any difference between the two but some people make a big production out of one when in reality, logic puts them the exact same.

We stopped teaching the basics and without it nothing else seems to matter any more. The elders had the basics and learned to build on it so that everything that mattered was looked after. The elders knew that faith is far greater then money, that some things can be a blessing in disguise and to never loose your faith while waiting for a blessing. They knew that the way home was through your actions and not your bank account and that your intelligence will take you further than stupidity will ever allow. The elders had been there, gone through this, that and everything in-between and gave us the shirts off their back and to show our gratitude we leave them out in the cold while disregarding everything they had been through to obtain their wisdom.

The ironic thing is we are not only leaving them out in the cold but we are leaving the human race and it's Creator in the same predicament. We leave people out and allow the gadgets to come pouring in and the elders did just the opposite so how hard would it be to fix all of this? Well let's see, Dad teaches

153

one thing while man teaches another so I guess it all boils down to who you want to listen to. The elders listened to Dad and were much happier for it and now people listen more to man and have become miserable because of it. (The elders had a saying, until you get His teachings correct do not come preaching to me.) Basically it goes with that saying, if your friends all jumped off a bridge would you follow? Dad is the parent and man is the friend and right now we have more listening to man then to Dad.

I know that my mum has said that more than once and Lord knows how many times the elders have let that phrase cross their lips. They never fought for power but for the survival of their loved ones. Now we have wars all over the place including inside our own homes. We have wars for all seasons and for all reasons. The war on illiteracy, religion, drugs you name it and all it is doing is pulling everyone apart instead of finding a way to bring them together. Instead of arresting people for doing drugs why not spend that money going after child molesters and putting a permanent stop to them. We arrested innocent people for smoking an herb that Dad put here but had to let out rapists and molesters to make room for the herb smokers and this is your tax dollars being put to good use. They have us bickering amongst ourselves and that is keeping us distracted from what is really important. I do not care if someone wants to do drugs, it's their body that they are screwing with but do not touch my kid. We have to learn and teach and not go bossing people around and controlling their every move and thought.

Faith is a feeling inside of you and it belongs to you and only you. My elders would tell me all the time that people and life will test your faith and protecting it can only make it stronger. Putting things right with your mind is a good place to start and then sooner or later your heart will follow. The same goes for putting things right inside your heart sooner or later your mind will follow. You have to figure out the difference between right and wrong because it clarifies the difference between good and evil to an even greater degree. You may make mistakes along the way but as long as you are paying attention you will get the hang of it. Keep in mind that making mistakes does not make you evil, what is set in your mind does.

The elders would all say that in the end it all boils down to good vs. evil and picking the one that you want to be and seeing it through to the end. The elders were already one or the other so I was not too sure how they grew to become that way. Now that my mum has helped me to connect what the elders have taught me about everyday life I am learning that the path is not as hard as I made it appear to be. It does have more to do with your mind set then anything else. I know that there are a great number of kids who do not want to grow up like their parents but thankfully I am not one of them any more because I have a great set of parents. If you listen to someone who has an evil heart then they could put your mind down that path without you being the wiser. The elders I knew all had good hearts but I was too busy being pissed off because of the no parent thing for it to really sink in.

I am learning now that every generation is not separated by anything except for knowledge. I also learned that what made the elders so great is that they could talk to each generation as it came to them and they could fit in with anybody. Now people have become so hateful that they do not even like themselves much less someone smarter than them, we have learned to make fun of people far too long and to destroy them at all cost but do not like it when it happens to us. We have to learn how to break certain cycles while learning how to hold onto the values that matter. If we do not learn how to be proud of who we are and the skin that we live in then we will never be proud of anyone standing next to us. I learned this by watching the way the elders would say grace at the dinner table. None of their heads were bowed but rather held high because they looked up to Dad and knew which direction he was. They were proud to be in their bodies because they knew that no one else had been given the same one....ever.

They were proud of their laugh lines because they had earned them and would never have given them up for anything in the world. They were not vain by any stretch and knew that their health and what was on the inside was far greater than anything you could find to replace it with. One of my elders was born without a bridge in her nose and she never had it fixed because she said that there was nothing wrong with it. Everyone made comments about it but you could tell that it never affected her in anyway because she knew that this was just one way that Dad made her different from the rest. She adored not looking like everyone else and I always thought that it made her look unique. Now you have people doing the most grotesque things to their body thinking that will make them happy. Changing the wrapping paper does not change what is in the box. Instant gratification will end up costing you more in the long run then what you may realize. This goes back to man preaching one thing and Dad teaching us another.

He made us in His image and some of us are telling Him that it is not good enough. I know that humans make fun of things that they are not but let that fall with them. Did you ever stop to think that the reason they are making fun of you is the fact that they are jealous because they are like everyone else?

Look at what makes you different and be proud of it because Dad gave that to you and you should not let anyone take it away from you or get you to change it yourself. Holding on to what makes you different makes you stronger. Wanting to be nothing more than what they call eye candy is not only shallow it is annoying. (Also people who just want eye candy will never allow you to be who you are or want to be so be careful about what line your hook is on before you swallow.) My mum has never been shallow and is one of the most gorgeous angels I have ever seen in my lifetime but it has nothing to do with her outer appearance and everything that she is on the inside which makes her outside glow. This holds true for everybody. I even thought that all of my elders were sexy good looking because of who they were on the inside and the smiles they would share on the outside.

Maybe that is all my elders were trying in different ways to teach, how to look for depth on the inside of people and if you cannot find it in someone you may never will. My mum has a tremendous amount of depth to her and the more she shares with me the more I enjoy being a part of it. Going through life bum backwards is not all that bad now that I look at it. Some people have a good home life but later on learn to grow bitter because of what the world puts them through, and then there are the ones like myself who went through hell early enough that it can still be taken out of us. I used to not wish my life on anyone and would have traded anyone in the blink of an eye but look at what all I would have missed out on, knowledge, wisdom, love, understanding and someone who loves me so unconditionally that it is hard to loath the people in the world giving you such a hard time. (I say loath now because my mum does not like or allow the "H" word to be used and she can box my ear-hole. She would not but just knowing that she could makes me stop doing things that gets on her nerves.)

Most people never realize what is really important until its to late to do anything about it but thanks to life giving me such a rough ride I know what I want in life, but most of all I know who I want to share it with. The elders never having met my mum and the rest of the family have somehow tied in with each other and I get to be a link in-between the two. We have all spent our life time separating ourselves from each other but in the end it is who you stay connected to that makes all the world of difference. The elders were superior in their knowledge of this from having survived long enough to make it to the top, but the secret is not letting it go to your head and instilling it inside your heart along side your Faith. Keeping these two feeling together keeps you stronger when somebody tries to break you.

The elders were all about strength in so many different ways and that it was more than about numbers. They each possessed all four strengths; physical, mental, spiritual and strength of the heart. Each of these started out weak but throughout their journeys they replaced what they had to in order for them to become strong and that to me is admirable. They had four out of four and that is what made them elders and I have since noticed that these four are what are challenged throughout your life. My Grandfather was teaching me how to be physically strong so that I would not stop myself which in turn made me mentally stronger. My mum gave me the heart to come home and that is where I am now. The cool thing is that since it is my mum's heart I find myself being that much more protective of it. I am not in a hurry to speed through this stage in my life because I want to enjoy and explore every moment of it.

I learned that I never really could have loved anybody even as hard as I tried because I was never shown the good kind of love. I am figuring out that the way my mum loves me is the way I want to be loved and I can feel my heart growing stronger, it stills has a long way to go in order to catch up with the other two but my Family is not on a time clock. I am figuring out that there is a big difference between being used and being unconditionally loved and that just because someone needs you does not mean that they love you. A full family circle consists of: I love you because I want you, I want you because I need you and I need you because I love you, just make sure that it is not hollow when you complete it because it will make you feel empty. (The one for a lover is different and should go desire, pleasure, crave.) You complete the circle so that it can be filled and not with hot air coming from someone you are trying to encircle. My elders encircled me without me being the wiser and when they went home I thought that I was left with nothing but I am discovering that they left me with the keys I would need to find the heart in which I would be truly calling home.

The elders are needed now more then ever because they pass onto us their four hidden strengths through their words of wisdom and understanding. Life is about testing all four and sometimes all at once but in the end you are the only one who can stop you. If you will notice age does not account for any of this because just like my elders believed and have taught me it has nothing to do with life. I think that is daft to base your whole life around a number and to tell people that they have to achieve whatever stations in life by a certain age. If you do things in your own time you will have a better feel for them and therefore a better appreciation for them. Maybe you are not ready for it now, plus I was always taught that it was rude and highly ill-mannered to ask any one their age.

To tell someone that they cannot do something any more because they have a certain number attached to their birth cheats everyone involved. A birthday is meant to celebrate someone's life not the number and should be considered sacred. The elders never put the age on a birthday cake and never wasted their breath filling up black balloons like they are mourning something. It was to be a festive day filled with laughter and not making someone feel bad and like they want to die when they make their wish.

If you take away age and gender then what do you have left? Simple, the things that truly matter. If you take this away and instill only age and gender then you rob people of what they were meant to be, themselves. Dad gave all of us emotions not just to the female gender and along those same lines He gave us all strengths not just to the gender of males. If you do not believe me then look it up for yourselves, we are called His children because He does not separate us into gender. He never says that one is the weaker one while the other is forced into being the stronger one that is man pulling that crap. He knows that human beings have to have all their emotions in order to become well rounded balanced people who posses inner strengths. You can never achieve all four when you leave even just one out. People after all are human beings and we all need the same things in life even if we cannot admit it to ourselves.

Life is not just about having Faith but learning how to put strength to it and heart and putting it all together gives you the mental strength to go through anything. Life is tough but you have to learn how to be tougher and giving that strength to your Faith gives your heart the courage to go through anything. Dad gave us everything in life including the elders and we need to stop acting like we know better then He does about what we need. Our wants and desires should not cost us our Faith even in the human race. He gave all of us the means to be who we are and just like the elders we should be proud of that fact and do something with it. The people in society will always try and make you feel less then who you are and if you believe them over Dad then it will always eat at you.

Society wanted me to feel like less than who I was because I did not come out of a loving home but I have learned that instead this turned me into a talented survivor and gave me the means to find a family who survives life through love. You have to not only be tough you have to have a balance between all four of your strengths and doing this will always keep you safely guided to what is right in life. Remember: Anyone can go off the deep end but can you get yourself to make a come back! Life is about taking knocks and learning to do something with them besides using them to knock other people down. Life is about being handed the torch and holding your head up high even if you have mud all over your face because you are part of the human race. If the elders can be proud of who they are because they earned it then what is stopping us from being glad that we are at least getting there? Everything comes in due time but putting the elders back in charge is long over due. I found out that I may have been lucky enough to grow up with my elders but that not everyone is. They may have been luckier in other ways but without the knowledge to know the difference how will they ever learn to appreciate it. I learned through the elders how to appreciate a good family without having one of my own. Now that I have one of my own I have learned to appreciate the wisdom the elders passed down to me in order to realize when I have one. I also learned that not being given something right off the bat can be better for you because it gives you a chance to better yourself in order to become more deserving of it. (I may have entered the world through the bum but at least I am coming out ahead for it, better then the other way around.)

I am figuring out that life is not necessarily what is handed to you and what you do with it but more so what you make of yourself because of it or allow others to make out of you. I could have let the world turn me into a poor me baby or allow them to make me feel like I could not do anything right but why! The only feeling that comes from this is pitiful and if Dad tells us that what does not kill us makes us stronger why would we let others convince us to believe otherwise? Who is smarter Dad and the elders or the ones trying to play like they're a god! Life itself is not twisted; it's the people in it trying to make it appear that way because they themselves have stayed that way. Lies can be twisted with the truth to make them more believable but you have to be smart enough to figure it out for yourself. Keep in mind the old wise saying: Some of the most simplest and necessary truths are the last to be believed. Why because gossip is juicier and since the truth cuts right to the bone it gives you something to gnaw on. I personally would rather gnaw on a bone then chew the fat any day. One makes your jaw flap and the other gives you something to cut your teeth on, the wisdom is learning not to bite the hand that loves you.

I may have cut some of my teeth long before I met my mum and I may have shown them to her a couple of times without meaning to but the one thing that I will never do is use them on her like so many offspring are inclined to do. I know my place with my family without having to be put there. There is no need to challenge anyone in the family because we all have our own rightful place and that makes a world of difference. I have also learned that I did not have a place with the elders but that I was placed with them. The difference is when the group is disbursed so is your place among them and that is not where I belonged anyway. I do not mind that my mum is the one who found out where I truly belonged, the important thing that I love keeping in mind is my family is not going to disburse so I will always have my place in the family.

I learned a great deal from my elders and will always give them credit for turning me into a proper kid my mum thought was worth adopting and holding onto. I had learned a lifetimes worth of Honour, Loyalty and Respect but until now I had no one to share them with. Now that I have a whole family to share with I am finding out that my families morals are the same as my elders and that everything that was taught was not learned in vain. I learned that sometimes you have to hang on even if you do not know what you are hanging in there for because it could be bigger then you imagined. I hung in there for a mum but ended up holding onto a family that I never realized I so desperately needed.

My elders kept me mentally stable (well, as best as they could with me,) but my family is the one who gives me proper balance. I no longer over compensate for anything because all of my needs are being taken care of through the love and support of my family. My elders taught me what to look for but I had to figure out the rest. "This is what a proper family is about," is a lot different than, "This is a proper family." My mum never tried to take away the old world teachings that had become a part of me; she just helped me to modernize my way of thinking and is showing me how to include real family as part of it. You would think that when you get family you would know what to do with them or how to love them but that is not always the case.

I learned through the elders how to filter out all the bad ones before they become imbedded and so far I have done a pretty good job but I could not figure out what to do with the good ones. I learned how to be a fighter and a survivor but it threw me off when I did not have to be this way with my mum. I thought that if she did not need me to protect the family like I was taught by my grandfather how to do then it was a waste of her time to include me. The strange thing is between what my elders taught me and what my family is teaching me I am going to get it through my head one way or the other and I know that my heart will follow.

I am learning that there is a difference between being protective of your family and protecting the family. My mum never adopted me to protect the family but somehow knew in her heart that I needed a protective family and they are just that and more. The elders taught me what to look for and my family is showing me how a real family protects through love. Anything outside of that is a village and I have had enough of that for several lifetimes.

There may be a great number of us who were raised in a village but the greatest thing is that we do not have to remain that way if we do not want to, but you have to be willing to let go of any grudge because bringing it with you will only hurt those who truly want to love you. I understand that we all come with some kind of baggage but when you move on remember to pack light and only bring what will help you to grow. You cannot expect someone else to help you through anything if you are not willing to let go of what you have always known. Despite contrary belief pain does not make you feel alive, as a matter of fact it does just the opposite. Pain was created to let you know that you have been hurt, that is all. Love or being loved is what makes you truly feel alive so why would you want to hold onto the other one for dear life? Starting any kind of new relationship will never work if you refuse to acknowledge that holding onto past pains is what is keeping you from being who you were meant to be. Happiness is not a long shot by any means and if the elders could find it on their way home then I know that we can while we still have time.

One of the simplest things that the elders taught me is that pain can be talked through and it has to be in order for any kind of healing to begin. I realize that the more I talked with my mum about what I had been through the less of a hold it had on me until it had no choice but to let go because she is the one in charge of things now and forever. I also learned through her that holding onto a past pain allows their side to win even after all this time. I do not know about you but I think that if my sanity was up for grabs I prefer to win it back than just to give it to them without a fight. My elders were all quite sane considering I was mixed in with them and the way I see it is if they could do it with me then I should have no problem getting through it too. Going through hell is not a bad thing, however keeping yourself there will keep you traumatized for life and there again there is no reason to. Hell is meant to either give you a life lesson or a reward but if you choose not to look at it this way then all you will end up with is a life long punishment.

Anything can be overcome if you are willing to put forth the effort and see it through to the finish line but it will never come to be if you give up mentally before you even start. You have to decide what is more important to you not to someone else. Being one of my mum's kids was important to her but until I made it important enough to myself it would not have mattered. I learned the hard way (like I usually do with everything in my life) that pain can and will make you feel not good enough for anything but letting go makes you feel worthy of not only being loved but loving someone else as well. You may feel like you are not good enough but the thing to keep in mind is that they are your feelings not someone else's and until you get over yourself you will never have the heart to be truly loved. I had to decide for myself what was more important to me; my mum, family and the elders' teachings or all those years of pain. Yes, my mum was willing to give me a one way ticket into her life but that is all she offered. She never said that she would change my heart, mind or life; she knew that if I wanted it bad enough I would have to learn to change those things for myself. Doing it any other way would make me a burden to her and why would I want to do that to someone who offered me a one way ticket prepaid out of a village life I never cared to live in, in the first place!

I made the leap of faith when I discovered the oxymoron about hell. Even though they show hell as fire and all I figured out that it is indeed an ice cold place and so are the people in it. When I figured out that my mum was warm and that I was the one being cold to her (a learned village thing) I could not wait to pull my head out of my backside to jump into that warm family blanket (after I showered of course.) I knew the moment I heard the elders echo in my ears: Those young ones always rush into things before they even know what their doing, who knows one of these days they might just learn to open their eyes. That was it, I learned to survive hell because I learned how to keep my eyes closed and feel my way through but jumping with your eyes closed is never a good thing. Well no wonder I kept landing in a village! "What is holding me here and keeping me away from my family?" When you learn that it is your eyes all you can really do is just roll them and adjust them before they come back around.

The elders were right all along, some of us go through things with our eyes closed and head first which can only lead to black eyes and headaches and I had done it my whole life so I swelled my eyes shut. You miss out on the beauty when you do that but since I was still living a village life I did not mind until I saw how beautiful and wonderful my mum's family is. I may be hard headed but I am not daft and I learned what I needed to do in order to join that side. I will more then admit that I was scared but I learned something far greater. Being scared just makes you a little bit nervous but fear will keep you standing right where you are. Fear without me knowing it had consumed me, no wonder I led myself to believe that I was not scared of anything. I figured out that the only thing I feared was someone finding out that I was born in a village, since my mum already knew this I learned that there was nothing to be scared of and the fear just disappeared. (Fear is nothing once it is exposed.)

Once my fears were exposed to the light, I learned that they were not as big as they would have liked to have stayed and they lost everything, including the hold I allowed them to have on me. My mum's love, all the elders teachings and my family were bigger then the fear. If the elders teachings of respect being a two way street was correct then why was I giving fear the respect it was not giving me? I did just like my Grandfather told me; I fired it without giving it a two weeks notice. The funny thing is that as big as fear may come to be once you see it for what it truly is you can make it beg. "Oh please, if you let me back in I will do...." and the lies get filled in. Fear is no more than a coward inflation of the unknown. Once you deflate it you expose it for the coward it really is and then you tend to feel silly that you were ever scared of it in the first place. Once you figure out that being scared of something just because you do not know something about it turns into light when you learn something about it you can go beyond that point that made you scared. When you look back at everything that made you fearful because you did not know something about it, look at how far away that fear is and how much further you were able to go without it. The thing to remember is that fear can be worked upon until it is preyed upon, it can also be instilled through the seed of a thought and you have the ability to make the fear stop growing. Fear is a weed in your mind and learning how to overcome your fears weeds your mental garden and allows positive thinking to take hold giving it a chance to grow.

Every one of our fears can be overcome when you learn to discipline your mind to such an extreme that your subconscious more than agrees. When someone tries to break you they first do it through fear, either your own or the ones that they want you to believe that you have until you believe that you should concern yourself with having them. If you do not learn to control your own thoughts you will never learn to believe in yourself so that others cannot break you no matter how hard they're allowed to try. Your subconscious knows how to think and you should learn to connect yourself with it because then you will have two things backing up your spine. Learning how to control your thoughts stops people from getting inside your head and rearranging your thoughts to where you learn how to doubt yourself on the spot. Instead of becoming surer of yourself and going further you waste time having to justify your actions while they're keeping you at a stand still. The more you learn about fear, the more your realize that people will use it against you so that they can waste your time and keep you held back from becoming everything great that they're to lazy to be. The more you can get yourself to work as a team the greater the feeling of empowerment you will learn to possess. Your mind is not a toy and should be considered a razor sharp instrument in the key to your self-esteem. You can use it to keep yourself cut down to size or you can use it to cut through all the smoke screens and begin to see what is truly there and has been all along. A smart, attractive from the inside out, can do anything that they set their mind to heart of a human being. Imagine that feeling pulsing from your brain to your heart through your backbone! Fear would learn not to come close to ever knocking on your door ever again because it would know ahead of time that it did not stand a chance in hell of putting you through anything so why bother.

The elders taught me a lot but the one thing that I learned for myself is that just because people want you to be a certain way, does not mean that you have to bow down and be that way. People want your greatest fears to come to the surface so teach your mind not only how not to have any but how to pull any before the have a chance to root. No fears, no worries and it gives you more time to figure out that, "You can learn something new every day!"

# Chapter Five
# "You Can Learn Something New Every Day"

You really can learn something new every day, even if it is just a saying like a small piece of knowledge or wisdom. Relying on knowledge takes courage of conviction, sticking with it shows gained wisdom.

Being a kid at heart and wanting to play and have fun does not make you less intelligent nor does it make you less of an equal human being. Keeping this in mind keeps you ahead of the game, keeps your head in the game and therefore you stay out of their mind game.

You can learn to either leave your mark or be an easy mark.

Knowing how to defend yourself and not need it is better then needing to defend yourself and not know how or even where to begin.

Some people will go out of their way to make you feel ignorant so that you will not realize just how intelligent you really are.

Sometimes casual conversation can be used for friendly digging, even if it is for someone else that is not there.

A key is worthless without a lock, a lock will stay that way without a key and nobody should be allowed their own skeleton key to pry into your personal mental closet. If they made one without your knowledge, learn how to change the locks so that it cannot be picked from the outside.

We need to bring back quality over quantity.

Setting your own bar keeps you from lowering your own expectations and standards.

The more you lower your intelligence level for someone, the more stupid villagers are allowed to get away with.

Learning to laugh at yourself is different then being force to think something daft is really entertaining and therefore funny.

Instead of keeping your friends close and therefore your enemies even closer, why not change it to keeping your loved ones close keeps the family even closer.

Intelligence can only be achieved when validated- stupidity when validated as intelligence allows the wrong people to think they know it all. Showing that you know how to think on your feet should be rewarded as intelligent. Showing that you know how to ride someone else's coat tails to the top should be looked on as stupid and therefore nipped in the bud and made to be corrected by the one riding the coat tails.

Stupidity needs correcting; intelligence never does unless used to make someone feel stupid that rightfully is not.

Stupidity never uses intelligence, not using your intelligence shows stupidity.

Making someone feel bad because they were not taught something that you learned, shows your hidden ignorance. Reassuring someone that just because they do not know something, does not make them ignorant and will help them to learn that they are smart. Helping someone to realize they are intelligent brings yours along for the ride and using them together brings about greater potential.

Whatever happened to: Live and let live unless they're doing someone harm?

Why are we so fast to be led to believe the worst about good people to the point where we want to publicly lynch them without a fair trial? However when evil people have more than proven themselves to be the worst of their kind we drag our feet at a fair trial in order not to lynch them?

It is a dirty job but someone has to do it. Then why not make the ones who created the dirty job do it, maybe next time they'll learn not to leave things that way!

If sex is such a violation of other people's human rights when seen out in public, why are we allowed to publicly violate people sexually in corporate run (scam the hard working people out of every penny that we can) businesses called a urine test?

166

Helping people should not feel like a slap in the face to the ones who need help, and a slap in the face should never be viewed by anyone as a helping hand especially by the one doing the slapping.

People should not be intimated by working tools, making yourself a working tool should not make other people feel intimated just because they're not the same. The right tool for the job is not always going to be the same flat headed screw driver and the best tools are not found in a junk drawer now are they. We need to learn how to separate the tools and appreciate the best ones and stop putting them in the junk drawer.

When someone asks for your hand in marriage where does that leave the rest of you? If the love of your life does not want to hold hands out in public then they should not be allowed to take your heart in private.

Brains without brawns gives you ideas that you will not be able to back up, brawns without brains may make you big but you will never have an idea worth backing up.

Making people feel stupid and telling them that they are so worthless; that they can be replaced just like that is good for production and moral how again?

Hiding the truth for long periods of time causes people to loose sight of it.

If brains and brawns are needed together for creative production, why are we taking creative production out of the educational process? We are taking away the creative process from educated people and making them feel less productive. If you want new and better ideas for a business then reward the ones who know how to be creative and not the ones holding up production.

Being naive is not the same as being ignorant and acting ignorant does not mean that you are actually naïve. Babies are born both and could care less. Why, they know that they can learn as they go and both can be overcome by being exposed to knowledge. When someone makes fun of you because you have not been exposed to something it shows how naïve they are to their own ignorance of never exposing themselves to knowledge to learn how to overcome it. That makes them a childish baby and you just a babe in training like the rest of the people exposing themselves to knowledge. Let them cry a tit fit while you learn.

Corporations use modern technology to take jobs away from humans. Family-owned business (mum-and-pop shops) did not take away human jobs just so that they could afford modern technology.

Since mum-and-pop-owned business believed in family values and corporations take values away from family owned business, why not bring back mum-and-pop shops at the expense of corporations? After all people thrive when something is making a comeback and everyone gets to benefit from it in someway. That would be poetic justice.

What happened to people fighting for justice instead of having to pay out the (I will say nose) for it? A law that is fair to all should not need manipulators stringing themselves to your account and calling it fair justice. If you want fair then only the criminals should have to pay and they should be made to work while they're paying for their crime and the fruit of their labour should be paid to the one who received the injustice.

People believe in propaganda without questioning a word of its truths like it came straight out of the Bible. Some of these same people question the Bible like it was full of government propaganda and therefore not a word of it can be true.

When we find letters to loved ones that we have never met written long ago we claim them as treasures. When we open them up and begin reading them we cannot help but to feel a personal connection to both the writer and the receiver and even begin to picture it in our minds of what it must have been like and wonder where they are now. We feel the love, the pain of them being apart and do what is in our power to find one or the other so that they will know that someone loved them so much that they took the time to put it in a letter. If neither one can be found we still hold on to these sacred treasures, and never question the love that was felt between them because you could feel it through written words.

If you wish that you could find treasured letters such as these or that someone would take the time to write you letters like that someday do not worry because they did. If you do not believe me just open up the Bible, in it you will find nothing but these exact same letters. It should not be considered less of a treasure just because they went and put them all together and called it a book.

Learning to like yourself to where it becomes second nature will cause you to love who you truly are without being conceited.

Second nature is just another name for the subconscious.

People who want to dredge on the horrors of your past just so that they can force you to dwell on them do so because they want to keep you from being successful. If you allow them to succeed at getting you to dwell then you let the horrible people become successful in the pain they put you back through.

Being disruptive should not be considered funny, and being truly funny should not be considered disruptive. One breaks the tension, the other keeps it building.

If someone gets jealous because someone else is just being nice to you it is because they know they're guilty of not truly treating you as well as they should be.

I am never going to be good enough for you am I? No, you later find out that you were to good to put up with them in the first place.

You are smarter than what you think you are but only if you learn to give yourself credit for being smart, so learn how to give yourself credit before someone else can take it away and put it in their account and blow it.

If we learn how to spend time with the ones we love and therefore create fond memories, then time will not turn into wasted moments that are noticed as years. Then we will learn how to see that it was just a moment ago and another one has just past.

It was once said but never uttered again that a true leader honours their followers and takes care of them because they're the ones making your living. Now they have replaced it with people who cannot follow much less know how to lead honourably and take care of you by helping themselves to your hard earned money?

We pass safety laws that protects us from ourselves but who is going to protect us from the people passing laws that violate our safety?

Street smarts prove that you can be taught something hard on the spot. Book smarts shows that you can learn something over time with the only pressure being when it comes to applying it. Both should be learned so that you are not taken by someone who only knows how to use one of these to their advantage. Then you will learn how to have and how to apply knowledge on the spot.

When we keep our brother hanging on the cross we keep Him suffering and loose sight to why He suffered. When we see past the suffering we see how He was able to move on.

Holding someone's past against them is ludicrous, did you not expect them to have a life before they met you? Is it not after all better to be a part of someone's present then to be mentioned as part of someone's past?

Mum-and-pop shops were warm and friendly and worked right along side of their help because they did not hire lazy people. They knew that catering to stupidity would cost them their business. Corporate owned are cold and distant and refuse to work along side of their help. They do not care if catering to stupidity costs good hard working people their jobs. Not until the lazy stupid people is all that they're left with.

When a kid has a talent that someone can make money off of, they become a prodigy. When they put their talents to good use and never ask for a dollar they are told that they are wasting them. When they make money off of their own talent they become a threat. We somehow feel threatened when someone has the potential to use their talents to earn an honest living.

When someone is made to fix a mistake that was not theirs it puts them behind in their own work that they were doing correctly. When the one who made the mistake is not made to go back and fix it they are taught that they can make someone else do their job for them correctly so why bother learning how to fix your own mistakes.

I do not mind helping someone out when they need it as long as they are putting forth more of the effort to take it from there. Otherwise I am just taking on a debt by myself that was never mine and was someone else's responsibility. If they want something bad enough they will learn to work just as hard for it as they wanted you to work hard at getting it for them.

When people learn how to ride the fence between the lesser of two evils they do so to benefit themselves and will never stand for the greater good even when called upon.

The younger you are at heart, the less you care if lines show in the glow of your face.

It has been proven that you have to have a break down before you can have a breakthrough but in order to have a breakthrough you cannot keep yourself broke down.

Learning to laugh with yourself makes it harder for others to gang up on you to get others to laugh at you. At least you can make yourself laugh, they only know how to keep themselves miserable because they keep one thumb in their mouth and I am not sure of what they do with the other one, maybe their using it to point at what they want you to hand them.

Kids will laugh at themselves and with their mates; adults will never have mates because they poke fun until it gives them something to laugh at.

Over protecting your kids because you never want anything bad to happen to them causes them to stay hurt by any little bad thing that will happen to them and it makes you not want to look. Exposing them to what is in life gradually keeps them from staying in a constant hurt or being constantly hurt.

When we give kids educational toys and leave them to it we take away human communication and are not a part of their learning fun because we left ourselves out of it. If we would learn to stay beside them while we see what they're learning, we would feel like a part of their education and feel how much fun it is to learn things together. When you learn things together, they will

170

always know that they can come to you and you will figure it out together, just like you always have.

When you stop asking your parent for permission you give them the impression that you are their equal partner. When you start asking your partner for permission you give them the impression that they are your parent. When you play house see if one of the roles are being concealed.

When someone thinks that you are doing a good job just to show them up and it is proven that you were not you need to be careful because they will always harbour this false resentment towards you even though you cannot prove it. They will then get others to think that they are helping you while pretending that you are the one not doing your part.

Has Amsterdam not been around long enough to prove that using herbs is good for your health since they do not have a massive crime waves going around or starting wars they have no intention of finishing. Herbs have nothing to do with your I.Q. your learning new things does.

Spending your time gripping does not get anything done, taking care of business exposes the ones who want to do nothing but gripe so that they get nothing done.

If you cannot beat them join them, be careful of joining something that beats you down. The fine line is beating someone down to force them to join you places someone in your mists that does not agree with how they got there. When someone wants to beat down your door urging for you to let them join you, they more than intend to cause a full fledged mutiny so that they can take over the ship you built. Joining together to beat people at their own evil games helps you to regain control of the destination of your ship.

Allowing someone to ride your coat tails to the top will soon make you discover that someone is padding their pockets.

Over crowed classrooms leave little time for individual one on one teaching.

When did spending loads of money on someone take the place of showing how much we care about our loved ones?

Building a stairway to Heaven on good deeds and good intentions should make you wonder which way its heading?

Preaching is not good teaching and teaching right from wrong is not preached but shown through the life you lead.

People will try and talk you out of what you know is right to keep others from finding out that they have been doing wrong all this time, and getting you to question yourself gives them time to cover up what you knew were wrong doings. Always follow your gut reaction rather than listening to someone else's.

A fig leaf is all that is needed to hide the truth behind the deceit; the fig leaf removed exposes the naked truth behind their deception.

Sometimes, going after someone to expose them, can expose your true nature. Discrediting someone that has helped you will make you feel like less of a credit to yourself.

Wanting to know everything about someone all at once takes away from spending quality time getting to really know someone. If they want it all at once you should wonder about their quality and if they're really worth the waste that will be your time?

Having someone give you a bad feeling when they are in front of you should tell you something, having them give you a bad feeling when they're standing behind you should tell you everything. Getting a bad feeling from someone from the start should keep you away from them completely.

Admitting your mistakes shows wisdom and fixing your mistakes shows applied knowledge. Acting like you never make any shows ignorance. Trial and error should not be misconstrued as grounds to put you on display for making a simple error. A mistake is one thing and an accident occurs when the same ones are allowed to keep making the same mistakes because someone else will always be made to fix them. The ones who err all the time without learning how to fix their own mistakes should be the ones on trial.

Good people pay dearly for an honest mistake instead of bad people paying dearly for a premeditated motive.

Being exposed to certain things all the time makes them a part of your nature but learning how to swallow an injustice should never be a part of your true nature.

Mental strings can be used to pull at your heart strings to get you to open up your purse strings. When you feel your heart string being tugged through your wallet your mental string should know to keep them all closed up. If your purse string was never approached then your heart and mental strings will be all that is needed.

When the purse string is used in anyway then you have to wonder how much they are going to string you along before placing you on a permanent hook so that they will always have something to play with as they're waiting to reel something else in. They will always use your purse string as bait to lure you into the water. Knowing this makes you the one doing the fishing and knowing how to fish and not bait.

I would rather stand against man then stand with him against Dad.

Why is there such a defined separate line between church and state when they should work as a balance to power? Man would learn that punishments need to fit the crime so that all may be forgiven, not to be repeated and the church would learn that when someone commits a crime they need to be held accountable for it otherwise they punish someone else for it.

They say that the road is paved in gold, and if you look closely at it it's the same road walked upon with good deeds and intention on the road to hell.

A religion that is a fad is just a passing fancy and another way to waste time. When religion is taught so that it becomes a way of life to loving Dad then it is not a passing fancy that you will waste your time on if it does not involve loving Dad.

Just because papers have been created to make something appear to be right, like stringing someone along at a higher price does not mean that it is true. When we learn to dig at injustice we can uncover the truth that they tried to bury. Learning to get our hands dirty is sometimes the best way at uncovering the hidden truth.

Some people cannot handle or stomach the truth, leaving those that can to deal with the lies of handling unstomached truths.

Not knowing anything about something does not make you less intelligent, acting like you know everything does.

Outwitting someone evil exposes them for the little people they have always been. When they are not exposed they can cause good people to feel like they are small and evil.

Using your wits to outsmart someone evil is not diabolical, being evil and using your smarts to outwit someone less intelligent then you should be considered extremely diabolical.

Some people feel so out of control that they take it out on others. Some people feel the need to control others so they will feel like they are in control of their own lives.

Do not knock it until you have tried it yourself, do not knock someone that is at least trying.

We start out liking someone until we can find a reason not to, or until someone's jealously gives us a reason not to. Very seldom do we ever stay long enough for the reason to come from them, it never will because it was never there to begin with.

When we dislike someone we will find every reason that they are not to be trusted. When we like someone we will find every excuse in the book why they are not as bad as everyone says they are. The sad thing is that we are suppose to like the people we feel close to but very seldom do we ever take up for them like that.

Learn to fake it until you make it has carried over into the needs of our life. We learn to fake outrages injustice at the things that do not have anything to do with us. When we really need rage to put a stop to the injustice we tend to give into the side being fake.

Calling a child molester a pervert takes away from their crime because they are not perverts they are molesters. Calling gays perverts does not make them child molesters. They are not molesting their sexual partner; a child cannot be considered a partner in a sexual act and therefore are being violated. Having a partner agree to have sex should not violate their rights. A child molester should have their rights taken away since they molested a child. If you put half as much effort into putting an end to sexual predators and rapist as you do putting a stop to two people having consensual sex then less children would be preyed upon.

If more people learned how to stand for justice instead of outrage courage could stand alone and be all that is needed for justice to prevail.

Hooked on phonics does not work for dyslexics, think they were confused before, try that stuff on them!

War causes both sides to grieve over the loss of their loved ones.

Sexy is not having everyone paw at you sexy is feeling so good about yourself that you do not want people pawing at you.

Sometimes you have to go through life the hard way to get a better understanding of what you're trying to grasp.

There is no longer a difference between right and wrong; you just know that this is the right thing to do even if it looks wrong at the time to everyone else at the time.

Why are some trying to destroy the world that they are so eager to rule?

Letting people take over who are not leaders will allow them to do just that; take over. People who are born leaders will lead by not taking over.

The "Power of Thinking," can only be good for us.

**Oh I Once Saw.**

Oh I once saw things so glorious that it would make your heart sing. The birds danced and the heavens opened to the kindness being passed around. There was something called harmony and it was found in the family but where did it all go now!

Oh I once heard a grandchild being respectful to the ones looking after them, they listened and learned and took great pride in all that they had and learned how to share more then their toys with the ones less fortunate than they but where in the world are they now?

Oh I once heard a baby call out when they were scared and being held ever so close and dear. They knew they were loved and wanted by those that had created them. They did not have to look anywhere but in the mirror to know they were part of a heart that could beat as one anytime of the year, but once again where are they now!

We used to hear: If you mess with my family you mess with me so do not even try to think that you can get away with anything but somehow we opened up the door and let morality just pass us by. We held firm to what we believed and could not be talked out of anything but now money somehow became our family tree. Oh where are we headed now?

I found a mum who saw the things that I once did and brought them all back to me and now I am with her and the family and no matter where we go or what we do we are together inside her heart. Now I remember all of the things that brought me a smile and instead of saying I had once seen I traded it in for I am seeing again the true meaning of a real family and the beat of our family starts in our mum's and dad's hearts.

# Chapter Six
# What If?

What if the soul mate that you are looking for is not another person at all? What if it were as simple as there being two sides to your soul, good and bad and whatever you do throughout your life adds to one side or the other? It is thought that some people are born inherently bad and everything that they do in life will eventually make them turn pure evil. The flip side to that is some people are born so pure that Dad automatically takes them home early so that they will never suffer for any reason.

Then there are those who were born with the scale tipped just slightly more in one direction then the other, but you are not informed which side is the good one you just have to learn to be observant as your dealing in life adds up. You learn that when you do something good it adds to your good side but just a negative thought can withdrawal everything that you have saved up on the positive side. You feel that your heart has a lot to do with keeping you in balance and that your mind should have a firm handle as to what constitutes for better judgment. You feel like there has been something with you all along but because you cannot see it, it tends to elude your thoughts and seeps into your dreams. You see yourself doing things that you would not normally do, or possessing abilities that you never thought that you had but in this one brief moment there you are. You do not have to picture yourself doing it because you see yourself in front of you. Then when you wake you think to yourself,

"I just had the strangest dream." What if it were not a dream at all? What if that was your souls way of communicating with your sub-conscience trying to tell you that if you can dream the unimaginable then doing the impossible is as simple as just setting your mind to it.

They say that the more you can tap into your sub-conscience the greater the understanding you will have of your most inner-self. Deep down some of us are hiding the coward who controls us instead of learning how to control the coward hiding inside of us. Deep down some of us are hiding a knight of true valiant honour instead of letting it sit upon the dragon's back. We want to be something more in our lives before we learn how to be more to ourselves. We start out in life where knowledge is grey and learning how to separate everything right or wrong into black and white losing ourselves somewhere in the mix. The struggle within ourselves is finding out which one we are and building a connection to the one we want to be. We want our soul mate to not only complete us but to completely agree with everything that we do and when you begin to realize that your soul mate is you connecting with yourself you find that you no longer have to reach outside of yourself but now you can reach deep inside the dragon of courage because you have given yourself the ability to do so. Our soul mate is the one looking back at us through the mirror knowing we can do it and setting our conditioned minds up for the challenge ahead and giving a shaky heart the nerve through a steady hand. When everything is both half light and half dark, when you turn the light off and on, one can appear to be different then what it truly is. When you connect yourself to your soul you will notice that you are completely one or the other and you will never again second guess yourself for any reason. Nor will you find the need to question yourself about the feelings of others.

You broke yourself down in every way that you had to in order to find any part of you that may have been lost. Your gut instincts, your minds reaction time, your heart knowing that it can are all a part of you being who you are. You should not hide you from yourself and knowing who you are keeps others from cracking you much less getting close enough to break you. You learn to have two sides to yourself and being true to both of them. The one you show the world, strong, tough, courageous and the one you are with your family, soft, tender and needing pep talks that gives us the courage to be courageous. We learn how to have that fire in our bellies, light the fire underneath us while figuring out how not to jump into someone's frying pan. A soul mate is like a ghost of yourself and you have to learn how to make that part of you appear upon command and you do so by creating it little by little. Some people may say they feel like a hollow shell inside, but it is just different sayings drawn to the same conclusion. No one person will ever complete us; they can only add what they can to the journey of the completing ourselves.

Applying knowledge will gain you insight to wisdom and wisdom is the key to unlocking greater understanding when applied. When we take our mind, heart, body and spirit completely through each of these steps until it forms a full circle separately and then together, as one, we will solve each one for the mystery that it is. We like having mysteries to solve and find certain things as intriguing clues and get excited when big pieces come together to start forming the picture. What could be the greatest puzzle life could ever have to offer each one of us individually as a great mystery worth solving? The mystery of who we are to ourselves when nobody is watching as well as when all eyes are on us. Do we befriend ourselves in our own time of need or do we stick to our guns while befriending others? Are we our own worst enemies when the chips are down or our own best mates when the deck is not stacked in our favour?

What if life were different roads to who you are and the only way to find the keys that you will need on your journey is by going down different paths that have not been travelled by you and you alone. You can spend your lifetime learning to quote the letters of the Bible inside and out but without applying it to your life you never see the knowledge that it possesses to answer the other questions in your life. You leave out the wisdom needed to unlock other doors. Knowing what the good book says is one thing, learning how it applies and applying it to your life takes a different path of strength.

Learning to gain knowledge from every book that we can get our hands on is good for us. Not doing anything but learning from them will never allow our wisdom to show. You can be a walking form of facts but you will never know what it takes to apply them to life or where they apply. You will never know the difference between needed knowledge and unwanted opinionated hearsay.

When you learn to walk down only one road, after a while you should begin to notice that instead of planting you have stripped everything away until it becomes bare and too fragile to do anything with. In order to sustain life a living thing needs air, food, water and sun. When we look at ourselves for the living beings that we are we need food for thought. Meaning that without facts our brains have nothing to digest, starving our brains takes away our thirst for knowledge and using that to quench the thirst found within our souls. When our soul cannot warm itself by the sun it can make us feel like we have to fight for every breath and it can destroy our bodies.

The test of inner strength is not only testing who we are but can we stand ourselves when the other half of our soul appears in the mirror. If given a test on yourself would you pass, fail, cheat or just hope that you can just squeak by? Who would you cheat off of if the only other person in the room is a reflection of you? If all you can see is a fog it's because you never took the time to get to know yourself. If you do not like what you see in the mirror it's because you kept your scales unbalanced and never learned to give yourself credit after something bad had occurred. If the reflection comes in clear but you see yourself glaring back you have made yourself your own worst enemy and see no need in ever helping yourself out. When you can smile at your own reflection before it has a chance to smile at you then no matter what happens you will know that you gave it everything that you had inside. No matter what, if it was a test of nerves at least you found the nerve to show up so that gives you some credit.

What if we could find all the keys to unlocking life's mysteries and it led us not only to the fountain of youth but to the garden of Paradise. That the stairway we need to learn how to build is the one out of living hell and then we can begin our journey through our life's garden. The road less travelled is the path to your life and leads to everywhere and you have to go down all of them sometimes from the opposite direction but you will find your way here using sure determination. Instead of feeling like people have outgrown us or be afraid of letting go to keep from moving on why not feel like we will meet them later on down the road. When we see them again why not learn to see how much they have grown and appreciate their road to change instead of making them walk it in front of us all over again for our amusement. If we can teach ourselves to change how we once thought about ourselves then maybe we can teach ourselves to change our mind about the way we see each other.

You go to church every day, make a lot of money because you have a higher education and can talk about a political point of view but that does not make you better then the rest. You can know everything about one and very little about the rest but without proper balance you do not have a leg to stand on. You can cower behind each one of these and each one needs three things to go with it. Religion shows us a way to both good and evil, without applying that knowledge in everyday life we will never gain the wisdom we came here to seek. You apply what you have learned until it becomes a way of life. When you do not educate your mind you tend to believe that getting less then honest pay for honest work is good for all involved. When you do not have enough money to take care of yourself, your bodies health beings to diminish. The political party claims to be governed as one under God and should have its people's best interest at heart. When the workers cannot take care of their bodies, people loose money. When you do not have food for thought you know that the political parties separated themselves into church and the people's money. The best interest of the people should be feeding them in everyway so that they will be not only allowed but able to take care of their families. When they feel good about taking care of their families they become more productive because their job shows appreciation through being well paid. When we produce more we have more to share and the political party can take that and pass out even more to the needy making them less needy. The political party shows its love for Dad by the way it takes care of His people. When you leave God out of the equation you leave man learning to bow to one another until they have you praying on your knees to them for mercy. We should not feel the need to bow our heads to anyone because even Dad tells us to hold it high when we approach His throne.

The road to ourselves is the same one in our life; heart-political, body-money, mind-education soul-religion. What if all of these had to have the rest of them agree before proceeding and then filtered through knowledge using wisdom as your guide? None of these should be left to their own devices, because they can learn how to cut the wrong ones out and its harder to catch them when its an inside job. When they say that the needs of the few should not outweigh the needs of the many you should look at the deeper meaning before you agree with your answer. The needs of the few rich ones should not come before the needs of the many workers. The needs of the few struggling for power should not out weigh the needs for the ones struggling to keep their power on. There is a difference between acting like you are an adult and manipulating people into believing it and just being grown up about something because you have the maturity to do so. What if the pen is mightier then the sword? We wasted all this money that should have been spent on a healthier way towards education and put it towards being destructive. It could have been more constructive learning how to write a letter that not only knew how to knock down someone's defenses completely on paper but was written with the back bone to prove it. It would be so powerful that the problem is talked about openly and the solution is right there in the palm of their hand. Some people get so caught up in something that sometimes the easiest of solutions is not always on their mind. It is so fair that it leaves room for compromise! We learn to stand up, admit that we were wrong and learn how to move past it.

When we take all the enjoyment out of everything, we take with it the enjoyment found in life. We learned that some of the greatest things were discovered by mistake, yet we force people not to make any mistakes or someone might find out that the company they work for is not perfect. We could not discover how to turn machines into workable robots but we learned how to work people like machines, beyond their means until they're mindless robots. Dad did not give us differences so that someone could make us feel lower because of them. He made us human so that we can learn to enhance our gifts through our differences and blending them with others making them eccentric. Sometimes all of us need a hero so that we can learn how to become one. Sometimes we need to learn how to be one to learn how to save us from ourselves personally and from others.

Sometimes you cross someone's path to gain their insight about what they're going through right now. You can carry it with you until you come across someone going through that same thing but this thought never occurred to them. Sometimes the insight to their scary life can help you to realize when you're living in your own. Listen for key words, "I am still going through the same thing," "I went and used my family to get out again," "This is how I put an end to it." Listening to someone else's life could help you to live yours and maybe learn to save your own. What if listening to someone's problem and the way they went about their life connected you to someone that you would not have walked up to before? What if learning how to listen to solve a problem was the connection we needed to keep in touch with human contact? A problem brought everyone together, learning how to solve it kept everyone closer. Everyone learned that there was not a problem that could not be solved with close thoughts being tied together.

Sometimes things happen to you to get someone else's attention and sometimes you need the right rock for a deeper ripple or a bigger splash. Keep in mind that if it were not for the waves created none of us could find our way back to shore. Riding a wave could be the difference in finding your way home or staying lost out at sea. When you learn how to fish in deep waters sometimes the harvest could be so great that you never want to leave. Sometimes you stay out so long that by the time you come back there could be someone else living in your home. Sometimes you haul in so much that it brings about scoundrels and thieves and they take everything and leave you stranded. Then there are the wise who know when its just not a good day to go anywhere near the water but you can still go out and play out in the rain.

When it rains it is just like taking a shower only we are not the ones at the controls. Rainy showers are used to keep us clean and everything around us fresh so why would I want to spend my cents learning to come in out of it. I would rather learn how to come in out of the cold and spend the two cents that it took to come in on cocoa. When I said that my mum makes everything right as rain, she lets me come to her when the world makes me feel like crying and then she has this way of turning into my rainbow bringing hope with her. I learned that my grandfather was my role model of a true father, he loved me enough to make me rough, tough, tumble and strong enough to survive in the outside world. He taught me what it takes to be a decent caring person and how to go about learning to keep myself that way. My mum is showing me right from wrong in all different things and is teaching me how to stay that way or when to just stay clear. She is teaching me the right ones to care about and which ones are definitely the wrong ones to have in your life. You need two strong pillars in your life to show you the path, after that it is up to you to continue the path that they have chosen or the opposite direction of your heading. We know when we are grown up because we learn how to diminish fears through our thoughts, we learn how to make our conscience our own personal thoughts and our inner voice no longer sounds like that of a child. Your mind has to grow and your heart needs to mature so that they can work as one. You should only belong to your mum and Dad as a kid not to the people in the world.

When we hold fast to our Faith we will begin to notice certain things about ourselves that were always there but we were never aware of. The more we follow our gut reaction or follow our instincts the stronger and more powerful they become, that in turn opens new areas that were once closed off to us. The stronger we build our Faith in Dad, each other and ourselves the more it will manifest into the appearance of others. When first appearances are everything through Faith we can see people as they are and not what they want to mislead us into believing. Through tests of Faith you learn to build your four pieces of protective armour; a helmet, body armour, a sword and a shield. If you do not have all of these with you in any battle, a strong heart, control of your mind, a steady hand and your Faith as your shield you will get hurt every time. You can have the swiftest blow but if you always loose you head in times of crises it will not do you any good. This is where: "You are only as strong as your weakest link," comes into play. If you use your body in place of your shield, it will not last you as long as it could have. If you do not have your heart protected it can receive a direct hit and sometimes it can be the deadliest of all blows.

You have to remember that it is all yours to protect while you're awake and you know that it will be guarded when you close your eyes for rest. Think about how great it could feel to know that it is not only your bum being covered but all of you when you step out into that world of a stage. No matter what gender you were born you can kick some bum when it comes to standing up for yourself and can back anyone down if need be. The best place to start is in your eyes, because you can change what is in your soul. Learn to have at least a little knowledge in the important things, and then you will notice the wisdom in everything. If you want to know something go out and find it, if you want to learn something find a way to teach yourself. There is more then one way to go about things and one of the best mysteries is learning to find your own way. Keep in mind that every problem does have a solution even if it takes a set of fresh eyes and a different approach to the way things have always been done.

People want you to expose your soul any time they want to know something about you but that is like going out in public without your body armour on, it leaves you naked and feeling exposed. You can be tough when you need to be and as long as your actions did not murder someone or bring bodily harm to someone why would you feel the need to have to justify or explain yourself when you did nothing wrong. When you keep your armour on except for when you come home you will not expose any of your weakness when you are out in the world. If you feel the need to still wear it when you get home something needs to be fixed.

What if you are the one who builds your armour and your soul is the one who wears it? The stronger and heavier you build it the bigger your soul has to be to carry it, the weight of the world that they could pick up off of your shoulders. The odd thing is with all of this armour on what in the world are you supposed to do with it? One thought is that may be you learn how to be a straight shooter in all that you do, say, stand for and will defend. Could be that you learn how to set your sights and lock on. A thought could be that you figure out who your alliances are, who will inflate themselves to look like their helping and who could very well cost you your life. If someone is not shooting from the hip they could very well believe in friendly fire while lining you up in their sights. Learning to put your best foot forward does not mean the one in your mind or heart, your best foot should come to mean you because you are what you stand for. If you are putting your best foot forward why would inner appearance not be everything? You want people to know that if they cross your path you will not tolerate being taken advantage of and yet you will help someone in need.

You cannot be intimated in any way because your tests proved that you have what it takes. You cannot be scared off because you passed through every hell known to man and never backed down from it. What if life was about learning how to build your own armour and helping to teach those around you to build theirs? You do not have to tell them in great detail how your armour works just show them what it looks like on. Armour protects previous scars from being shown in battle. It is far better to let old wounds heal properly then to let them fester because someone will not stop picking at it for you. The injury was done to you not to someone else, and when it comes from someone close to you it tends to runs deeper. The best way I learned how to heal a wound is to allow someone close enough to help you with it. I know how to take care of myself in a lot of ways but I also learned that some things are beyond my control and better left up to the specialist of the world like my mum and the elders. I learned that for all my knowledge and learning to apply wisdom there is still so much that I do not know and that is o.k. too. I mean after all look at how big the world is and to have to store that much in your head, what would be left to learn?

I learned that some wounds only my mum can heal and she knows how to take care of you when you,re feeling worse then bleu, (even if it is just your feelings that got the wind knocked out of them.) I have listen to different people throughout life and the one thing that I noticed in all of them is that they're all struggling with life too. The one thing that everyone tries so desperately to cover up is the one thing that everyone has in common. If we think that no two snow flakes being alike is awesome then why does it differ for people just because we are not as pure as the falling snow? After it hits the ground it blends in, but instead we waste our life blending until we too are left as background.

What if life were about finding the ones who love us and learning how to heal our wounds with them? It is hard to doctor a place that you cannot reach, and you learn that the ones who truly care about you never rub it in that they stayed at your side. All of us have been knocked unconscious at some point in our lives and there is more then one way to get knocked out, but it is up to you if you really want to come to or not. The more we learn to come to, the harder it will become to knock us out again, because we learn to duck and move. We know who is in our corner and we are tough enough to take a punch, but know that we have it in us to deliver one as well. We have to have the fight in us before we start picking our battles, otherwise you could just very well be at war with yourself and causing other people harm. When you have the fight back inside of you nothing can stop you from truly living and feeling like you're alive. You learn that being just another pretty face is not as important as having a spirit of being that sets you apart.

All of us have to face something that is bigger then we are but when we learn to allow Faith to be our shield then we learn not to become human shields ourselves. We learn so much growing up right or wrong that it takes time to decipher all of it. We are in such a hurry to want to be out on our own and in our own charge that we do not realize what all it entails. You can learn how to live or not live life by watching how others live without saying a single word. I learned what I did not want to be when I was surrounded by villagers, the problem with that is you cannot find out what you want to be because you are so busy not being them. The flip side to that is that sometimes you can spend your world being everything to everyone that there is nothing left of yourself when it comes time to give something back to you. What you learned is how to loose yourself anytime someone else comes into the room.

I lost myself in my mum a couple of times because I wanted to be just like her until I discovered that only my mum can truly pull off being her and that she accepted me for who I was even though I did not know who I was at the time. She helped me to figure out the meaning behind the Serenity Prayer: strength, courage and wisdom. It has everything to do with yourself and your surroundings then it does about anything else. Strength to change who you are, the courage to keep your differences and the wisdom to be able to tell them apart before anything occurs. I wanted to be me, but before that could happen I had to throw out everything that had ever been given to me. I learned how to pick out only the treasures that I wanted for my being totally who I want to be for my Dad, mum, family and myself.

In order to be anything to them I have to be something to me and learning how to travel down different roads shows you who you are to everyone else first then later on to yourself. I think that do not knock it till you try it means more then one thing but they find a connection through being compatible. Some of us have never had to walk a direct path to hell and will not understand why others find themselves in the predicaments that they do. All they see is the hell your life is, but never take the time to look right at you and see that you are the one going through it. They do not realize that knocking someone is just a contemptuous way of poking fun at someone. When you make fun of someone you later find yourself in the same boat, the only difference is how you got there. Sometimes we can fear or loath something so much that we become what we dislike and never see the impact it has made on us. Sometimes you can wonder about something to the point that it just takes you along for the ride. You learn though that sometimes things just happen so fast that all you can do is hang on and wait for the dust to settle before you can start to pick up the few pieces left by the aftermath. I learned that when you cross someone's path it has nothing to do with coincidence and everything to do with trade, a sharing of your journeys. Just because something happens now does not mean that you will not feel the effect later on.

I had become mates with someone for a long time and we were fine until she brought a villager into her life that had convinced her that I was lower then they can come. My actions up until that moment had been looked upon as decent but all villagers come with the gift of twisting and they can do it with words or actions that have already occurred. After she told them all about me it was then decided without me being present that since I gave and never took that I must be after something more after all this time. The villager had taken what we had and twisted it into something that it was never meant to be. She accepted the fact that I like being weird enough to make someone laugh and she never asked me to justify any of my actions until the villager came into the picture. He had gotten her to turn on me by pointing out the things that I have never done wrong. I tried to tell her that I got a bad feeling from him but she did not want to listen to it because I was attacking someone that she had just met and developed feeling for but was going to learn later on if she could trust them. I pointed out that she never got a bad feeling off of me before and she replied that she just needed someone who cared about her enough to help her find it. I tried to flip that back and tell her that is what I was trying to do for her but that did not work out. The more this went on the more I felt like her life was in danger and told her straight out. She joked about it when she was talking to someone she knows and they told her that they were getting the same feeling but did not know how to tell her. I took one of my mates over to her house and even though she believed them over me she still would not believe that it was not coming from me.

There was nothing that I did from here on out that was considered decent by her even though all I did was go after the villager. It got to the point that I had to defend myself against my mate because he got her to attack me. See if she does it then he does not get the blame for it and he still gets what he wants. If he can get her to get me out of the picture herself then he does not look like the evil villager that everyone says he is, plus he makes her feel good by convincing her that she defeated someone evil.

The sad thing is that she chooses to believe the villager over the ones she knew never hurt her or wanted anything from her. I do not know if she had felt embarrassed over allowing this person to come in and take over full control or if she was bound and determined not to be proven wrong, only she knows that. All I know is that sometimes you can do all that you can and still loose but at least you did all that you could have. Sometimes the other side can win for now, but learning when another situation comes up and not doing the exact same thing will more than help to even the score. I learned that villagers take all the fun out of life and replace it with nothing but misery. I learned a tremendous amount going through that with her but the effect was not felt until moments later. She blamed the ones who were trying to help instead of blaming the one who caused it all. I found out through an acquaintance of ours that she still blames me to this day for her life turning into a living hell and that the villager still controls her every move but that she still refuses to put it together. It is just easier to blame me then to deal with what is going on. I told them, "I left long ago," but before I could finish they said, "We know because we told her the same thing, that all you were trying to do was be helpful and that very few people would have helped to the extreme that you did. I guess her blaming you gives her something to hold onto." I could not understand that at all. She had me to hang onto but she chose to cut the rope not me.

I came across someone else just like her and the same situation was taking place. We were mates for a while and then she falls for a villager. I knew this time to slide back until the villager revealed themselves and in a matter of time they usually do. I remembered what I did that worked and what I did that backed fired in my face and adjusted my actions accordingly. Instead of tearing him down or pointing out the obvious I just listened to her tell me how bad he was treating her. I stayed away so that they could not hide or use my actions against me and I stayed clear so that I would not have to defend myself against someone that I cared about. This time I learned from my mistakes and I figured out that sometimes you can have the same different outcome but better than before. The same in the fact that I still lost someone I considered a mate but different in the aspect that the villager had to slither back to where he came from empty handed because there was nothing to feast upon.

Sometimes a family can house a villager in it and not even know it and sometimes a village can hide a member of someone's family, or they can try and come in to take one of yours in the night. Keep in mind that the darkest of night can happen in the brightest of days. I also figured out what my mum was telling me, that even though someone considers you something does not mean that you consider them anything. I just never applied that to myself, I may have considered some people mates but that did not mean that they considered me one of theirs. When someone is looking for any reason that they can to discredit you while needing something from you they always will. These are the ones who make you feel like you will never be good enough for them when you should realize that you are too good to put up with the crap they want to dish out. When credit is due and it is due to you then there should be nothing left to debate about.

Going through both of these moments separately helped me to realize other situations in my life and connected me with other moments. I came across someone who told me that she set expectations for me because she wanted to see me do more with my life. The problem was when she learned of what all I had been through, where I was in my life looked even more unbelievable now. I only appeared to be at a stand still because I had come a long way. This time I learned to stop and pay attention to who I ask directions from, the path that you go down first started at either a fork in the road or at a cross road. I was at one when I first got a chance to met my mum, then I could not find her when I came up to another one. I finally figured out that my mum has always been on the same road, I was just the one who missed the turn. I figured out with my mum's help the difference between the two when I remembered a moment that I had with her before any of the above took place. Something happened one time that I could not find the humour in (and still do not) no matter how much she kept whole heartedly laughing. The company we worked at together has a rule about no climbing and well when everything is out of your reach you just use what is there because you do not have time to get ladders and chairs all the time. I needed something from way up there and I am the type who will do it myself unless I really need help, since I know how to climb I saw no need to ask for help. I looked to my left then right then back to the left again and waited a second before I looked right again. I looked up to see where the camera was and since I was behind it I knew that I could get away with climbing up the shelf and being back down before anyone was the wiser. I looked left and right about a million times apiece before I proceeded. I knew the coast was clear after I looked left and right a couple more times and then I made my move. I put my hands on the shelf and was just about to put my leg on it when I hear; you guessed it my mum clearing her throat. I have never in my life hit the ceiling and floor about a million times apiece so hard at the same time before but I did at that very moment, it was not coincidental by any means. She scared me so bad that I now know that I am never going to reach puberty!

The exact same story from my mum's point of view: "I walked up to see you looking left and right and left and right, I know that you were not going to steal anything but I could not figure out why you kept looking left and right. You kept doing it until I thought surely any minute now she will turn around and see me standing right directly behind her but no you just kept looking left and right. Then when I saw those two little hands and that little foot go up I knew that you were about to climb." My mum laughed the whole time she was walking towards me telling me this and I am surprised that I heard a word she said because my heart was beating so unbelievably loud and so hard that I thought it was going to pop right out of my chest and run off. She asked me through her laughter, "What did you learn from this?"

I was still breathing frantically hard but somehow managed to get out, "To look behind me at least once!!"

She just dies laughing and says, "No, your not suppose to climb."

"Oh, that too." (See I told you that I always get two lessons from the same error in judgement but this one seemed way different from the rest of them let me tell you.)

She is still laughing when she tells me, "I have never seen anyone jump that high standing on one leg before."

"Well I thought that the coast was clear," and I really did too, if I had any doubts you know that I would have looked left and right again before proceeding!

The worst part about this whole incident is that my mum just reaches up and pulls down what I needed, she never even used her tip toes or had to straighten out her arm. She was still laughing when she hands it to me. If I had the ability to read minds I know that she would have been shaking her head saying, "What am I going to do with you."

I told my mates what had happened that day and they all laughed with her, "Excuse me, are you not suppose to show me understanding first then wait until I leave before you side with her laughter!" The nerve of some people! They missed the point that my mum literally got me to jump way past where I was going to climb to in the first place.

There was something more to this that I never realized no matter how much I would think about it. I learned that putting things on the shelf because you do not understand something or you think that there is something more to it then meets the eye is o.k. as long as you get them back down. All of these people had things in common with each other but not with my mum. None of them believed a word I said even though they knew I was not lying; they all said that I was either imagining it or just making it up to get attention. What attention do I need your life is the one in danger not mine? They all sold me out the first chance they were given and got mad when this made me more instead of less. They would ask me to help them in hopes of setting me up to become untrustworthy and when this did not happen they went out of their way to discredit me. When the chips were down the ones they thought that they could count on are not to be found but after the chips are gathered you are the one who is asked to leave. When I needed them none of them would even watch my back. Everything good or bad that has ever happened to me my mum has always been on the side of my back even when I never thought to look. She never told me that I needed to get some sleep when I get a feeling and she never tries to talk me out of one. Instead she talks me through them until I can better my grip on them.

I have never felt the need to ask her to please believe me like I did with all the others. When I talk with my mum and tell her things she does not look for a way to use them against me later. She has always had my back and it made me realize something else. That some people do stay in front or beside of you intentionally because if you felt them from behind you would truly know to beware. I never get a bad feeling when my mum is behind me and I noticed that I felt the need to keep people in front of me and allow very few beside me because I never trusted them. I never trusted them with backing me, getting my back or watching my back, I just never realized it before. The game that came to mind is red light green light only when they get next to you they take either a shot or a stab in the back because they do not believe in trading places. The thing with walking down paths alone is that you never know who is along for the journey because they found a free ride with you. Some people learn to hide behind your imagination so that you will believe that it is the one getting the better of you instead of them. Some people strategically place themselves behind you and hope that the fear they try to instill will overcome you and hold you in place.

Some people still play that game where they distract you so that someone else can get on their knees behind you while the one in front knocks you over. Some people have just never been taught to play fair I guess, the worst ones are the ones who sneak up behind your back. Keeping people in front of you all the time makes you forget to look behind you to see if anyone is sneaking up, it also makes you less aware of seeing if you have your back covered. Very few villagers will ever do anything face to face because their bluff is easy to call. They only know how to do things behind people's backs and appear to look innocent when they were just about to be caught. Nothing my mum has ever done could be considered underhanded. Watching her up close I noticed that she is a straight shooter, taking a step back to observe her I realized how she became that way. She does not have an itchy trigger finger, nor does she use people as target practice. She does not hunt people down in hopes that they will make a mistake so she can pounce and she has nerves that make her hand steady. The part in the movie where it gets to the showdown and you know that the one who remains calm is going to be the most accurate and therefore become the most dangerous, that would be the part that my mum could win an Oscar for every time. She does not get rattled but she will get fired up and there is a big difference.

No matter what my fight was, she remained calm and collected to the point of where I could feel it too. There were times when I had every right to panic because the situation became dangerous before I could realized it but like she taught me that is when you need to keep yourself calm the most and remain that way. She knows that I have been through enough hell to know when something is wrong and she is helping me to figure out when I need to stay and help and when I just need to leave. You cannot help all of the people all of the time until you figure out what you are really helping them with. Sometimes when you help someone else it makes you realize that you are going through the same thing.

I learned that I had someone in my life that wanted to break me in order to follow in their abusive villager's foot steps, when that did not occur it filled them all with rage and no fair fight was going to insue. The villager tried everyway there was to attack me, mentally, physically, played on my emotions, and even got me to take their word over mine. Then it was time for the village of sabotage and this is where they tried to get my heart to come along. He called and tried to make it sound like he was going to take his own life and something told me not to call back that it was a trap but I dismissed my gut instinct even though it had been right every time up to date. He knew that his reign of terror was about to be ended by me but tried to hide behind his village and thought that it would give him the ultimate control. When your gut reaction tells you to remain calm but to slowly turn around you realize that you cannot afford to let them see you jump for any reason. One false move and you can be held in sheer terror for the rest of your life. The thing that bothered me the most was not so much that the danger was coming from behind me but that the ones I considered to be mates where the ones holding me in place. I thought that the reason they were holding me so close was to protect me when in turn they were just trying to make sure that I could not turn around to see who would deliver the fatal blow that would have cost me my life. Sometimes it is better to figure a way out of something before you realize you're in danger.

Some people will use you as a sacrifice but there are people who will get you down from there. I learned the hard way that villagers not only can disguise themselves as family but as mates to. I also learned that some people will never learn from their mistakes because they can get someone else to pay for it dearly. When I told the people in my group about the bad gut feeling I was getting they all sided with him and justified why he needed to be a controlling bully to me, because none of them had it in them to be one with me. I made the mistake of talking to villagers instead of my family and that is what put my life in danger. When I told the villagers what my thoughts and ideas were they discovered how my brain works and learned how to use my better judgment against me. I was told that maybe he did not know what he was doing, then I made the mistake of telling them that I knew his father beat his wife until he learned how to break her and then beat her some more to keep her broke. When you witness something from one side you do not mistake it because you will never forget it for as long as you live, you just do not recognize it when it comes in from a different point of view.

I knew that he was going to his father for advice and that he was getting mad because it did not work on me because I tried to stay one step ahead. He needed to beat me down so that he could have his father's approval when the time came to break me. I never realized at the time that I was using the villagers to help me escape from their clutches. Your past comes up to haunt you when you do not learn how to get over your fears. I had always lived with the fear that one wrong move would send me back to the village I escaped from. When the truth of the matter is that fear kept me from making a move at all. When you feel the need to tiptoe something is deadly wrong even if you cannot see it at the time. I do not feel the need to tiptoe around my mum any more and it made me realize who all I had been tiptoeing around, people from different villages.

I now know that it takes all kinds to make a village and that you may not realize that their idiot is the one they're making out of you. Thinking that something is going to change if you just take enough crap. Thinking that you can change someone who wants nothing but to take over control and being led to believe that if you give up control it will make you wiser and therefore better off.

There comes a time in your life when you figure out what role you have been type cast for and have been playing all this time and the hard thing to learn is that it is not the same one that you tried out for and thought you got. I like being my mum's jester and doing things that bring her laughter. I however do not like playing the part of the fool in a village where staying made me the idiot. They are not the same role at all even though they can be made to appear that way. I was typecast as the village idiot and was foolish enough to believe that I left

192

long ago and therefore it could not happen to me over and over. I learned that you can either make your village your home or you can make your castle your home. One leaves you exposed to everything and the other surrounds you with protection made of stone. One brings you in closer so that you can be fed to the wolves, the other keeps their lambs protected and keeps the wolves at bay.

Counting on someone not to be something that they are, can lead you straight to the slaughter. I was led there through the belief that I would find real family; instead I was led away from there by the ones who claim me as a member of the family, they're more exclusive. When my mum warns me of something or asks me to take precautions I listen to her without question because she has more then proven that she has my best interest at heart. If she were to tell me to duck instead of asking her to tell me why, I just would, because I know that it is a warning. Sometimes when you ask a question that you should not you can end up getting hit. The difference between a real castle and a village trying to appear that way is that there is only room for one Queen and King and the rest of us are different subjects of their court and I like that. A village always has people fighting for top position and in a castle there is only one but there is never any question about who holds it.

Keep in mind that anyone can put a roof over your head but it is the ones who learn to put up protective walls that keep their loved ones safe from harm that know how a true family is built. Castles use their walls as protection not members of their family and everyone is doing their part to keep the roof over their heads. I love my family because they're like the fairy tale after the story has ended. The Queen and King have children who get to share in their happily ever after saga. I know that I talk more about my mum then I do my other family siblings but they're all bigger than me and know where I live, plus they're all nuts and refuse to come to terms with it. To hear them talk they will make you think that they're the normal ones but I know that I am not the only nut in our mum's fruit bowl mix.

See the thing that I notice most about my mum (besides the fact that she usually is standing right behind me when I do or say something,) is that she defies logic and there is just no reasoning with her when you are clearly wrong. My mum was nuts to think that she saw something more to me then what was really there and I tried to tell her so, (not the being nuts part the way she acts I thought that she already knew but the part about the other thing.) Since my mum never met my elders I could not understand how she could think the same way as them but it slowly came together. They believe in us so that we could do better and let us come into something in our own time. My siblings know that they're good kids and that they're loved. They have to come to terms with

193

being nuts in their own time, hopefully they're not as hard headed as I have been about certain things. My mum knew that I was nuts when she met me so that was not something she had to help me with. She helped me come to terms with the fact that I was a good kid who is going to be loved and allowed me to come to terms with it in my own time.

I was clearly wrong about myself and my mum knew it and that is why I found her to be extremely unreasonable about not wanting to be reasoned with. She maybe nuts but she is also hard headed enough that you cannot put a crack in her shell. She makes all of us feel like diamonds in the rough and that we are going to have to go through the process of getting cut and shaped in order for us to properly shine. We get to become a part of the treasure chest that only rare gems are placed, even if the gems at a closer glance are a bunch of mixed fruits and nuts!

I learned that no matter what abuse or traumatic moment that you have been through someone can help you though it, the difference is what you do with it. Your life can head many directions down the same path. I know what it is like to have someone in your life that hurts you but you do not see it, that causes you pain and can leave you feeling traumatized. I have been around people who want to see you get hurt and who want to take your life because you will not give up control. I have been around some of the worst people imaginable and even brought them into my life without giving it a second thought because I had nothing else to go on. If you do not know what you are looking for it can make it hard to know what you are supposed to be picking up.

I figured out that my mum clearing her throat and making me jump that high is a good thing, even though I still do not think it is very funny. She helped me to go further than what I had in mind and was there with me through the whole thing. She was watching my back the entire time and never made a big production about it or helping me to get what I needed. She may have scared me out of puberty but she did not scare the life out of me and that is what the villagers are all about: scaring the life out of you. I also noticed that when she came up from behind I never got a bad feeling from her and even though she could not or would not stop laughing it was not an evil laugh. Sometimes the fine line between good and bad is how you perceive the moment. Sometimes good and bad people can say the exact same things but their actions are what make them become good or downright evil. I knew that my mum was not evil from the start even though that was a wicked thing to do to someone who knew for sure that the coast was clear. I am ever so slowly beginning to figure out that no matter how slick I think I have become when it comes to the villagers, I am never going to be slick enough to get anything past my mum because their rules do not apply with her. She has the gift of fine tuning and if I have learned anything in life it is that you do not mess with someone's gift. My mum has a great number of gifts and the sweet thing is that she shares them with us. The only gift the villagers have is the gift of gab and grab. One of her gifts that she shares with us is her compassion of wisdom and understanding of how knowledge is obtained. She knows that sometimes you can know something that you are not aware of and that it takes time to get it to come through. Going through different things in your life helps you to form the thought behind your opinion, learning to guide your thoughts takes a controlled mind and when you learn how to combine them you will learn how to control your thoughts before you make an unbiased opinion. You learn not to be so fast with your judgments, or your criticisms or your condemnations. Sometimes you can have bad people in your life because they just appeared but did not first appear to be that way. Anyone can have bad people amongst their mix but not everyone has the strength to get rid of them. I learned that you can have all the strength that you need when you come into contact with the right family of people.

Some people will see you as something worth conquering because they see your strengths and want to gain possession over them. Some people have seen what you have been able to conquer and know that you are worth more then your possessions. Others will see you being conquered and know that you are worth saving. You have to be not only aware of your surroundings, but who is in them as well. I will admit that I have been set up to take a fall of many kinds before but now I have a true family who will help me to conquer all. They are loving and tough and do not hide behind the castle walls but know how to defend them with combined strength. All of us possess great strengths that may be unknown to us at first but when they become ours we can feel it. I have spent most of my life's journey learning how to stay away from people because I could not figure them out until it ended up costing me everything. What I ended up receiving in return is the guided strength of family that took the time to teach me how to love them. We share in each others strengths, weaknesses, miseries and joys and that brings us closer together instead of tearing each other apart. Now my family may not go around head butting people but they know that if they need me to I will because my head is more than built for it, (that is one of my strengths.) If I need one of them to reach something for me all I have to do is ask. My family is not at my disposal nor is any member disposable but our strengths are at each others disposal.

I also figured out that no matter how freakishly huge for my size (because of my spirit) that I may feel I am or how tough I have learned how to become my mum is always going to be bigger and tougher because she is the Queen Mum. She finally got it through to my thick head that I do have a big spirit but that I was just inflating some of it to make up for what the world knew I was missing but never had the heart to tell myself. I had spent everything that I had inside of me convincing myself that I was doing just fine without any of the people from that nasty village and up to a point I was but I learned that my mum has gently taught me that every kid needs the right mum so that they can be allowed to go even further because we have them. I may have been one of those kids who started out with a dark past but thanks to my family I see that I do have a bright future because I have all of them.

I heard a villager once say that little people are mean and it went all over me at the time so I was going to defend them. "Sometimes people do not pick on someone their own size and sometimes little people have to inflate their size to get the bigger ones to back off." The thought that never occurred to me at the time is that mean people do not expect the ones they're picking on to become big enough to put a stop to them. They want to feel like the bigger person because it gives them inflated power over the weaker ones, they inflate themselves for control and we inflate ourselves to take back undeserving power. My mum knows what I look like when I become completely inflated because someone pissed me off beyond my control and what my actual size really is and deals with me accordingly. I have never inflated myself towards my mum but the cool thing is that it never scared her off when I was. Everyone that I have ever come across has always said, "I just do not know what to do when you get like that," but my mum has never flinched or jumped when my temper has gotten the better of me. I realize more and more about the differences between the villagers and my family. My family knows that I can get that way because someone was messing with me, the villagers did not realize that I can become that way when they have messed with me for long enough. The great thing about observation is figuring out what makes things different, not just that they are different. They taught me how to tiptoe around them but I learned that if you scare them just right you will cause them to walk on egg shells around you. My family does not scare me nor are they scared of me so I do not walk on tiptoes and they do not walk on egg shells and that gives us balance. I learned that when people feel the need to walk on egg shells around you the reason could be that you were supposed to be an easier mark than what you truly are. Right before they moved in for the kill I would inflate

196

bigger than the size called for and make them scared. Now they have to think twice as hard because they did not realize your defenses before they made their move on you.

When people tell me that what does not kill you makes you stronger you can tell by the look in their eyes that they do not apply it to themselves and therefore no one else should either. You are supposed to stay little inside and not grow into the grown up that life wants you to be. They want you to stay defenseless and feel like you are helpless so that you have nothing to rely on but them. If you figure out that you're strong and can do things on your own then you will realize that you do not need them because all they are doing is keeping you from yourself. When I was told that expectations were put on me I was fine with that because I never looked for the deeper meaning. They expect certain things done their way and if you do not comply they try to convince you that you are going to go nowhere because you did not listen to them. You were not willing to give up control of your life and hand it over to someone who has shown that they have no control over theirs. They figured out before you did that you have ambition and if they can control yours and turn that into expectations then they can make sure that you never reach them.

When you become predictable then the villagers can attack you from all sides because they know what your next move will be, when you become highly unpredictable they do not know what to do next. Everyone had known the old me and everything that I would do but nobody ever expected me to change. I learned to change the way I thought about things which in turn gave my actions a different outcome and surprised everyone around me.

"The true sign of insanity is doing the same thing over and over again expecting different results." If you do not change things about yourself then your life will never get any better. If you want your life to get better then you have to expect to change things about yourself. There comes a point in your life when you have to decide to take control of your life instead of allowing it to take control of you. There comes a point where you can for the most part control your life and all that is around you. There comes a point where you will have to go at it all alone because everyone that you asked for help is nowhere to be found. Nobody ever expected me to leave everything that I had ever known behind and nobody ever expected me to grow past where they wanted me to be. I had to dig in and learn to pull myself up and which hands were safe to hold onto. Life can be dangerous and yet mysterious as well. I have been in some dangerous situations and the thing that I noticed more then anything else in the world is that people are behind it, not Dad or the boogie man but people. The better you get to know yourself the more you will be able to decipher between good and bad and good and just plain evil.

I was once told that if I was one of Dads kids then nothing bad would ever happen to me but that is just simply not true. Dad does not control us nor does He control our lives, if He did then there would be no need to go to church because none of us would ever sin. He does give us free will and it is up to us what we do with it. I was free to leave the village that spawned me and that is exactly what I did even though I was no where near prepared. My mum and family were free to allow me to keep on moving instead of taking me in. Every decision that you have ever made was in your control, now there may have been outside influences but boiling it all down it still was left up to you and you alone.

I could have been one of those kids that does not want to get past what I have been through and spends my life blaming others for everything that everyone has put me through but I would have lost out on so much that was rightfully mine. Remember that when you go to hunt for treasure you have to look for clues, you have to hunt and dig and you have to be willing to face a certain amount of hidden danger to get past where you need to go. My adventure started when I wanted to find myself a real family and Dad supplied me with certain tools that would help me along the way, and even included a map. (I just never thought to tell Him that I have no sense of direction and therefore had no idea of how to read such a detailed map of my journey.)

If we could look at the map to see where we need to head, how many of us would give up before we started because the terrain looked too treacherous or we thought that the journey would take too long? How many of us would rather sit in the back seat and holler, "Are we there yet," after every stop? You are allowed to have someone drive you and your life but what you are not allowed to do is to go and blame them for the direction that your life took. You have to be bold enough to stand up and say, "This is where I get off, this is my stop," and if they do not want to slow down then you have to learn to jump. Yes, you can and will get hurt and knocked about but look at the big picture, you will always heal back up as you move on. You would have never been allowed to heal while someone else is driving you. I am not one to use other people as guinea pigs and say, "You should try this and see if it works," while I stand in the background and make notes about what did and did not work. I made myself my own guinea pig so I really do know what will work and what could end up costing you everything.

When I first took off the only thing I had was basically the clothes on my back and a tremendous amount of hate to keep me going. It will get you far in life but not on the side that you want to live your life. When I met my mum she was standing right in front of me but I learned that I was on the wrong side of the road to just walk over to her. I had to find my own path to where she was and my mum knows in her heart that I have it in me to be ambitious once I get everything set just right inside my head. I will get to where I am going, even if it takes me longer to get there. You do have more control over your own life than what the world wants you to know but you also have to be willing to go at certain things alone.

What if you found a map of who you are meant to be but nobody wanted to go with you? Would you look for the greatest treasure all alone or would you give it up for the safety of all you have ever known? If you are one of those who does not want to give up the safety do not feel so bad, I was just like that for the longest time. My mum knew that I would have jumped to her had I not have been so scared but she did give me hints on how to get to her. Think of it like this; you are on your treasure hunt and you are standing above where you need to be but you are there. Now all you have to do is climb down that rocky road until you come across the hidden cave and trigger the traps before you go all the way through. Life happens just like it does in the movies, nothing is easy, you are going to loose people along the way and you are going to have scoundrels trying to stop you every step of the way. If you notice in the movies they do get hurt but they do find what they are looking for and forget about all they went through to get to here.

You have to be willing to go against the grain and to make your own path to find what you are looking for. Yes there have been others who went looking for that same treasure as you and never found it so they made others give up their search as well but you have something in your possession that they do not, you have determination and you know that this is the one thing that they lacked. I have always believed that some people were never meant to find certain things because it did not belong to them and they were the type who would have destroyed it right after they found it so do not give up. The easiest thing in the world to do is give up; the hardest thing to do is keep the drive going.

Living with the villagers any longer and they would have ended my life so I had to take the chance and leave and yes my life got harder and harder as I went along just because I led myself to believe that there was only one evil village. When I finally learned that villagers are scattered all around us and they can hide behind a kind word or a smile or a deed then life became a little easier with every step that I take. I learned that I can do a number of things that I think are in my best interest; I can stand completely still, run, stand my ground, defend myself or just choose to walk off. With the village I came from I had no choice but to tell them one thing while secretly planning my sneak out and run plan. I may have been filled with hatred but being that little against all those people I would not have stood a chance trying to defend myself. I was only head strong and nothing more and you can only head butt so many things before you give yourself a headache. Could I go back and defend myself now? To be honest and I mean really honest it would not be me defending myself any more. I would only be going back to seek revenge and because of all that I have been through I would take their life just as they took mine only I would take theirs permanently and would have no reason to ever feel remorse. The way I see it now is I am not the same person who left that evil village and the one who left is the one who deserves revenge. The way my family has supported me and helped to guide me I realize that I have already gotten my revenge simply by being more than they ever could. Sometimes the best revenge is just breaking free and never being pulled back in.

I learned that breaking out of a village is not all that hard if you keep logic right out in front of you. I knew that they could not hold me forever and that one day they would have to stop beating me because I would no longer be there but I had to fight to stay alive if anything good was going to come from this. I fooled the world into thinking that I had come out unscathed and fooled them so much that I had believed it too but the one person who was not going to fall for it was the one person who cared enough to look deeper…my mum. Having the right mum does make all the difference in the world because they can save your life even if they do not realize the danger you were born into.

Nobody knew anything that I had gone through and the ones that did I left behind because I never wanted to be reminded of it. I left more than just the villagers; I left anyone who cared because I never wanted them to learn how to care for something like me. I never saw the potential that they were trying so desperately to break but I knew that I was too hard headed to let them slowly kill me. My mum knew that I had the potential to finally break free after all this time because she knows that even when you leave, it can still have a hold on you. How do I know that I finally made it back home safe to my real family? Easy, I no longer have the desire to go back to any of the villages and show them what they lost. If I would have just made more out of myself to show them up then it would not have lasted this long, also my mum is smart enough to see a fake. A fake is someone who has no intention of living up to their potential, they just want more to show up those around them and that can never be good.

I have had people throw things up in my face like, "Well I have a mum who loves me no matter what I do," or, "I will always love my kid no matter what and I apologize that you do not know what that feels like." I could tell by the way they were saying it that it was nothing more then a complete dig at me. I even had someone I cared about at one time tell me that and yes part of me wanted to point out the obvious, "But your kid does not give a toss about you and that is what you should care about." I never did say anything because I knew that I was going to be out of their village soon and that it was no longer going to be anything that I would have to concern myself with. I realized that when people would say things like that to me that it would indeed piss me off but now it no longer bothered me because I could see past them. I finally figured out that when someone knows your weak points they will go after them softly so that you will not see them attacking with a vengeance. I have to admit that they are good at what they do; they're just not good people and have no intention of ever being one.

I noticed that the difference between now and the way things were then is how I choose to look at things. When people come at me with the rumours that they have and the little snide remarks all you have to learn how to say is," I do not care," or, "So," as long as you do not feed into them they have nothing to go after you with. Everyone knew that I did not have family because of the way that I would react to their words and once they found a way in it is hard to get them out unless you switch your frame of mind. When my mum first grabbed me I had someone tell me that she was only humouring me and sadly enough I believed them over my own mum. I did not realize that I had just insulted my mum and the worst part is I even told her, "For how ever long that it lasts Thank-you for being my mum." Sometimes you can learn so much or feel so much that it takes a while for it to completely sink in. In a way I also wanted to make sure that if my mum did indeed want out that she would have one without having to feel guilty.

I also figured out that rule of: Those who live by the sword die by the sword. Right before I broke from the other village where all hell broke loose I noticed the decision that was right in front of me. "Do I want to die the same way I came into the world? I had to defend instead of learning to live." I have spent all of my life with my head down ploughing through whatever I needed to until someone needed help. More than likely it was usually life and death help because the situation was going to become down right dangerous and Dad knows that I tend to thrive on things like that because I had to learn how. Oddly enough someone threatening my life was no big deal because I had to put up with it on a daily basis growing up but suddenly it had become a big deal because I was set up while I was trying to figure out how to help two people who were not in their right mind to help themselves. One was a mate who later on turned out to be a friend and the other was myself realizing I would loose my mum. The thing about grasping at straws is everyone is standing around waiting to pull one out and you never realize what their grasping at until you realize that it is you. The best thing to do is find a rope, tie a knot in it and hang on. Better yet you can swing past them or hang on while the rest of them fall.

I have had people tell me that there is no such thing as evil or bad people but then there would be world peace if that were true. Any time there is a crime committed was there not an individual involved? If you can arm yourself with knowledge so you can see something before hand would that not be better than debating whether or not there are evil people in the world? When people snap it is not always going to be in a good way and you never know when you will be in a situation where someone else does the snapping. Before my mate came with me to warn her I had to convince them to come with me and it was not an easy thing to do. We argued for what seemed like a life time until we reached a compromise that I would take a nap if they would come with me and if they did not get the same sinister feeling I would drop it. (You spend all that time gathering information to help someone just so someone else can convince you that you're either tired or you do not know what your talking about.) They did feel something sinister as soon as we stepped out of the car so we took it even further. When I get a gut feeling like that I refuse to be talked out of it and will do what ever I can until I can get someone to listen to me. Sometimes the wisdom under a bad circumstance is knowing when you can handle it on your own, when you need to quietly go get help or when to try to put in a good enough bluff that it cannot be called.

When you get a bad feeling off of someone the best thing to do is not stay long enough to figure out why. If they are with someone that you love I learned how to talk with them too. See they are already conditioned to defend because they have to defend themselves against someone being abusive so that is already instilled. In order to side step them defending the one beating them down do not tear down the abuser. When you take this step out of the equation you throw everything that is suppose to take place out the door and this gives you a fresh start. The important thing to keep in mind is not to focus on the abuser but rather the one being abused. They can either feel like everyone knows and they feel ashamed or that they're all alone because nobody knows. If you suspect this is going on you have to talk to them softly and hold them so that you're not face to face. This keeps you from feeling the need to go head to head. You have to talk softly to the one who has been abused and save the aggression talk for the villager.

It goes back to the way my grandfather would protect me, he would grab me and pull me behind him and he would be the defender. The only thing is that nobody ever took the time to console me so I never knew when things were o.k. When I went to help someone I did the same thing that he did, grabbed them and pull them behind me. I never tried to comfort them or tell them that everything was going to be alright. Going through life like I have, abuse does look different depending on what view point you are looking through. Some people will ask, "How do you allow people into your life that are going to hurt you?" You do not know how someone is going to react to you nor can you predict how you are going to respond to someone's action. I never would have thought that I would have someone in my circle who wanted to end everything for me but there they were. I have been told that, "Well they just need to see it for themselves," and in most cases that is true but if you were to see a child getting electrocuted would you wait until they noticed what was happening to them before you offered to help? Sometimes the best thing to do is not always considered the most reasonable plan of action. If you have to grab someone and weather out the storm to keep them safe and they get mad, well at least they're safe enough to bitch about things. Some are told that you should wait until someone asks you before you help them but it has been proven that sometimes it can be too late because they never knew that their life was in danger.

If I had not have gone through life the way I have then I would still be under the impression that everyone is good and therefore trustworthy. Going through life thinking this way will leave you open to all kinds of scum and scoundrels. I noticed that no matter what I tried to do to shake off the bullies I had been born into it took someone else standing up for me in order for me to learn how to protect myself. We have learned how to expose people's weaknesses but what we should be teaching is how to protect one another. Kids need their parents to protect them when things are beyond their means and since more parents are living at work then that leaves the kids learning how to protect themselves. I would still be running in my mind had my mum not have stepped up and said that she would protect me from the villagers. The fact that she said she would protect me from them made me feel stronger. Words are a powerful thing, they can be used to defeat you or make you stand tall.

The more you get to know yourself the more you will be able to decipher between the ones who are hurting and the ones bringing harm to others. You have to have two sides to yourself so that you are not showing compassion for the wrong ones. It is easy to say that you would do things differently but if you were put in the same violent situation could you make it out unharmed or would you have ended up costing yourself your own life? When you help someone help them, do not give them just another debt to have to fill. You never know when you just might someday need it yourself and if you already cashed in the help that you gave then it will be you that owes. If we all changed our way of thinking to include the environment around us then we would all realize that we are a product of its influence. Everything about the environment that you surround yourself with has influence on you, your state of mind, the way that you react to something, if you listen to your gut instincts or not. The more you begin to realize this the more you will begin to notice your influence in your own environment and the changes that follow.

The only way to have influence anywhere in your life is to start on the one person you know will try and fight you every step of the way, yourself. I was taught early how to stand up against the impossible but later began to realize that I found it near impossible to stand up to myself. I would let my mind wander, my conclusions jump, my heart get taken and my legs swept out from underneath me all while believing that I knew what I was doing. No matter what I did or seemed to try I was still putting myself in the same environment while never realizing that I was setting myself up for the fall just in different ways. I somehow managed to seek certain people out because I knew how it would end. I never realized that the reason that I could not just come to my mum and family was that I was trying to fight enough people in my life to account for all the villagers I had to endure when I was little. I have gone after the same types of people in different surroundings the same way they went after me. I know how I will respond in certain situations when a threat is imposed and so does everyone around me. Everything that I have learned be it from the elders, my grandfather, my mum, family, teachers or someone that is just passing through has given me a basic walk through of life. I know what to do when I enter into that realm but oddly enough when I am placed where nothing is wrong I freak out and become so nervous that I am surprised that it does not register on the Richter scale. I do not know what to do with myself since I have always had to survive and fight.

When you change your environment from evil to good you become shell shocked at the fact that you no longer have to jump and it does take time to adjust. The same holds true for the opposite of changing from good to evil, it takes time to condition you. Anyone who has ever gone through either one or both will tell you that. They never let someone just bully them and the way it was done was never noticed at first. What do you think sweet talk and flattery are used as? Like I have said the way to the heart is through the ears so use them to make sure that they are not telling you something that you want to hear. Then instead of falling for something that you wished that you would not have you will be able to catch yourself from falling into a trap. The one obvious observation that I noticed in every situation where someone was being hurt is they make sure that you do not like yourself. I never realized the complexities that come from my mum having said that. If you learn to wear your mind to where it fits you then you will notice how beautifully your body works and your heart will always feel good about that.

The better you like feeling about yourself the more you feel like you can take on and accomplish and come hell or high water you are going to get things done and take care of business. You will notice so many more things in life because you will have exposed yourself to life and learned how to become a part of it. I was always just surviving and knew how to just get by because I stayed around people who would always make me feel like that. I learned that sometimes you can be directly involved in something that you do not have to be and how you can help without becoming directly involved. The thing is that you have to be involved in every move that you make or at least be a part of your own decision making. Every form of your life involves you so you should concern yourself with what goes on in your life.

No matter what the people in the world throw at you do not let it stop you. We are not victims of anything; we are indeed survivors and have learned how to overcome incredible odds. Calling people victims takes everything away from us that you have no right to take. One of my mates who had been raped asked me how in the world I went on after all that I had been put through. Her exact words were, "I was only raped once and cannot seem to get past it but you went through this your whole life and it never seems to have bothered you. How do you do it?"

"Have you never notice how pissed off I can get and the walls I can go through when this occurs? The only difference between the two of us is how we choose to look at something. You look at the world through your heart which is not a bad thing but you learn to feel sympathy for the one who hurt you instead of giving that feeling to yourself. I have always looked at the world through my head and when something happens that is down right wrong I get beyond mad. If you will learn to pull your heart back and let your head into the

205

game then you will not be broke down into feeling sorry for yourself." Oh the look she gave me would have killed me if I would have let it. "I never said that you felt sorry for yourself I said that if you allow others to break you down they will make you feel sorry for yourself. Look, you were here when everyone found out my dark secret about being abused and what did they all do? Try everything in their power to use what they had just found out to get me to break myself. They cannot stand the fact that I am tougher because of it and if you will notice since I left the village no one has ever been able to put their hands on me again. They want and need for me to feel weak so that they can move in for the kill. Did you also notice that nobody outside of my family ever said that they were proud of me for making it through, glad that I am alive to tell about it. No and they never will. All they saw was someone who had powers that they did not possess and they wanted them for themselves at no cost to them. If you will also notice, none of them are around me any more. The difference between the two of us is anytime something happened to me I got pissed off and you did not. The hardest thing in the world to do is hold up someone who looks like they are going to explode. I will bet that if we talk about your rape…." and she stopped me.

"I do not want to talk about it."

"Why, because it still bothers you?"

I knew it did, so please do not think that I was being sadistic. I kept at her until I finally got her to cry and yes I did it intentionally. Sometimes people hold onto something to keep from breaking and if my mum has taught me anything it's that sometimes you have to let go of a deep pain before any healing will occur. I held her tight while she cried violently in my arms and I whispered softly in her ear, "I have you kid so just let it out." She cried for as long as she had been carrying that around with her. I never told her, "O.K. that is enough now." How am I supposed to know when they have cried long enough, I just let her cry until she felt better? Afterwards we talked. "Now who were those tears for, you or him?"

"What?"

"Were you shedding tears for you or for him?"

"For myself."

"Good, because what none of them ever knew is I used to cry into a pillow in my closet to make sure that none of them could hear me and know that they got to me. Honey, despite contrary belief I am human just like everyone else and even I have my breaking points. Now how do you feel about what happened to you. Are you happy that it happened?"

She looked at me again like she was going to kill me. "You know that I am not happy about what happened so why would you ask such a thing."

"Do you want it to happen to you again and again?" Oh that one made her see red but she still just sat there. "It really does not bother you at all does it," and that one made her jump in my direction. She finally reacted the way I needed her to. "Now you're pissed off huh?"

"You're damn right I am," but before she could misdirect her feelings I got her head to jump out in front.

"Everything that you are feeling right now, give it to your head and let it stay there."

"What?"

"That feeling you have right now of wanting to kill me for what I said. Change it into thoughts, you cannot feel thoughts you can only think about them. Get pissed off enough to get it through your head that this is not going to happen to you ever again until you feel it in your heart of hearts. The more you think about it the more pissed off you become until it becomes a part of you. Then and only then will you have the same gift that Dad gave to me, you cannot stop me no matter what you try and do, but keep in mind that I will not tolerate a whole hell of a lot before I snap."

"So that explains why you trigger so fast." The tension that filled the room was now replaced with wholehearted laughter.

She told me that she use to feel terrified at night when she was alone and now when she thinks back to what happened it no longer bothers her like it use to. "You may have gotten away with it once but it will never happen again because now I am on my toes." She got to the point where I did when I went out into the garage and beat the crap out of my punching bag but she has never been the type to raise her hands like that. She actually had good parents who loved her tremendously but never showed her how to defend herself. I could not see instilling that into her so I figured out a better form of therapy to fit her needs. "You know how you could tell that I was picturing one of them as I was popping that bag, well do the same thing, only let your pen and paper be your punching bag. Put everything that you want to say to them down on paper and for the love of Dad do not go easy on them after all they never went easy on you. Give them both barrels at full force and when you are finished put it in the mail. I know that you do not know where they live but either make up an address, or send it here, but get rid of it."

I received a forty two page letter that would have made the devil beg for mercy. (I asked her that if she sent it to me if she wanted me to read it or not and she said yes.) To tell you the truth, I never hit that bag as hard as she hit with that letter so please believe me when I say that the pen is mightier then the sword and fist which I never knew before. She said that when she let it go she noticed a difference in her "friends." They were not trying to comfort her but rather using what she had been through to keep her feeling broke. "I thought that they cared but all they cared about is what they could help themselves to. When I told them what you did they told me that you had no right to do that and now my brain is working like yours because I noticed that they never said that about the one who raped me."

I told her that when all of my dark closets were getting opened that I actually had a villager tell me that she knew I was depressed. When I told her no I was not she went out of her way to try and get me to feel like that. "Well, I know that your depressed I don't care what you say," and she said it like she had some kind of authority over my mind. Instead of having to justify my action she was telling me what my actions had meant and that she was not going to tolerate that from me. She had become an expert on the way I felt, thought and thought that this would give her control over my actions. When I stood firm and told her that I was not depressed and that she did not know what I was thinking she became irate. "Well I am not going to tolerate you calling my house all pissed off."

"I never called you when I was pissed off."

"Yes you did and I am not going to stand for it. I know that you're depressed." And that is when it hit me, son-of-bum grabber a villager can actually disguise themselves as elders and the sad thing was I am the one who gave them that title.

The sad thing is that the more she went after me to "expose" me the more she indeed ended up exposing her true nature. See I even know that I am much easier to deal with and manipulate when I am not going head strong into something. She wanted to expose the fact that she found someone daft and a burden on the world and she was going to be the one who turned me around. The thing that blew her out of the water is she went against what my grandfather had taught me and even said that he had no right to. What she ended up exposing was my intelligence and my stubbornness and it came right back to bite her in the bum. Sometimes you might want to leave well enough alone if it's not bothering you because as it has been said many times before: You may do what ever you can to go out of your way to break someone but they may not break the way you want them to. When she went after me every way that she could think of and I would come out better for it she went after me in a way no one ever has. She went after my work ethic and that pissed me off beyond what I have ever been in my entire life. You can attack me all you want because you know that sooner or later I will make a come back but to go after my job performance is beyond dirty. She had hired me for a job that she had no intention of allowing me to finish and thought that because she had read it in a book that she was the expert. She is the type that becomes an expert at everything she reads and does not think that she has to apply it to prove it. I found out through a series of people that she was telling people that I left the job like that and that she had to fire me because I was slacking off.

I have never been fired from a job and damn straight was not going to let her be the first. She more than went out of her way to make sure that I was not going to get the job done and even screamed that I was not looking at her. Now I do not know about you but when a villager throws a great big tit fit you know that someone is going to get screwed over and it sure is not going to be them. I could not understand why she would not leave me alone and let me do the job that I was hired to do. All she kept saying was, "Did you not hear them say how perfect you are, that you're a gem. You're so perfect." Someone she knew saw my handwriting and said that it was perfect and never once said that about me, but all she heard was the word perfect and that I was attached to it and it sent her right for me. I even tried to tell her that but you know how villagers are, they are never wrong in their own mind. I was perfect in everyway and it was up to her to put a stop to it the only way she knew how. To hire me to do work on her house and then deny me access to it then she can play the pity poor me act. "I tried to help that ungrateful little bastard and she just took the money and ran. I should have known better then to try and help scum but look at what she put me through. Oh everyone feels sorry for me." I am just grateful that I am not like that and did not pick up any bad habits from trying to work there.

The funny thing is that between the two of us I was not the one going around pretending to be the perfect know-it-all and when her bluff was called she folded. She is the type of villager that wants all eyes on her and if they're not, somebody is going to catch hell for it. Yes, there are a number of jobs that I have been hired to do and when I am finished I get told that the job was done to perfection and that I pay a tremendous amount of time to detail. I have never taken a compliment that was for my work and kept it for myself. I was taught to do any job right the first time and to go back and correct your own mistakes before you turn it in, just like in school. It is better to correct your own mistakes then to be too lazy to and get handed back a failing grade. If you do the same job over and over you should have it down to a scientific perfection. Remember practice makes perfect and the step beyond that is to practice until you cannot get it wrong.

I know that I should have seen all the red flags going up and every alarm being triggered but I had everything else on my mind and because she was there when other things were being triggered she knew it. You know your screwed when they tell you that they are not going to allow you to meet your dead line because that would mean that you had the job down to a perfection. I will admit that there was a big huge part of me that wanted to slip back into my old ways of taking care of people like her and just beat her within a meter of her life and sad to say it came real close to happening and no I would not have felt bad about it. I will never raise my hands to one of my elders but old villagers have been around long enough to know better. "Never under any circumstance should you attack a stray." When they tell you things like, "I am trying to take that animal instinct out of you and make you less of an animal," there is going to be a battle that could end up turning into a full fledged war and I will not take any prisoners. Yes it is true that I have perfected animal instincts but they were developed over time and throughout every battle. Now I am not so much of an animal that I have ever found myself drinking out of the toilet but abandoned kids will learn to develop their animal survival instincts every time we have to. That is just how Dad made and intended for us to be.

Maybe that is why my mum never flinched when she heard me growl and watched me show my teeth. She knew that I had to learn how to do that in order to survive and abused animals of any kind are prone to do it at anything that moves in their direction. She knows that you do not walk up to a wounded animal because they do not know if they can trust you and their first built in reaction is to run. Oh you can beat an animal until they're scared of you but if you beat them long enough they will indeed turn on you when you least expect it because they know when you left your guard down. The weird thing is that my mum never considered me an animal; I on the other hand knew that I could turn into a wolf when you came close enough to pull the wool over my eyes. When I discussed this with one of my mates that are still here after all this he gave me a book that he said fit me to a tee and that he never realized that it could not only be true but that he met one when he came across me. The part that stuck hard was now becoming clear: From time to time throughout history, apparently wild children have appeared in society, children who seem to have grown up by themselves or to have been reared by animals. They go on to ask if an infant could survive alone in the wild? Could they be "adopted" into a group that is not their own? If nature's children were brought into human society, would they be hopelessly daft to the world around them and a constant reminder of the bestial part of human nature——-or a noble savage, free of the corruptions of civilization? They called people like us, "simply orphans" because we were abandoned of all human contact. Uh, we did not abandon ourselves so why are we being considered the animal? (I guess putting it that way makes us easier to deal with and to dismiss.)

Maybe that is what that one villager thought when she came across me, that she was going to take a wild animal out of the wilderness that they have always known and turn them into what she considered a human being so that she could parade me around in front of her society friends. I would get to be, "Look at what I have done and therefore created experiment." She was impressed with the fact that I could sit up and play dead with just a look in my direction but what she refused to see was that I was already capable of doing this. The fatal mistake that she made was backing me up into a corner and then trying to beat me so I did what came natural, I attacked her. Granted most of it was verbal but that can be abusive too. Maybe that is why she kept trying to beat it into me that I was depressed, to keep me from attacking her. When someone is going out of their way to make you submissive there is a hidden agenda and it is not in your favour. The mistake they made was trying to beat down an already wounded animal and doing so makes us become highly aggressive and the one thing we learn above all else is to go directly for the throat. One it keeps them from hollering for backup and it keeps them from being able to get to yours.

To answer their accusations; a wild child was first part of the society that created them even if it was just long enough to spit us out and then we were left for dead. Some of us were indeed raised by what you could consider animals but their breed is that of human society not of the animal kingdom so do not confuse the two. If you force us to have to go outside ourselves because you feel like it is someone else's responsibility to care for us then do not be at all surprised when we come out of the jungle ahead of you and are more alert then you could ever dream of being. Have you not ever noticed that animals can sense danger while the society of humans all runs around in place screaming and asking, "What, I do not see it for myself?" Yes, infants can survive alone in what ever situation you put them in because we have no concept of fear only survival. To us this is just how our lives are so we take what we have and learn to thrive. Can we be "adopted" into a group that is not our own? Well my mum and family sure seem to think so and every animal can adapt to their surroundings, which is why it is so easy for us to move on. Death is not considered a loss to us, just a fact of life.

If nature's children were brought into human society, would they be hopelessly daft to the world around them? To put it quite simply, no just the opposite is true. We are very much aware of the world we live in and cannot understand why society making the world what it is has no clue of the life they created around them. Chaos ensues when knowledge is banned. We know more about the world then the self proclaimed scholars who think they're worldly and we can figure things out before everyone else is finished reading their books. We possess something far greater then street or book smarts, because we are societies not nature's forgotten children. Dad gives us clairvoyant vision that He helps us to develop. Wonder why animals like us learned not to be afraid, because we can sense the danger before it is actually there. All we have to figure out between now and then is how to avoid it before it gets close. Babies who have grown up in a breed of society panic when they hear the word danger and loose their minds before they can figure out what to do since now it is right on top of them.

Are we a constant reminder of the bestial part of human nature? I cannot figure out for the life of me why they wrote that because the definition of bestial is: inhuman- lacking normal human feelings of pity or remorse. Sexually depraved: sexual in a depraved or purely physical manner. It also says brutish: lacking intellect, reason, or culture, or relating to beasts: relating to or characteristic of a beast. People have more of this characterization than animals ever could. Now from my animal intellect point of view, wolves will howl together as one when one of our own dies as a part of life. We do so out of pride for the ones we love not pity. And you never see animals abandon their offspring because they need to get laid and you sure as hell do not see them beating their kids into submission or telling them to marry the squirrel who can hoard the most nuts. If we remind you of anything it is that we know how to live in our world without trying to destroy it. We know how to survive even though you sent us out into the world to die. All we really remind you of is survival of the fittest and you know that since the wild could not kill us then you sure as hell do not stand a chance. We also remind you that animals can control their instincts and not allow someone else to run off with them.

Animals teach their offspring how to survive and show them how to hunt and what to do when danger gets close. Society babies goes after anything that moves if they think they can feed off of them and will stand in the same spot when the danger is more than present.

Now what eludes me is how the question was put. Do you think that if you got rid of our kind that everyone in your society will think that greed, lust and envy are a way of life? Maybe that is why they try so desperately to force us into becoming human so that we will forget what is right and what they're doing is clearly wrong. Maybe we remind them that animals do not act like that in the wild or when we are brought in from the cold.

I also do not believe that we are noble savages either. That in itself is a great example of an oxymoron. To be noble means having a magnificent and excellent moral character. Savage means undomesticated, living wild, beyond the control of people. (Beyond the control of people, I like that.) If you took out just what you need then all you are really left with is it is more noble to be uncontrolled by humans. If you add what you need to it then, We are noble because we allow Dad to place us where He needs His business taken care of and we will not question why we are placed here. That could be why Dad gave my mum to me and why He gave me to Her, because I am a part of His business and He knew that She would more than take care of me and because of doing so I would always be Loyal in my Respect for my mum, in giving her respect and in showing her the utmost respect. Mums deserve more than respect but that is a good place to start.

He knows that both of us are free of the corruptions of civilization and my mum was raised as a human. Mum Nature taking in a child of nature, how sweet is that. Did the villagers really think that I would settle for less than the Kingdom of Heaven when I knew that Dad made me an offer I could not refuse? They are all corrupt in different ways and that is why I left, but now after all this time has past I was somehow supposed to become daft living out in the wild and just forget what they are all about and go back. Please, we are not the ones who lack intellect and we prove it every time one of them comes near us. We may be "simply orphans" to you but we have become more complex than you will ever read about. These same civilized people will ask me if I believe in God and freak when I tell them no. I do not believe in my mum or family either for that matter and they have never pulled what I said out of context. In order to believe in something you have to accept that something is true. To me my mum and Dad are facts that come with life; it does not matter if you believe them to be or not because it will never take away from them. Everyone starts out believing in the tooth fairy and it crushes them when they find out that it was all made up. I will never put my Dad or the members of my family in that same category for any reason. I have faith in my dad, mum and family and because of that it gives me faith in myself. In order to believe in something you first have to question if it's real or not and I knew the minute I popped out that Dad was real. The only thing that I questioned was if I was one of His kids or not and He went out of His way to prove that I am because He gave me the best family He had to offer because He knew I would eventually find them. He also knew that by the time I found them I would need them out of more than desperation; I would need them out of desperation for love.

I feel both empathy and sympathetic for those who question His existence or hide behind His letter to all of us. I may have fought Dad from the start just like I did with my mum considering the circumstances I was under but I never questioned whether or not He was real. Some people will tell you that they do not believe you and then you are supposed to go out of your way to prove them right or wrong, one way or another. I myself have learned not to care what other people think and that if they want to tell me that I am wrong then they need to go out of their way to prove me wrong and not just make something up. All they have to say is, "I do not believe you," and leave it at that and you are supposed to stop everything that you are doing until you pacify them. How ludicrous. I never could understand that one, "I do not believe you," so get off your bum and go look it up for yourself and stop expecting people to spoon feed you. I have witnessed lots of things in life that were, "not supposed to happen," but they did and instead of doubting what I just saw I looked deeper into it.

You have to understand that there are some people in life that will never believe anything that they see themselves and want you to stop seeing something that they refuse to acknowledge happened. If they want to loose out then let them, but do not put your life or thoughts on hold for someone who is going to go out of their way not to believe you. I had an ex-mate stand right beside me when something occurred and came right out and said, "I did not see what I just saw, nope I am just not going to believe it." I saw it too but never denied it. What happens if you go back home and Dad asks you not if you have been good or not but if you believe in Him. What happens if you say, "No, prove it with some parlour tricks." Dad just looks at them and simply replies, "No that was on earth where I would do things to convince you that I was real. Now you're up here and you have to prove to me whether or not I should believe you exist. If you do not believe that I exist then how am I suppose to believe that you do so please go make some place else your home."

Some people tell you to just have Faith but never say anything more after that. They never tell you how to acquire it just that you are supposed to have it. My favourite is, "Faith will come in time." What? No it does not. If you ask me Faith is something that you build yourself and you can build it out of doubt and understanding all at the same time. I built my Faith out of pure doubt and I am grateful that I did because I would have never learned that there are two sides to Faith and it is not until you combine the two that the veil comes off your very own eyes. Full Faith comes from when you believe in yourself and when you realize that you would have never gotten this far in life without Dad giving you some of His Faith when yours falters. You can have Faith in Dad all day long but if you doubt yourself then something is going to go wrong. I have noticed that the more I have Faith in my Dad the more I show how much Faith He can instill in me because I will do something with it. The more you learn to have Faith in yourself the more you show your Faith in Dad. (Faith is a deeper version of trust.) The more you have Faith in Dad the more He will show how much Faith He has in you. Think of it this way, who would you give the most Faith to: someone who will do nothing but doubt or someone who will take care of business because they have Faith in you and you in them.

Faith is a feeling that the impossible can be overcome when you learn not only how to reach out but to reach up and ask Dad to hold your hand as you're going through something. Your mum holds your heart; your Dad holds your hand. I would have never been able to stand up to any of the abusers that I have come across had I not have been honest with Dad and let Him know that I was at a loss as to what to do at times. Love is the same feeling as Faith; if you believe in love then you open yourself up to Faith. The more you can feel Faith the more you can feel not only earthy love but His spiritual love for you. Faith is a bond of trust.

Remember the saying; And the soul felt its worth, a thrill of hope…? Before your soul can begin to feel anything, you yourself have to know that you are worthy. It **is** hard for anyone's soul to feel worthy if you feel like your worthless. I know that it is a simple thought but when you feel it you know that it is not all that simple. The more I think about my life and how I went about things, the more clarity I am beginning to see between myself and my spirit. When the two come together you can actually see yourself standing inside your soul. I know that is an odd thing to say but what has not been so far!

Let me see if this will try to explain all three sides in detail. When I was being abused, although I stayed beyond pissed off (because it will keep that fight in me going strong) the inside of my body never healed like the outside and everything that had ever been done to me was always right there. When you look for a scar or a bruise on the outside of your body it may have disappeared but the inside keeps everything as it had first appeared. You walk around feeling like everyone can see every mark that has ever been applied and that includes the ones to your heart and mind. (When people loose weight I have heard them say that they still feel like they are the same size. The same thing applies, we still feel like we are that small.) That was me, one knocked about forgotten orphan who people insisted on treating like a side show freak. Although I never showed emotions it did not mean that I did not have feelings. I learned how to keep myself locked inside a closet long after I left. One because I never wanted anyone to ever hurt me like that again, and two I never wanted anyone to see how bad I did get hurt. I figured out after all this time that keeping that door shut did not mean that I was safe, some people would come in and do what they could to help keep my soul alive before they had to sneak out again. The rest would do the same things to me that had always been done, and then act like because they were not caught means that it was not a big deal.

The thing is that my spirit had other things in mind and was not going to go through life getting picked on or beat up, not mentally or physically anyway. When I was shrinking inside it was using that to become bigger and it was definitely not going to feel inferior against anything. When I get fired up my body stays the same size (I never noticed that before) but the rest of me does not and now I realize that it was my spirit that could go through brick walls not me. My spirit became invincible because I am the one who held the fear and the feeling that we could get hurt with me. Had my spirit had any doubt there is no way that I could have lived through half of what I did and still come out to be as sane as I think I am. The cool thing is that I learned that there are two sides to my spirit, the overwhelming side that comes out when someone needs to be protected (through love, I remember.) The other side is the brick wall that comes out, mess with my family and this is the only thing you will come up against. Pretty sweet to think that you can have enough spirit for two powerful parts of your being. Kind if like the two pillars in your life. My grandfather helped me to build into a solid brick wall; he showed and taught me how to go through anything when you set your mind through it. Then my mum comes along and tells me that my wall is knocking the ones I love out so she taught and showed me how to build a loving, soft protective side that only they get to see.

When my family took me in and treated me like they do each other, I got to do a lot of things right before their very eyes in a manner of speaking. I wanted to change having a trigger temper and I have. I wanted to heal from all the pain I had held in for so long and in order for me to do that they gave me a safe place to let go and recover. I know that some people feel like when you save someone's life they become indebted to you, and all village children believe this way. But when your family saves your life you become bonded and hold together tighter than ever. With their help I learned that while I was trying to help someone out I would some how get traded into becoming a servant to someone in their village be it through their kids, animals or whatever they could find as pawns. My mum has never used her hugs as weapons on me nor does she hold back her love in order for us to do her bidding. She knew that sometimes I could not see the full picture because I had seen too much of an undesirable corner and would fight to keep someone else from getting placed there. She never once told me to just let it go because they cannot hurt you any more, because she knew that they did indeed tear me up. Instead she took me in, showed me the kind of fruit bowl I was going to be getting mixed up in and let their love do the rest.

None of them have ever tried to contain me nor control me but they instead helped me to become master of my own spirit. Now instead of my spirit leading the way, we get to stand together as one. I have always been told that I was too small to do half of what I have already done, and if it would not have been for my spirit taking charge I would have believed them. Your spirit can actually be ten times bigger than what you think that it is. I learned this when I left everything behind to start a life with my family. I had always walked around feeling freakishly huge for my size, you can ask all my family not just my mum on that one. I had always gotten hand me downs so I never paid attention to clothes, that is until I lost all of mine. The sad thing is all the kids that use to give me their clothes are long gone and I have to go and find my own now. You think that you would notice things about your body since it is yours but the only thing I really paid attention to were scratches and things of that accord.

The only thing that I ever noticed was the size of my spirit, not my actual body size and you just get this feeling that you cannot shop in the grown-ups section because all the trousers hanging on the rack are taller than you are standing. When you have to go out and find new everything otherwise you are going to freeze to death it makes you pay close attention to great detail like your actual size, not your spirits. For example my spirit wears a fifty nine and a half boot, (I know because I measured when they were not looking.) I go to find a new pair of boots and instead of my normal size; I now have to wear a 1 and ½ in little kids. I discover that my spirit has more than a bit of an ego when it comes to leaving big impressions and it freaked out when it discovered what size shoe I was now going to have to wear. Now when you feel your spirit looking down on you saying, "How in the world did you ever keep up with those small feet?" Then you find yourself thinking, "Well, I did wear a two when we were in all those battles and journeys together if that helps you out any." You know you connected with your spirit when it looks at you as if to say, "Just how big are you really? I know what we can look like together as but just on your own. How big are you by yourself?"

The funny thing is that my spirit was not the only one freaking out about going down a size in boots. I called my mum freaked out, it was not the physical part that was getting to me, it was all mental. The reason is that right before I broke the zipper on my boots forcing me to get another pair I said the same thing I always say when someone comments about my small feet. "I had them special made that way when I put my foot in my mouth I do not have a lot to swallow." Then bam out of no where the universe takes advantage of the situation. I was trying to tell my mum that ever since I had to put on a ½ size smaller I was feeling like I was now a half of step behind of where I would normally be. I told a mate about what this was doing to me mentally, she paused for a moment and then said, "One way to look at it would be like a reward. Hold on before you ask how smaller feet would be good. You know how you like discovering little pieces of life's puzzle and then figuring out how they fit? Maybe taking a half a step away from you is all that was needed for you to stop putting your foot in your mouth, since your foot is no longer in your mouth it keeps you from biting your tongue and since I know you like life in threes it keeps you from biting off more then you can chew. The last one you do all the time but you do follow through I will give you that. You know what the freakiest thing about all of this is?"

I started laughing, "No, what!"

"That I have been hanging around you for so long that your weird way of looking at things is sinking in." (Now how in the world could I not take that as a compliment meant for my head but felt in my heart. I could feel both of them laughing so it must have been in our favour.) Then she had to go get all philosophical on me. "You know how you told me that when you would figure something out that your teachers would tell you not to stop, keep going and then your mind would build on top of it and run. They would allow you to go so far and then tell you to shake your head so you would loose your train of thought. Then you would tell me how they would tell you that you took it far enough and now it's time to enjoy what you just learned because you earned it?"

"Let me take a deep breath before I say yes to all of it." I just knew I was going to get nailed.

I did and then she said, "Maybe the universe was knocking you in the head so unbelievably hard because you went too far in your "Figuring things out the way you were taught to" frame of mind and you forgot to shake your head so they did it for you. They just had to do it so many times because of how extremely hard headed you are when your mind gets going. Maybe knocking you in the head and making your feet smaller was the universe's way of forcing you to take a long over due step back so that you can appreciate everything that you have been learning. I know that sometimes when I am around you I feel like knocking you in the head because you are so stubborn, I can only begin to imagine how stubborn the universe knows you to be. I will admit though that when you get a feeling that nobody else sees at the time you hang in there even when it's your own mates doing the attacking. Then when the world proves you to be correct about your bad feeling you have never once said I told you so and you know that so many would. Yes, that would be one way of looking at things. If I were to think completely like you then I would say that your reality is a figment of our imagination and our logic is a figment of your imagination brought on by your reality. Yep, I have been hanging around you to long." I could not believe that she said that last part with such a straight face, I was so proud of her for that. The odd thing to me is that everything that she said made logical sense in reality and in reality it was all logical.

It was not until I took a good soft look at myself that I discovered what made some people laugh when I would go on the attack. They saw my size go after someone, not my spirit; I felt the size of my spirit when I was going head to head with someone not the size of my body. When I take a step back and look at the size I really am when my spirit is resting, my mum's right, I am little. Good thing I never noticed that before otherwise someone might have stepped on me way before now. My mum never emphasizes this in any way except for when she came right out and said, " When I saw those two little hands and that little foot go up." So, my mum knew my secret identity all along and never blew my cover, which is pretty loving if you ask me. She kept it so secret that she never even told me that I was to small to take on what I do, I guess it's like the nuts things you think they already know.

Maybe that is what part of life is, learning your own secret identity and being true to it. The people in the world will always see this tough brick wall that will not stop at anything to defend someone in trouble because we are to freakishly huge for anyone to stop us. My family gets my secret identity side, the side of me that realizes everything about me is small except for my tongue and that is because I stick it out all the time. (Just to stretch it.) They have the softer side of me because they took time enough to care for me and about me. I figured out that just because you feel protective of someone does not mean that you feel anything past that and protection is not a form of love. I knew that I would be highly protective of my mum and family but that I did not need to protect them all the time and that scared me. I have always cared long enough to help someone out of the same village that I was in but now when I honestly look back… All I really cared about was getting them out. I have become involved in situations in my life because just like my mum I knew that they could not see it for themselves and needed me to hang tough until they were clear. I tried in an odd way to reach back and pull the ones I had left behind out through other people. Some people will have you to believe that it was a death wish of some kind but both my heart and head disagree.

In a subconscious way I was conscience about all that I had been put through and was trying to right wrongs that I felt like I had done. I was too small to rescue anyone besides myself and that in my eyes made me guilty because I was not the only one. I learned later that they call it survivor's guilt and it never runs out until you face the truth. I was always told by the villagers that I was too small and going after them meant I was not too small any longer. My grandfather taught me that just because you have a gun in your hand does not make you a fighter, all it makes you is the same as everyone else someone with a gun in their hand. True warriors use themselves as weapons and that is exactly what he made me. I could either use my eyes, my words (just nothing I would want my mum to hear) my body language, my spirit and if all that does not keep them at bay then more than my fists come out swinging. I learned, "I have been through enough and I am not going to take it any more." The odd thing is I thought that if I stood up for myself like I did for others then it made me selfish. I learned from my family that being selfish is not learning to stand up for yourself because when you hurt so does the ones who see you go through it.

I knew that I wanted out of the life I had been born into and always thought that every step I was taking was leading me further out of it until I realized that all I was doing was walking around in circles until someone would need my help. When my life was put this way, "Stand your ground and loose your life or keep your life and loose your family," I noticed something that never occurred before. I had a choice to make, usually all I get is live or die and nothing more. I learned how to see all the positive and the negative and how to pull what I need out and leave the rest. He knew that he could not get to me with, "You look depressed, you look depressed, I am going to tell you this over and over until I can get it inside your head so that you will start to feel depressed." Only my family is allowed to have access to my head in that way and he was finding this out. Then the heart with, "Call me," and as you know I did until I realized that I no longer cared because I could see his true nature and I no longer wanted to look at him. He tried to break me in everyway through my business, my home, my family and all that stood in his way was me. When someone denies that they said anything even though you have them on tape saying it and they never keep their word believe me they never will. Physically I had proven that I may be small but that does not mean that I am weak nor fragile so he knew that if we took it outside I would be pissed off enough to beat him within a millimetre of his pathetic life so he went for the chicken way out of things.

I noticed that every thing he went after was a piece of my armour; head, body armour, shield and sword and when I was putting them on as he was attacking them I noticed my spirit handing them to me instead of the other way around. My spirit had always taken care of things and now it was time for that little kid to come out of the closet and show them what we are made of. Just because you think you destroyed something and got rid of it does not mean that it did not turn into something else. I learned that you cannot have everything in life be one way or the other because you will never learn how to piece things together for yourself. I can take on bad people myself but evil people; well Dad helps me with those and always has even when I am too stubborn to know that I need help. I finally had to break and say, "This is too much for me, I cannot do it alone." That is the very moment all of my family came into my heart and I knew that if defending myself was going to cost me everything I was going to decide what that everything was going to be.

I made them think that everything was fine and that I was going to be put back under their boot and left it at that. I went inside my house, locked the door and went through everything that I had and pulled out what belonged to my mates, a couple of things that I wanted for myself and gave the rest to the people who were going to move into my house. That was the way it was suppose to work out. Instead I just lost everything because some people turn out greedier than what they look but I never had to pack up what I truly love and hold dear, my Family. It was not truly until then that it hit me, I do have family and I need to start thinking of them and not these freaking villagers.

Helping someone go through this is different than going through it yourself. I started over and left everything behind without giving it a third thought, (the first two votes came in the same) because even though some of it was sentimental I did not want material things to be put above the love I feel for my family or my safety. See there are always going to be bullies and bad people around so there will be another day but now I no longer look for them and am not in plain eye sight for them to take pot shots at me. It was then that my soul felt and realized its worth. I was worth more than being beaten down and I had proved it….to myself. I realized that when you become involved in someone's life without realizing right then, "This is a moment that is about to become a part of my life and therefore a part of who I am." Everyone that you meet will influence your life somehow, now they may not always leave an impact of an impression but you will always take something away with you just like them. You may not realize the impact or impression you leave with someone because they do not realize it themselves until later.

Everything in life has duality even if you do not see them appear together, you could learn one part now and save the other one for later. The definition says that they can either be opposed to each other or be complementary to each other and I have spent more of my life being opposed to what I went through. Now I am looking at things in life that complement everything that I have learned and achieved going through all of this. I replaced resentment with compassion, loathing for longing and my world of hate with a mum who brought along with her, family as back up. Who could say no to all of that? The great thing is when you learn to break both sides down and head straight down the middle. I searched the world long and hard for my mum and hoped that if she ever found out that I did not have a perfect life before her that she would show me just a little compassion. Instead I received a world full of compassion from my mum who knew I had always longed for her and went through hell and back to be a part of her.

Life is never just going to hand you something, not a hard life and not a good one. When you learn how to combine things the answers become clear enough for you to see but not to where you can necessarily point at them to show someone else. A great deal of life takes place inside your mind but it is up to you whether or not you include your heart and your spirit along. When you do though… You begin to notice the metaphysical realm of pure thought and the philosophical side of life.

## A Love So Great and Pure.

A love so pure, that the angels did sing the Holy word of her name, and upon my lips I did bear a cross, that should have fallen. So tender and great this love shall be, that all of Heaven sings her praise, and though it shall come I waited just the same. In my darkest hour I did hear the angels weeping and whispering, for I had missed her once when she came calling. My spirit soared up high to catch a glimpse of this great pure love and I knew that in my heart my darkest days would soon be forgotten. There it was so tender and pure that I knew for sure this must be her. The Heavens cried and made my heart ache for the one that was going to be so great and no tainted love would she give to me or to another.

She would fill all hope that was lost and tenderly hold you so dear and give you inspiration when all you could feel was despair. This greatest love I did find when I finally broke and called her by her Holy name. I was now a part of the choir and could feel for myself why the Heavens and all that it holds thinks so highly of the one we call our mum for she is the purest and greatest of all the loves that your heart can ever hold. She is the one true light that looks towards Heaven as she holds her children dear and gives us the eyes to see the same.

There will be no other to stand in her place and no child sane or otherwise will ever feel the need to replace the one that holds them dear because we all know that the love they give to us is so rare that we value highly the love so pure and great that comes from the only one we will ever call our mum, the Holy name sent from Heaven to guide us on our way. Thank-you Dad in Heaven for giving us mums and for letting us call them by that great titled name.

# Chapter Seven
# The Metaphysical Realm of Pure Thought and the Philosophical Side of Life.

Duality is the metaphysical and the philosophical sides combined to form an outcome. It is the reality and logical sides to your thoughts that bring you to form your actions. In order to have complete control of your mind you have to open up all of it. Doing this means being both left and right brained at all times. I am left handed but I make my right hand do things to exercise that side of my mind into keeping aware of what the other side is thinking. Waking up the other side of your brain opens the door to new thought provoking thoughts of realized ideas. If we only use one side of our brain when we are either left or right handed and get ten percent out of it then surly getting the other side to develop should by all rights give us the use of twenty percent. That is being both realistic and logical at the same time.

Maybe opening up both sides will help us come to conclusions instead of jumping to them. You will be able to see both the outcome and what needs to be done in order to achieve it. You figure out the difference between I learned how, I know how and I can teach someone else how. When you open up the other side of your mind you can teach yourself how to over come certain obstacles by using total recall that fits the situation. You learn to think completely one way and how to think completely in the opposite direction and then pulling out what you need in order to reach your valued conclusion of wisdom.

Learning how to open up the other side of your brain makes the other side recognize it as a companion even it they disagree from time to time. Opening up both sides brings religion and government working together as one. You know what is right and wrong and keep yourself walking a steady path in order to achieve your highest mind set. When one side of your brain has doubts the other side jumps in and talks you into finishing. You have positive and negative all around you in life and your mind is set up to receive these waves. If you keep both sides open you can find a healthy balance between the two. When the negative side of your mind is the only part allowed to develop you will be more susceptible to all that comes with it. Your mind will think that everything is too good to be true instead of realizing a good thing when it sees it. You should be able to take a situation and interchange the positive and negative sides until you have a complete fit of everything that can happen and still keep your wits about you. You can see everything negative that could happen before it does, and you can see all the positive outcomes all in your mind. By combining the two together you know what to avoid and if it is not unavoidable how to solve the problem quickly before it gets out of your hands.

By opening up your mind to both the metaphysical realm of pure thought and the philosophical side of life you teach yourself how to take the good with the bad. Your mind learns that positive thoughts get you further and actually stops the other side from having negative thoughts because it knows that it is just a slow form of unforeseen suicide and is there to help. You have taught your mind how to listen to you and now you are showing it how to listen to itself. You got your brain to listen to you by learning reasoning and logic and it talks the other side out of walking down that lonely path by using the same method of understanding. "I know that you are feeling bad right this moment but if you look at it this way…"

I actually tried to force myself to think negative about something that was occurring and I could hear that side of my brain stop itself. I could have sworn that I heard it say, "Why bother, the other side is just going to reason us out of thinking in a negative way by being logical." When you open up the negative side when all you have listened to was the positive it forces you to see things for how they really are, and not what you would like to imagine them to be. You loose that, "But I want it done my way," to this is just a better way of doing something. Logically it should work like this but in reality it came out like this. When you combine logic and reality you learn how to figure out what not only is there but what can be strived to bring achievement. You learn to see hard roads as ways of improving your skills instead of diminishing them. You learn how to take things in stride and when to step out of the flow. You figure out that being crazy and confused is one of the best ways to live life. You're crazy enough to go through the hard times and confused enough not to let it get you down. By the time you figure out what really happened you are already long gone mentally and physically out of harms way.

The key to anything is first made in the mind because a thought had to bring it up. The more you develop both sides the more keys you can create and develop, which leads to further exploration. I learned that the only time I was ever positive was when I was making someone laugh but now I have developed a side that can stay positive simply by rearranging my negative thoughts around to where they get acknowledged too but not have full say. I realize that without the logical side of my brain nothing in reality would make sense. Without the realistic side nothing logical would ever be obtained. When you stay positive and exclude anything negative you loose sight of the fall and tend to drop harder when the situation lets you down slightly. When you give both sides of your brain a say it gives them proper balance, and since the mind controls the body it then teaches you how to not only feel better about itself but how to think better about yourself. Self-esteem and self image are linked through two different parts of your mind. People can look good on the outside but that does not necessarily mean that they feel good about themselves on the inside. Their self image is fine but their self-esteem is empty. The people who feel great about themselves on the inside are made to feel bad because their beauty is not going to be found on a magazine cover. Their self-esteem is fine but they have a hard time with their self image. What if waking up the other side of your brain by developing the hand that you do not write with gives you that other part of you. I know that you are probably thinking to yourself, "I cannot write with the other hand." If you remember you could not write with the hand you are now at first, you had to practice. If you're thinking, "I cannot do it." Your correct, you are never going to because you told yourself before you started that you were not going to so you stopped yourself before you even tried. It is all in your mind set and if you set yourself up to fall that side of your brain will go out of its way to make sure that it occurs. If you tell yourself, "I am going to enjoy this," you will. You have to take control of your mind, yes you can let it wander off without adult supervision but you cannot allow it to tell you what to do.

When you come across something new or a nasty job you tell yourself that you are going to get this and that you are going to enjoy doing it and before you know it the crappiest of all jobs is over with trash, chores, whatever is over with and you feel good about yourself because you're finished with it. You did the job and it did not get the better of you by causing you to moan. This is a way of outsmarting the negative side of your mind. I am left handed when I write but I practice getting my right hand to draw, they are weird drawings but to me that just means it matches the other weird side of my brain. Oh would that not be weird, to have one side of your brain be weird while the other side is normal, how would you go about looking at life?

"That is so weird!"

"No it is not!"

"Yes it is!"

"No it is not!"

"Well, I am not going to listen to you."

"Good because you're being too weird to give you much thought."

I never gave that one much thought until now; I just assumed that the other side would be as weird if not even more strange then being in our right mind turned out to be. I asked one of my teachers about that, "If I am in my right mind then how come everyone makes me feel left out, but the ones not being left out are not really in their right minds?" I never did receive an answer just a really strange look.

When you start to develop your other hand you will begin to notice changes in not only your mind but in your attitude as well as your demeanour. You cannot really say that you are open minded if in reality you are really not. I have always let my conscience mind wander where ever it wanted to but I was always more aware of my subconscious thoughts. One time I got dinged in the head so hard that I wanted to black out and consciously I did, but I could hear my subconscious part talk me into coming back around. That is the part that kept me coherent and I walked away just fine.

There is an odd way to develop your mind but it does work. Submerge your head in water because drowning is the easiest thought to panic over. Get a timer because there is a visual part of your brain that has to see improvement through whatever means but it thrives off of numbers or words. Hold your breath and see how long you can hold it but not only that keep in mind what is going on through your head. Normally, you're concentrating on your breath and the water around you. Keep track of your numbers but only when it comes to this. Now when you do it a second time think about something before you submerge your head and think about that for as long as you can until your thoughts loose track of themselves and look at your time. Even if you just improved a second you did improve and this will register inside your subconscious. The third time you do it you have to force yourself to stay until you panic because you need air and then you have to picture inside your mind you're telling yourself, "Its o.k. we are inhaling (and picture yourself doing it) and we are exhaling (and again picture yourself doing it) if your mind believes that it is it will calm down to the point it actually believes that it is breathing normally. Now when this was done to me they held my head under and when I struggled they tapped me on the head. It may sound like a bad thing but what went through my mind was, "Hey, why did they do that. I do not know maybe we should ask them. Not a bad idea, do you want to remember to ask them or should I?" Before I could answer them my head was being pulled up. I had held my breath by distracting my thoughts a full minute past when I first started struggling to raise my head in panic. When you control your breathing you control the need for panic, and when you learn to control your breathing you can actually control your own heart rate. Slowed breathing and controlled heart rate equals no room for fear or panic. In addition you realize that because you remain calm you are more in control of the situation.

This is the greatest mental exercise you could ever do for yourself. The worse time to panic is when you're drowning and when life comes at you and you feel like you're drowning your brain will come in and stop it. When your brain registers the improvement in numbers it feels good about the improvement throughout the whole body. Your brain knows that it did it, it passed the test and believe it or not it will start to look for new challenges because it feels good about itself and it will make you feel good about yourself. The brain will share what it feels so do things that makes it feel good about itself. Another good one to practice is plugging your ears for a whole 24 hours with either ear phones or plugs but you want to make sure very little sound comes in. You would be absolutely surprised at how movement will enter into your realm and your eyes will be aware of so many more things and be able to zoom in on something that you never gave a second thought to. A good one to do is cover up only one ear and notice the difference.

Every kid has to have done this at some point in their life but when you close one eye you notice the change, when you go back and forth. If you cover up one eye for a day it forces the other one to be keener, the same for covering up the other eye and doing the same. Cover up both and just sit still, allow the sounds to come to you. Does your mind wander or is it paying attention to what is going on around you? When you cannot sleep at night because your thoughts keep you up, start listening to them, because they're trying to tell you that you have unfinished business. When you do not pay your thoughts any attention they have their own way of coming forward. The more you train your instincts

228

and become aware of them the more you will have them to command and take charge with.

If fear is all in the mind and you teach yours how to not only overcome but not to buy the seeds that start it you will learn not to give fear any existence over you or through you. The more you empower your mind the more it can and will empower you. Give yourself a situation and picture it to where you turn it into a worse case scenario and walk yourself through it from beginning to end. Make your brain figure out what needs to be done and how to go about doing it and picture yourself doing it. You have to picture yourself doing it otherwise you do not get the full benefit. Your brain is both visual and audio, that is why you can picture things in your head and hear your thoughts. I figured that out when I was thinking about giving the corn eyes and listening to them talk to the potatoes.

When you open up the conscience or subconscious part of your other half you will notice that it can figure things out ahead of time. One part can figure out from start to finish how to accomplish anything, the other side looks for things to go wrong and how to correct them ahead of time.

One time when I was driving I thought I would play a little mental game with myself just because I thought it would be fun. The situation was I had just robbed a bum bank so I was wanted for hauling ass. There was an actual car coming towards us that we made "the coppers" but it was a good two meters ahead so we had time to figure out what to do.

My first thought, "Do not panic," my second, "We need to turn off."

"No, because that will make us look suspicious, instead ever so slowly roll up the window."

"Why?"

"Because with the window open it's causing a breeze to flow into the back seat and now they're flapping in the wind."

"Good point." I rolled the window up and thought, "O.K. now what."

"Now just let them pass and keep your eyes straight ahead because if you turn around you are going to freak." The car was passing us and you are never going to believe this but it was an actual cop car and because I had remained so calm they never pulled us over for hauling bum across international waters while driving on the road. I could not stop laughing after that happened, life was playing with me too. The more mental games you play the more you would be surprised at how life will play with you.

There are all kinds of mental exercises that you can do to prepare yourself to handle anything that comes your way. The reason you want to develop the hand that you do not normally write with the same way you did with the one that you do write with is because it forces it to pay attention to great detail. Make that other hand wake up so that it can activate the other half of you. Everything in life has a connection even if you cannot see it at first. One side thinks the other feels. Instead of being full of fear you learn how to trade it for caution. Cautious thoughts keep your safe, fearful ones keep you in place. The more you use both halves of your brain the more they will come together as one and then you posses a collected mind and thought pattern. You might hear, "This is going to be hard," and just as firm you will hear, "Yes it is, but we are going to make it through," then together as one you hear, "Yes, we will."

Now I have had people make fun of me for saying, "We," but the way I see it is it includes Dad and everyone else that has given us something to think about so nobody gets left out. Plus it makes you feel less conceited when you say "I" all the time. I would not want to listen to me either if I never included the rest of me in anything. Me, myself and I become we since we are all in this together. It also makes you feel like you have back up even if it is in your own head because that is a good place to start. I have argued with my thoughts because something needed to be done and I did not feel like getting up off my bum to do it. All I heard was, "We are going to keep on and on until you do it so instead of hearing us nag you about something you should be taking care of just go and do it. They're right though, when I got up and took care of it I did not have that nagging feeling hanging over me any more and I did not have to have it brought to my attention every half second. No offence to my brain, it wants to say none taken but it's too stubborn to think that that was a compliment for making me get up and do things. Oh, now it says thank-you. (Between you and me, I think it just got what we meant.)

Your mind is a wonderful thing to explore not exploit and so is your body. Sexy is not having everyone paw at you; sexy is feeling so good about yourself that you will not be pawed at for any reason. When something happens to your body does it not affect you mentally and vice versa? The better you feel about yourself the less you are looking for someone else to make you feel better. Someone can make you feel good but you learn that only you can keep yourself feeling great. You learn the difference between doubt and misdirected thoughts. Even when you see something bad you know how to adjust your thoughts to where you can see how to change things and turn something negative into something positive. Anything negative can be turned into something positive by finding a way through. I had to do something that I have avoided and every chance life has given to me to do this I would find some reason out of it. Now I am forced to and instead of being negative I flipped my thoughts and now think about it in a positive way. I would have never got to meet some of the nicest ladies you could ever find all together. I decided that if I would not have done this I would have never met them and that is so much nicer then dread. Your brain is smart enough to come up with thoughts and ideas to make things go one way or the other. I could come up with the worst case scenarios just right quick but thinking positive well, that took some thought. Now I can combine the two and think of the worst things that could occur, the best things that I want out of it and by taking a little from both of them I can go right down the middle. If it turns out to work in my favour great but if it does not I am not let down because I had already figured this into the equation.

If things in life are a mind set, then learn how to set your mind. If you are always thinking negatively your mind can be set to self correct itself. The less you stop yourself the less willing you become to allow someone else to stop you. Remember the more drive you give yourself the less you want to be just the passenger. I learned to figure this out when people were driving me up the wall. When the villagers saw how much drive I could get going they wanted to be the driver, oh I was supposed to carry on like nothing was wrong but I cannot drive when someone else does the steering. When you allow someone else to take control they will never leave you room for error, you will because you have your mind set. I always allow myself room for error because you can have one of those days when absolutely nothing goes right and if something is going to go wrong then it will.

You can figure things out faster in your head than you can with it all spread out in front of you. When you try something new or different for the first time and it does not work out exactly like you had planned pin point where it went wrong and adjust what you need to in order for it to go further. Just because something does not work like you had figured does not mean to scrap the whole thing, learn to keep adjusting. The more you exercise this part in your mind the more it will do it subconsciously and all you have to do more or less is tend to the thought. Your brain learns to decipher between needed knowledge and just plain old criticism. It learns to separate into needed not needed and will not be tolerated all in the blink of an eye.

The more you learn to play mind games with yourself the faster you can catch someone else playing one on you because you can tell the difference between make believe and just an odd fact that nobody ever paid attention to. Anytime I have ever felt some form of danger near the first thing my brain does is snap to and all of my senses are on alert, then it scans everything around us. All of us have built in alarm systems if we would learn how to put them together and hook them up. Your brain is the best place to start because of its capabilities, and lets you figure out how to drive the helm. The more you figure out how your mind works the better you can create an environment around yourself. Learning how to open the other side of your mind will indeed open up a whole new world to you.

Both the definition of metaphysical and philosophical includes each other in their definitions so that should mean that we should also include both of them in our lives? When you learn to be both sided fully you will notice that you are not judgmental to either side but rather more understanding and you can talk on either side without playing or picking sides. You figure out that pretty much all anybody really wants is to be heard and treated fairly, not a lot to ask when you get right down to it. If using half your brain got you this far in life and has you thinking a certain way then maybe opening the other side will bring you the adjustments that you need to take you all the way.

Metaphysical explains the beauty and good found in the world, philosophical is the deeper meaning of those findings. With everything that we have been through it would be so easy to have a bad outlook on life, but when you learn to see the beauty in life then you begin to feel it too. Think about life just like your second childhood, the twenties is kind of like your terrible twos and you are always getting into trouble even when you do not mean to but it happens and you learn from your mistakes and go about life from there. Lord knows I have done a bunch of things I am not proud of but I no longer do them so that means I did learn and paid for my mistakes. As you go through life you will notice that you do not stumble and fall as much because you have a better understanding of what is worth hanging onto and what you should never reach out for in the first place.

You have to want to better yourself until it becomes a desire. The desire to live, move on or to go further it does have to come from deep inside of you. Once you reach where you are going do not stop, keep going because there is so much more to life that meets the eye. You have two halves to your mind and then you have your grey matter. One side is basically the metaphysical, while the other stands ready to think about the deeper issues and combining the two is what pours out into your grey matter. This part holds known truths, but far too many people develop this area of their brain and nothing else. Using this part only leads you to question instead of knowing, using both sides together as one, answers more questions than man ever could. If you will notice you have two sides to every story, two sides to your brain, a conscience and a subconscious, good and evil everything comes in twos and knowing this is half the battle. It means that when you are in the thick of things keep going because there is another side. When you feel bad you can remember something good that has happened and hold onto that while learning to dispose of the waste so that you no longer feel like you are wasting your life, time or gifts.

Your mind can do all kinds of things for you if you will take the time to include it in your everyday life. Ask it what it thinks and how it feels about the situation and listen to it, do not dismiss it. Your brain is just like you, it gets lonely and unlocking that door to the other side gives it not only companionship but a trusted one at that. You know that you would never steer yourself wrong, but that is not to say that you cannot be misdirected. It happens; I kept spinning my boat in a circle until my mum found me. I did it long enough to where I was beyond dizzy but eventually you do stabilize just pay attention to where you want to go. I went through a lot of rough waters but you do have it in you to brave the sea because there is nothing in the world sweeter or greater than being there for the break in the storm. Just like when it rains and you're in the house with it lightening all around you. At times you get scared because it sounds close and everything is shaking all around you, and sometimes even big mighty trees can become up rooted but you wait it out and then…you step outside when the storm has passed and everything smells so fresh and the light seems brighter and the birds echo their songs in your ear. That is what life brings you, good with the bad and if you can tough out whatever storm may arise you will get to witness what very few do, the other side.

You have to see the good with the bad so that you learn how to blend the two and come out with a richer mixture. If it were not for the evil people I would have never been born and that was a nice thing to come out of all that mess. The storm hit and I was trying to find some kind of shelter in different villages all the while hearing my mum's voice. You can find something to keep you going and that is all you need just some thing and it does not have to be big, it could just be a memory of meeting your mum for the first time and wanting to get back. It could be a time that you alone remember just keep it with you so it can keep you strong. When the storm became violent as they sometimes will I tried to help any survivor that I could find but the greatest thing about storms is that sometimes you are the one being found.

Life is about weathering the storm and learning to come in before one hits or moving to higher ground. Life is about losing everything including your mind and seeing if you have it in you to get it all back. I would have completely lost my heart long ago had my mum not have put it up for safe keeping for me and taught me a very valuable lesson along the way. You should never give someone your heart but rather the love it can give, that way if anything happens your heart is still safe. The other lesson that came with this is when you are a giving soul and you are giving to someone else, the give and take thing is fine as long as they give back to you. I learned how to be giving early because of Kindergarten. When a kid got caught with a piece of candy and the teacher would ask if they had enough for everyone and they said no, they would have to spit theirs out. I got caught with a piece of candy and when she asked me if I had enough for the whole class I told her yes and showed her that I had enough for everyone to have at least two so I got to keep mine. It surprised her though when I gave her the rest and she asked me why. "Because you are my teacher, you taught me how to share." She knew that I was not trying to show her up, she knew that I had paid attention to why they had lost theirs, because they would not share. She also knew that I liked figuring things out like that because it was a thought left up in the air.

My mum taught me through the family what it means to be giving, I cannot give them my love if I am never there and they cannot tease me if I do not let them. (Apparently I am never going to be the tallest one in the family.) When you are truly loved unconditionally you cannot help but to learn how to love unconditionally as well but not only that you learn not to settle for less and that does include yourself. When you take your spirit and put it inside of you where it belongs you will feel your soul connect. Remember when your spirit breaks then you have no choice but to follow, but if you can keep it from breaking then you stay ahead of the game. A good deal of life is mental and you have to teach yourself how to be and stay mentally strong when everything is against you. Another way to look at it would be that your spirit is the thinking part of you and your soul is the feeling part of you. When you think that you can make it and you keep yourself going and you feel better when its all said and done then you add to both these sides. A good reason for depression is not dealing with your feelings or emotions, everything good or bad has to come out and the sooner the better. Your brain does keep track of unresolved issues even if you are not aware of it. Ever since I put to rest all the skeletons and feelings that they had I stopped thinking about ending my life and thinking the world was a better place without me. There was a part of me that will fight to stay alive and that was my soul. My spirit was the one who wanted to end it all when I could not see what was going on. Unresolved anything can and will take its toll on you and depending on how long you keep them that way will decide the price you pay.

In an odd way this time around I learned how to separate everything into the metaphysical and philosophical by learning to think completely one way and then another and seeing more than one way to go about things. There has to be a business side of you and a personal side and I figured out that I was giving my family the business side when it should have been personal. That may explain why I kept telling my mum that if she wanted to fire me as one of her kids that I would understand because I knew I was not doing a good job but thank the good Lord she did not see it the same way. I have to conduct my personal life like a business because my personal life is my business and I do not want someone to sabotage it or do a hostile take over that sounds good at first. I also learned that I have to conduct my business life like I would my personal life because business affects the way I personally live. Mum, Dad and the kids in a way is a family-owned business and if it is not good for business then it's not good for the family. They never allowed villagers to hide behind the name customers and let them run their home. Telling kids and people that the customers or adults are always right is bad for business and can get them hurt. Showing them what is good for business and the family will ensure that undesirable deals are not sought after as something good. They learn to speak up when something is not right and learn to confide in family because they will be believed, instead of telling villagers who try and distract them by deceiving them. If they are always right then let them run their own place, be it work or home. If you allow anyone to take over something that you started do not be surprised if you are the only one that supplied action when everyone else was supplying betrayal.

That could explain why I had no problem firing the villagers because it was bad for my business, then when I tried to merge with my mum and the family I did not want them to be burdened with my heavy losses. I learned how to liquidate all the damage through the villagers because they think they get something great from it. The way I saw it was personally hanging onto it was like trying to stay in a burning building, you can keep moving around but sooner or later you will be overtaken through either the smoke screen or the flames themselves. I made a trade with these last villagers and gave them all my crap and just told my mum what I traded them without having to go through it. With the villagers, it was nothing personal it was business and now I am out of the business of hanging onto and trading crap. See, when I first met my mum, a part of me wanted so desperately to tell her that I was a shit head and to stay clear. Personally, I was a wash out but in business I could keep a clear head. Thanks to being mixed in with their fruits I learned that I just had a great deal

235

of dung for brains which can never be good personally or in business because they are tied together. Yes, what I traded the villagers was all the crap they had given to me over the years and now they have it and I do not. I know what I gave them was used feelings and since then I have been cured of a deadly disease that I never even knew I had called Stockholm syndrome which explains why I always went back. (If you have ever gone through anything traumatic you will feel this so be aware.) Someone has to be the authority figure in a kid's life when they are going through it because they do not know. I never did and the kid on that talk show does not realize it either. It is a weird thing to do when you identify with your captors who have abused you from day one but that is the thing that we need to be taught, we only identify with them but that it is not our identity. Villagers are not a family run business; they are and always will be a highly disguised sweat shop.

I use to hear living among them, "Believe only half of what you hear and nothing of what you see." Apparently it stuck without me realizing it because I did just that with my family, I believed them half way about wanting me but left before I could see them. Now because of the new ground rules that my mum runs the family by I learned to listen to everything and see everything and then decipher from there. I learned that some people know your predictabilities and use them to get you to run into an ambush. Everyone knew that I had a mum and made sure that they used the word help to keep me with them even though they always tell me that my help is never good enough after it was given.

Now that I know what it takes to run a family and how to keep the business strong I no longer want to take shady deals and see if I can make them work because it is a waste of my talents that I could have shared with the family. The cool thing is that villagers hire temps because they can always be replaced at no expense to them. Families have members that hold a lifetime position and that is sweet to think that nobody will ever replace me as the nut in the family. I learned a lot, and was taught a tremendous amount and figured out a number of things and that is something to not only feel good about but to be proud of as well even if the only place it is documented is inside my own head. The hard thing I am learning is how to apply that knowledge while I am still learning how to figure things out.

Life is a complex system once you learn how to break it down but the roads that come with it are indeed incredible. I learned to quit wandering off without my family because that does make you an easy mark but I can stay with them and just let my mind wander. If my family needs or wants me it does not take me as long to snap to like it does when I am trying to find my way back to them.

I learned not only how to take the good with the bad but how to separate them and combine them and create something out of them. When I said that something good can come from any situation if you just change the way you see things, it can. If you have been abused, raped or whatever the traumatic event that occurred, the best thing to come out of it is you. They went out of their way to break you and take your life but you made it, do not let what they did stop you from being a part of the rest of your life. Only you can let it break you and if you allow it to then it always will, but if you will think yourself stronger for having survived then you become one of the fittest. Survival of the fittest sure does beat living among the corrupt. Everything that you go through in life makes you something at first, then when you add to it, it just makes you that much more and I would rather hold my head high knowing that I survived another day with everything good and bad mixed than to be forced to hold it down and be looked after like a victim.

Even though I was knocked unconscious for a great deal of my life, my mum knew that there was still some life in me and that I would come around. It is kind of funny thinking of yourself walking around in a coma but I had a lot of head trauma done to me, some people are in a heart coma, spiritual coma but a part of you will just not come to. They tell the survivors to keep talking to their loved one and that sometimes the sound of their voice will bring them around. As much as I wanted to awaken when I first heard the sound of my mum's voice I would have come to screaming and traumatized beyond repair but she kept talking to me and inside my head I was heading for her. When I would come to, something in my mind stopped me from taking another step, but she has this way of showing you that boulders, while appearing to be mighty, can simply be rolled out of the way with a little effort on both parts. My mum never met me half way; she stayed her course and gave me an hundred percent of anything that I needed, hugs, love, words of both encouragement and wisdom. She had enough faith in me to know that I would give her and my family the same things back, just trying to get back to them and would stay that way since that is what it took to get the life back into me.

I learned through them that I do not like meeting someone half way because you never know if they are going to have you reach over their side to make up for them not coming to the fair share of the fence. Then you have to deal with how much someone gave to someone else and then they still owe you for the last time but they will get you next time around if you will just do this one more time for them again. Now I just stick to one side because we all give the same and everything turns out to be fair that way. I remember that I told my mate that helped me through a hard time that I was not one of their allies, that I was just on their side just like they had been on mine in my time of need. Being allies means to give you question to their motives, being on someone's side means that even when someone looks you straight in the eyes and lies to you about someone you trust you hold firm to which one you believe in and have faith in. Life is about the mystical realm of make believe and seeing if you can tell real from true life fiction. A mum may read her children a bed time story but always reassures them what to believe in and what not to, what is made to spook you and what is to be a hard lesson learned. The only difference between some of us and them is that some of us know what the real world is like and desperately want to find our way home. Others know what a good home life is and are desperately trying to make it in the world. My mum's version of "Rock-a Bye, Baby" is, "And I will catch baby, cradle and all." There is no safer landing than being caught by family.

That reminds me of one of my most treasured mates who went home long ago. I was the thinker and she was the doer and together we would get things done. I was lost without her until now because part of her has always stayed with me like my grandfather. Sometimes you can think of what to do but you need help in starting the process, then there are times when you cannot think straight and you just do what you can. Then there will be times when you just hang on and the only thought that pops into your head is, "What ever you do, do not let go." No matter what happens you have to allow yourself time and room, time to grow and heal and room to expand and exercise poor judgment so that it will sharpen your skills for later. Life is about carrying on for those that could not make the rest of the journey and sharing what you have with those that did. Reflecting back is not a bad thing, but just do not spend your life looking back because sometimes you can forget which way you were heading.

When Lady Legs said, "Sometimes you just have to let things go," it never occurred to me at the time that it deals with life as well. Sometimes you have to let go of something that is bad for you in order to hold onto something that is great for you. Sometimes you have to realize that in order to start a new life you have to let go of the old one. Sometimes in order to grow you have to realize when your old life does not want you any more. There is a difference between leaving and ending, separately they can be overwhelming but when you combine the two of them you realize that something greater is waiting for you. I left a life that kept me fighting to stay alive and now that part is over, I realized at the last split second that I no longer wanted to fight to stay alive, but rather I wanted to live and love my family. When it finally hit me what I had always wanted and prayed for was right in front of me, I let go of all the hate that I had filled myself with and felt their love flow through. Sometimes you can fill yourself with something so much that there is not room for anything else and depending on what it is, it can either make you or break you. Now I am so full of love for them that there is not any room for anything else and it gives life such a nicer feeling.

Sometimes you can be dealt a bad hand but that does not mean that you are out of the game, sometimes you can hold your bluff and cause the rest to fold. The main thing is to find a reason to stay in the game. When the last of the villagers was on their way out and knew it they pulled out all the stops but this time I was not pulling my punches. I learned from my mate to write down what I was feeling and send it to them and they knew that they were about to get a letter from me. I said the word family and for the first time it made me get a lump in my throat and conceited as they are they felt it was for them and told me not to cry but that was the thing, I did not feel like crying. I got choked up because my family has come to mean everything to me and it took threatening to loose them for me to realize that. Sometimes being extremely hard headed can work against you. I wanted them over this life but I still had to get out for that to happen. I may have lost everything that can be bought but I never lost the legs that my mum gave me to stand tall on and that is what helped me to just let it go and walk away. That lump in my throat kept me from mouthing off and costing me all that I would have ever known to be good.

I am still going through the hard times but I do not seem to notice them as hard times any more, just ways of growing and taking the good with the bad. The great thing is that since my head is turned around I stopped letting things pile up so high that they get to me. Now I take care of things as they come up and I can feel my spirit inside of me now saying, "That is the way to do it," and before long it's taken care of. Life is a test of courage, will, strength and endurance and the reward comes to you in the form of your four pieces of armour. You can be one of two things in life, clay or steel. Clay gets broken and discarded, steel on the other hand, the more you fold it the stronger it becomes until its unbreakable to anything man made. My mum saw that I was made of steel, they just hid me in clay and every time a piece of it would break off to expose my true nature I though I was the one being broke. They say that clay and steel do not mix and they are correct, making a sword out of clay and steel will be lousy for battle because you never know when the clay part is going to be hit and destroy the blade. No matter how many times you fold it and fold it, clay will never be pure or strong. If I would have let my family be the clay the villagers would have shattered them by going through me because of the way I was thinking of my family. (They're not clay, they're steel.) Cowards always go for the ones in your heart, but remember that if you keep your armour on when you go out in the world they will never be able to see who is kept sacred inside your heart. I learned this by watching their eyes when they were trying to find a weak spot of mine. Before the word family would trigger me and cause me to want to fight; now the word family makes me defend. Some think that the best offense is a good defense but I think that the best offense is one that can be both.

I learned something through watching Lady Legs, her kids need her and that was something that I would not admit to myself much less give to my mum and that is what kept me from her. The circle of three should go I love you because I want you; I want you because I need you and I need you because I love you. I had two out of three but you have to have all three to get the correct flow. In those three, nowhere does it say that love wants to protect. If you do all three then the protection will always be there. When my mate and his mum needed help I remember writing them about all three but it came more from needing to feel this way because of the fact that I was so protective of them. The thing I never noticed before is that I had to chase them and was always having to prove something even if it was just my innocence to them, trying to get them to see that I was not the bad guy. When it was proven that I was not the bad one in all of this, she still made me out to be and I have had enough of that for beyond a lifetime. I never realized that I needed them to help me find my way home; I got caught up in a drama when I am more of a comedy person myself.

When it finally hit that I needed my mum and had all along, everything broke open and the full circle had finally begun to flow in my direction. The great thing about my mum holding my heart is that all the ones that she loves and holds dear I get to be a part of too. I get to feel the love instead of just feeling protective but I learned that loving someone as great as they all are makes you that much more protective of the ones you love. I love my family because I have wanted them for so long; because I have wanted them for so long I grew to need them more and more with every breath. The problem was I was never taught how to love just how to fight to survive. Since I know what real love is and how to love them through loving myself I realize how much a real mum's love is worth and felt. The more worthy the love the more worthy you feel for being a part of it. I may have come a long way without them being in my life due to circumstances beyond our control but I also know that all that time without them was pure hell. Now that I made it home to my natural family I learned that there is a form of unnatural love and it comes in spurts but real love from real family never stops flowing. I need my mum because I love her and I love her because I need her to love me and she does. The best thing about her love is that it makes me want more without needing to prove that I am worthy of being loved.

I no longer have to chase what I cannot have and no longer feel the need to do so, that is what ended for me. I grew up enough to realize that chasing something is just a game and that is not a game you play with someone you claim to love, you either want them or you do not. They either want you or they do not and if they make you chase them in order to prove that you love them then they're not worth the catch because they will always find some reason to throw you back. I did not chase my mum's love, I learned how to track it and now it keeps track of me and keeps me on track. I have lived a hard enough life to know when I have something good going and I have lived fast enough to go through a tremendous amount of people and what I learned in the end is that family should be your example, not villagers. If they are not like my family then I know to stay clear because my family taught me how to set the filters and only they can adjust them.

The great thing about learning when to just let something go and allowing something to end is that it does open up new beginnings to a better life. I was ashamed because I was born in a village but now I am learning how to be proud of it because it made me realize that I wanted a castle life and not only that it made me realize what I went through to find my family and what they went through for me. I have a tough family who holds together to stay strong and is bound together through love and support. The best thing about life is that even if you cannot look on the bright side of life just knowing there is one out there is half the battle and will carry you through some rough terrain. There will be times that you have to trade with bad people because they like dirt and giving them all that I had on me allowed me to get cleaned up on my way home, what they choose to do with it is none of my concern because it has no effect on me. Cleaning myself up allowed my mum to see all my wounds so that they could be cleaned and bandaged. Now that my war is over and I am no longer considered a causality of it I can see a world that I want to live in and be a part of because I have found beauty in it. Yes, war no matter what kind does cause both sides to mourn over their losses but they may not be grieving for the same reasons. Staying in a war that I never started would have caused both sides to mourn in ways that they should not have and I never wanted family so that I could have something to mourn and pine over.

That does explain why I stayed in the battle for so long and kept finding wars that were not mine to be a part of, I was scared that if I came in on leave that there would not be anyone to welcome me with open arms. When a solider of any kind comes in from battle and is surrounded by the ones they love and the ones who love them it makes them want to come home. When an unknown soldier comes in from fighting for what they believe in and the greater good for all and no one is there to surround them they feel like they are better off fighting because there is no place that they can come home to. I came in a couple of times wanting someone to pick me up, but when nobody was there I learned not to let myself down by coming in any more. I met my mum when I was dropping someone off and felt myself dying to come home to someone like her. I would never go back out if I had someone like her to love me but since I did not I stayed gone but always thinking how great it would be to have someone like her love me.

She offered me a family long ago but I had started too many things that were unfinished to come in just yet. I had to finish the war that was started before I was born to get that fight put behind me because I did not want it brought to them. The worst place for any battle is on your own home front and since I was being given a new home I was not going to allow it to be turned into a battle ground. I learned that from the short time I was around my adoptive Godfather. Pick your battles, do not let them pick you and believe it or not good and evil will pick a battle over who gets you but if you pick the one you want to be and the other side looses then be prepared for them to wage a war on your behalf. I started out on the evil side and waged a full fledged war on the villagers because I wanted to go to the other side and they would not allow me to go. They must have known that my loving family was over there waiting for me and knew what I was going to be capable of when I reached them. That is all I have ever known or had been exposed to was war and the carnage that comes with it and being surrounded by it does make you numb to all of it. That is why my mum and my Family have come to be the world that I want to live in because they do not make me feel, they get me to feel and I love the feeling of getting to be part of their clan.

I was the last of my kind and being that way makes you stronger because you have to be because you are the last but being the last also makes you realize just how alone you are because you are the lone survivor of your dark world. Now that my family has opened up a new world for me and took me in as one of their own I realized that I am no longer the last of my kind but rather a strong link in a solid chain. My mum knew that I had learned how to survive on sea legs alone and stayed out in the storms looking for survivors but never considered the notion that I might be one. Because I stayed around danger it kept me too busy to realize that I had witnessed destruction beyond repair and that I was the only survivor in the group that I had started out with to come out alive. I learned through watching them that the best way to get the feel for your new land legs is to give them a try. If you fall and stumble even if your mum is not there to pick you up someone in the family is strong enough to. I no longer trade with my family, I learned to stay home and share with them.

If they go through something hard they know that I can help walk them through and if I am having a hard time because something is good they walk me through that but through good and bad times we have each other which means that I am not the lone one any more. The greatest gift a lone survivor could ever be given is a new blood line to carry on with and I am overwhelmed that my new blood line comes through love. I may or may not be a number of things any more but the one thing that I no longer am is alone and with it forgotten.

The funny thing is that I learned that I was running from the wrong thing in my life and my mum is the one who pointed it out, I so love her. I thought I had been running because I was not one of Dads kids but when I look back on my life I realized that I would always talk with Him. I thought it would fix things if I knew for sure but because of my family I learned that I was always one of His. When my mum and I were having a heart to heart talk I told her that if it was not for her that I would probably be in jail for killing someone or them killing me and with just one sentence she finished the puzzle. She said probably the latter one and I laughed because both sides of my brain caught it. When someone says that I cannot do something I have always gone out of my way to prove that I could but this came directly from my mum who loves and cares about me. The funny thing is that she has always known me better then I have ever known myself. She said that, "Every kids needs their mum," and when it finally hit home that is what I felt most of all, the need for my mum and her love. Then to say that I do not have it in me to take someone out completely, that is what made me take off in the first place from the village because they did have it in them to hurt another human being and I wanted no part of it and that is what made me scared to go home to my real Family.

It never dawned on me that when I was in danger I would always find some way to knock them out so that I could just walk away. That explains why I would always go around head butting someone who was trying to hurt me; nobody expects someone's head to be that hard. You appear tougher because you knocked them out with one blow and they look weaker because it took them a while to come to and you are no where to be found. Oh, I have it in me to knock someone out or to clean their clock but that is as far as I myself will go. Sometimes you can be surrounded by the wrong people for so long that you see what they are all about and you feel like there is no way out but as I have learned if you keep your head good things happen and then when you get the hang of it great things will occur.

I still believe with all my heart that my mum has secret powers because she saw me coming a couple of meters away and gave me the proper tools that I would need to dig myself out of the rut and tunnel my way back to her. I may have been born into a village but at least I was hard headed enough to still believe in the fairy tale of castle life. Sometimes you can become stuck in your life, some people will pull you all different directions and shove you back and forth but the ones who truly love and support you will kindly give you a little nudge. Yes, my family is composed of fruits, nuts, and lost souls but they are mine and I am a part of everything that they mean to me.

They say that nobody loves you like your mum and nobody will ever know you the way she does and my mum proved both these things to be true beyond my shadow of a doubt. I finally grew into the kid that I have always wanted to give my mum, one full of love and who will always be loyal to her and my family alone. I learned that if I have any doubt to ask my mum first because she knows how to get through to both my heart as well as my head. I am proud to say that I am my mum's kid because I used to say, "That is my mum," the difference between the two is I excluded myself from one and am included in the other.

Sometimes people will cross your path that are just like you, trying to find their way in the world. Sometimes as much as you want to hold onto someone and call them a mate you have to realize that sometimes you are in someone's life to trade tools because they need them more then you do. I guess that is why I do not have a bad outlook on the way my life started out because I looked at it as business. Nothing personal, just a form of business and now that I have a new beginning with my family nothing is business, everything is personal and this causes me to talk from my heart with them and not my head where I am less likely to watch what I say. Sometimes I learned that you have to trade with villagers because they are holding onto something good and they will not let go. Sometimes you have to go in and put up a good fight and take back something that belongs to you and give them back what is theirs. I figured out that I went in and took back a spine that did not belong to them and held onto it until I found a good person that needed it. I took back pride and deflated them and gave it to someone who would do some good with it. I took back conceit because there was no need for it and gave it to someone who would use it to feel good about themselves. Villagers hoard things that do not belong to them because they took it in some way and I learn that I was little enough to go in and take it back. I may not have come out with it every time but I was at least a pain in their side. Everything that was stolen from me my mum and family replaced in abundance and now I get spoiled in hugs given in love and strong ties that give me confidence. A unique way of looking at it is that I was given the wrong blood line which made me have the wrong blood type and my mum knew this from the moment we met. You have to start the transfusion of one while draining the other until the last drop is out, then you make a full recovery. A part of me will always feel like I had been sleeping and the other half of me was in a deep coma until my mum found me picked me up and took me home. I stopped thinking that I was left for dead and now know that I was left so that she would find me.

I tried coming to a couple of times but lacked the strength to open my eyes. I feel like my mum has been at my bed side this whole time, talking to me, telling me stories and helping me to understand that when I come to I will have a family surrounding me but that I do need to wake up because everyone has been waiting. I learned that my past and how I was brought into the world was just that a bad dream and it took a strong family to shake me awake. I was fighting them while I was asleep. Maybe that is why I was more aware of my subconscious because I remained in the unconscious state of my mind. Now that I have come to I realize more instead of just learning it. I realize that some people came into my life and volunteered to be blood donors like my mate and her son. Our paths were to cross not tie and they gave me what they could as far as their good blood and traded it for my bad blood. Now their finding their path just like I am finding mine.

I realize that sometimes there can be bad blood between people and you have to filter it through yourself in order to understand which blood line you want to be a part of. In a way there are five lines: Good, bad, evil, the exceptions to the rule and the universal donors. Sometimes you can make the wrong decision for the right reasons but it turned out to be a bad choice. You can stand you ground and defend yourself and hurt them in the process but that does not make you evil. Sometimes you have to break a bad rule in order for there to be proper change. Sometimes you can be everything to everybody and not feel worth a dime. I have made really bad decisions and some piss poor choices throughout my life but I have made some really good ones as well. I have done some really daft and beyond dorky things but I have done some really smart things and achieved things that made me smile. I realized that if a line were drawn today around the world down the middle and one side was good and the other side was evil and there was no longer a fence to ride for just the bad which side I would fight on without hesitation and without doubt.

That is why I love my family and want to be a better person for them because they're on the side of good. There is a difference between having faith in man and worshiping them and following your family through thick and thin. I think that is what the letters in the Bible are trying to convey to us, Jesus did not come to earth as a super being; He came as a human being. He did not have worshipers He had followers and He never preached He taught and led by example. He lost His temper and turned over tables because He had His limits as a human. He reached out to His Dad and was strong enough to cry out. He never asked anyone to feel sorry for Him and He knew that He was going to have a hard life. Maybe He goes from 12 to 30 because in-between He lost His way just as we do and maybe He had to comes to terms with who He is. Maybe life made Him doubt if He was a good kid or a bad kid because losing your temper shows that you're human.

When you look at it through reality and logic and put it with you life everything begins to add up. I think we miss the boat when we worship Jesus instead of following the example He left for us. We miss the human side to His life and therefore cannot figure out how to put it with our own. He never says that the world was full of nothing but good people but He does tell us that there are good people in the world. He came across undesirables and people who would always be corrupt and tried to reach out to the ones who wanted it but never lived someone's life for them. He never forced any of His teachings or excluded anyone from them; even evil people were allowed a second chance at changing their direction. He taught us through His disciples that even good people can have someone in their group that will stab you in the back or back down when it comes to defending you. And you can have cowards and people who will carry on your teaching even when you are not there, all in the same group.

I think that is why He lost His temper in a place made to appear to be a temple, to tell us people will use His name to carry out their deceit but that it was not His way, He never killed people in the name of His Dad. I met some people who would hold the Bible in one hand while beating me with the other, (do not tell your left hand what the right one is doing because they might put a stop to it.) To me, I think that is what Dad wants us to keep in mind, that His

Son was human and stumbled and fell on His way home and that Dad still took Him home. We do not get reprimanded for making mistakes we get reprimanded when we did something wrong and we knew better. When we only take the part where He is perfect we loose the teachings in all of it and the meaning walks right out the door. Man says to walk in the shadow of the light, Dad teaches us that He is the light, man says listen to what I am telling you Dad teaches us to use our heads and to think for ourselves. Remember when you stop thinking for yourself you can and will follow blindly into anything. Do not go gently into the night; do not follow blindly into darkness, fight, kick and scream to stay a part of the light.

I think Dad wants us to know that He does not expect us to be perfect and that if we are truly one of His kids we are not going to be. When you are perfect you never fall and man is all about that and never forgives anyone for making a mistake. Jesus was no doubt one of Dads kids and He showed us that no matter how many times you stumble and fall and get spit upon and ridiculed Dad will still open the door when you come home because He knows that you're one of His children and not some stranger playing backwards Halloween. They knock on the door show you candy in hopes of suckering you in. I think that you can either be an example of mans teachings or an example of Dads and personally I would prefer to be one of Dads kids then mans any day. I think that is what my life was trying to teach me, that you can start out through man but that does not make you a product of them and that you at anytime can go home to your real family as long as you're ready to make a mental journey.

I also kind of think that is why my old life no longer wanted me and was putting people in my life to force me out, it was corrupt and I was not and therefore wanted no part of me. I was living in a corrupt world and was trying to help the good ones out of it just like my mum started doing for me but that is what I realized, that I was holding onto her and trying to pull anyone I could out but never saw that it was taking it toll on the ones I love. I was trying to hang onto my mum while holding onto a life that wanted no part of me and I finally had to let go. I realize that my mum held onto me this whole time and helped me to realize that I was never meant to be strong enough to go back for everyone but that I should feel good about myself for trying to help the ones that I did. When you cannot take care of yourself it is time to rest and readjust.

I learned that the best thing about something ending is that it means something new is about to take place but the thing to remember is that in-between you are given an adjustment period. I figured out that what my Grandfather was teaching me was how to be a fighter and maybe somewhere in his heart he knew I would fight my way through to finding my mum and that she would teach me which side to fight on by showing me which side I was fighting for.

Sometimes you do have to let something go. Even though my mum and family never let me go I let go of them and never thought that I would ever find their hand again. If you love something let it go, if it finds its way home to you it's because it is yours to keep, if it does not maybe it was not worth keeping. I realized from the time I let go until I grabbed hold again what my life was like without them and I no longer want to live without the love of my family. I also realized that the reason I let go was because I had unfinished business and did not want my Family anywhere near it. There was more then a good chance that I was going to get hurt and I did not want them to witness it. I was trying to tie up loose ends so that there would be no reason for me to ever return to my past life. I paid for the mistakes that I have made but I was also paying for crimes that I did not commit. I think that is why I never gave much thought to forgive and forget. There is not a bone in my body or a fibre in my being that will ever forgive them and I will not forget what they proved that they are capable of doing; I will leave that up to my Dad because only He can tell if they are being sincere. I on the other hand learned how to overcome what they did and therefore learned how to get over the hurdle they had placed in front of me. I am the one who chose to pay for their crimes now and I had to finish what I started. The ones who did me wrong will have to answer to Dad for what they did. The way I see it in my mind is that I paid for it they have to answer for it and own up to it.

To me, there are different realms of reality and sometimes you step into someone else's to see the logic in it. I learned that you have to learn to be more than one thing. What do you want to be when you grow up? A little of everything. You need to learn how to run, stand your ground, duck and fight. Sometimes you are going to be looked upon to run for help and bring it back, sometimes you are going to have to stand your ground when you know that someone needs your help. Sometimes your loved ones are going to be traumatized to the point where they take swings at you that are not meant and you have to learn to duck and not take it personally. Sometimes you are going to have to learn to fight because someone wants to hurt your family. I also learned that sometimes when you suffer from tunnel bum vision your perception can be off and the wrong ones look like your family. Good thing I know my mum's voice in the dark. Life is about walking into different realms of reality and adjusting your perception to see if something is missing or needs to be taken care of.

I love the fact that my mum knew that I was in a realm that I could not find my way out of and knew that I belonged with her. My mum knew in her heart that the only way to get through to me was to use logic and that by doing so I would see her reality in my realm and use it to get back to hers. I use to say to myself when I was little, "This cannot be my life," and you know what it was not. I was meant to have a life with them but I had to want it bad enough to fight for it and then learn how to stop fighting when I became a part of it. My mum knew all about my life before I ever said a word to her and she never made me feel bad or small for it. I love the fact that she opened up a chapter in her life and read to me that it did include me in it all I had to do was learn to read from the same book. I also love the fact that she opened up a chapter in my life and held my heart in her hand when she closed it for me. The chapter was titled: My life before my mum. I was ashamed of something because I had my facts all wrong. I was ashamed because I thought that they had instilled deep inside of me a hidden killer and when my mum read it to me before she closed that chapter in my life for good is that I grew to have killer instincts which helped me to survive them and that having killer instincts is not a bad thing to have when you use them for good.

She never left me the whole time I was trying to bluff that I was not scared when she knew in her heart that I was terrified the whole time. I was led to believe that I was a beast because I could survive out in the wild and I never wanted my mum to ever know that about me. What she taught me through her love and compassion is that I was a child when all of this began and instead of becoming corrupt I just learned to live in the wild among the animals instead of the beast of man. My mum never took the fight out of me and never tried, instead she gave me something better to hold on to and knew that as she talked with me I would let go on my own and instinctively knew that I would hold onto her. It was not until she held me that everything hit at once but I was going to be o.k. because I was in the safety of her arms. To think of all that I had been through without her, all that I had put my mum and the family through when they first reached out to me and everything that happened when I woke up screaming for them. All I can say is … scary.

Now that I lived through the yin part of my life and my mum was there to close it she is also the one who opened up the yang part of my life because that is where her life is and I so want, need and love being a part of it. I am a part of my family tree now and even know it is a fruit tree my mum does not seem to mind too much that one of her nuts fell because she knew that I did not fall far from her tree. I just hit the ground hard enough to ding my head and thought

I was somebody else's child. I had wrong term blood line amnesia, awful thing to suffer from; it makes you forget who the ones who love you really are. The funny thing is that they say if someone gets knocked in the head and looses their memory that knocking them in the head hard enough again should by all means bring it back. Now I am not to sure about that because I think Dad will tell you that sometimes you have to knock them in the head two, three, four or in my case five times before they come back around. I learned to hold onto my mum because the family holds onto her and together I learned to stop falling out of my family's tree. Letting go can cause you to fall into a reality that you might not find you way back from.

I also learned while being knocked out that you can time travel. Yes, you did read correctly "Time travel" and you can either go back in time or into the future. There is also such a thing called remote viewing and when you put it together with time travel you will be amazed at what all you can see. I learned that some people are still living in the past; the same lives they led when I left are the same lives they're living now because nothing has changed. I moved on they stayed right where they were in life. I saw when I was little a life that was going to be mine if I stuck with my lessons, studied hard and looked for that crossing ribbon. I have seen things before they happened and I have seen things clearly that were meant to stay covered up before anyone else could. I tried to warn, I tried to clear a path but I learned that I cannot save the world; I can only do as much as I can and then I had to learn when to back off because I was stepping on Mum Natures toes. Not a good thing to do because she can and will step on you if you get in the way.

I learned to see things in my mind, choose a plan of either action or attack and saw it play out in my mind, then when it came down to real life I learned how not to be self destructive. I learned how to play with my mind so that it will not feel the need to play tricks on me because it wants to feel included. I learned how not only to see the dark side but to find a way to the light not just wait for it to find me. I learned that when you're lost you had better learn how to holler for help and when they holler back to answer them so that they can better locate you. I learned that my decisions affect my families well being. If I would have stayed to fight the last villager it would have turned into a fight to the death and in my mind I saw me winning the war with them but losing my whole family in the battle. I learned that standing my ground was not as important as changing my mind. I no longer get provoked by words of antagonistic means and calling me a chicken or prodding me with, "I bet that you cannot do it," no longer works because that turns you into their village ass.

I do not know about you but my mum seeing me at my worst is not as bad as turning into the town ass right before her very eyes, they know that even though you're stubborn you will still do their work.

I learned that there is a realm of indecisiveness and that it leads to nowhere but making you go around in circles and all you get out of it is the fact that your head can spin. This is the realm that can cause your life to become a sewer because you will not decide one way or the other which way you want to go. This is where they herd you off in what ever direction you allow them to. I would rather make a bad decision because I can still think of how not to make the same mistake twice than not make one at all and have nothing to go on and be led around by my nose being swatted the whole way.

I learned that I saw my future the moment I looked into my mum's eyes and knew in my heart that she has always been the mum in my dreams, the one I asked Dad for from the start and the mum who would love me not just forever but for all eternity. I learned that if I cry to my mum she will not let the world know and will cover me so that they do not find out. I think that is what freaked me out is that I saw myself doing a lot of crying in my mum's arms but I could not hear why I just had to learn why. I cried to my mum because I would finally be safe enough to completely let go and through my tears she helped to heal me. I let go of all the tears they forced me to have but refused to let go of in front of them.

There are different realms of both reality and logic and the best world to be in is one that knows how to include both. I have always been more logical but I learned that I was not being realistic at all and that living in only one reality makes you one dimensional and that is not being logical when there are so many things to help make you become part of the three d world. Since I have been living in my mum's time I am learning how to be logical and realistic and my mum is the one who does the fine tuning. The funny thing that I learned most of all is that when you do not listen to your mum, Dad is going to knock you in the head for her so that she does not have to because it is not in her nature to. I am just glad that I survived the elders grabbing my ears and pulling me closer so that when I met my mum I would just straighten up so she would not feel the need to reach for my ears. When I was little people would always ask me why I had such big ears and I would always tell them it was because I never listened. Now I have grown into my ears and not only listen but hold onto every word that comes from my mum. I may be hard headed but I am not daft.

I found out in life that sometimes I learn things the hard way and share them with my mum, like one time I remember telling her, "Guess what I learned today!"

"What?"

"Not to use cloth as a thimble." Yes, my mum knows that I do not have it in me to sew but she does laugh with me when I learn goofy things like that. I also learned that it may have hurt when the needle went in but that you cannot just leave it there and hope that it will go away, you have to pull it out sometime and the sooner the better.

The sweet thing that I learned about my life is that it came with a moral but that my mum and the whole family had to tell me what it was. No matter what life you were born into or what road you are on just hang on tight until help arrives. That sometimes you will have to go at it alone to prove to yourself that you have what it takes to make it. That sometimes in the darkest of horrors the brightest of lights can be found. As hard as someone tried to break you be that much tougher to finish the race. Sometimes you will have to go on without someone because it was not their time to leave that same realm but you never know when they will break out on their own and come and find you. The two that I like best is that the sweetest love comes from a real mum and that the best thing you can do for yourself is mix reality and logic and teach your mind how to look on the bright side of life.

## The Nine Stages of an Angel and Then You Get Your Humane Wings

Everyone has stages that they must endure and this is true for all, including angels from above. They are first sent as angels, messengers from God and they must stand and deliver no matter how hard the job. They are not always going to be believed and some even become ridiculed at the sight of being seen but they do exist past the mind and through the heart to become more than what they are. They protect, and guide and leave without a trace except for the one that leads you on your way. Upon their graduation their name shall be turned.

Archangels stand on their principles alone for they know what it takes to be right and how someone could be led wrong. They are there to correct and challenge and do what they can to make the world a better place but for all their effort put forth they need you to take up their cause for even archangels know they cannot do it all. No matter how great their power they know that there is more to life then just what your principals allow you to have.

The sixth power to enhance is the one of principalities and this is where you are sent to school in order to learn the finer things in life. You are refined and tutored about all that life entails and that there is so much more than what meets your eye if you will learn how to have an open mind and embrace the cold world of left behinds so that you can stand your next ground.

Virtues give you morals and a better understanding about what is good and admirable and the difference between what is moral and pure and you try to adjust your life to the style that it unfolds. You can still stumble and fall but you know in your heart that it is better to pick yourself up than to allow others to keep you held over the fall. You try and live your life remembering that you were once a messenger but that you still have a ways to go but you must learn to become dominate over yourself before you can hold your next official office.

Domination gives you power and authority and a chance to become influential over an entire party but in order to prevail you must not abuse your position or the power that you can hold. You learn that you can tower above so many but that you should never look down on them because we all started out the same, some just learn faster than the rest but no matter what the road is there is always something more and that brings up to the next stage the one of the throne.

To sit upon this seat you must have a balance in your earthy powers for this is where you will hand out orders to all that seek your knowledge and skills. You must rule from this position with style and grace and have such a majestic soul that it is captured in all your dignity of grandeur and physic. In order to move on to the eighth level you must revert back to that of a child for all the world in every land knows that the next stage is a blast, that of a cherubim.

A Cherub is a well behaved child whose distinctive attribute is knowledge and how it is obtained. Their chubby face with hidden wings is meant to make you laugh and smile and feel more than oh so carefree. Their disposition is meant to remind us of innocence that has been lost but never forgotten although it can be retrieved. They teach us that in order to move forward we must revert back to our inner child and make them a loving part of our human nature. To be a cherub is to remember that life is full of mystical wonder and delight.

The Ninth stage of an angel is that of a Seraphim and it has been said that they have six wings although if you ask us I think that they traded it for a sixth sense. They are the highest of all angels in the rank and they see all and know all but never walk around with this in mind. They care for those below them and love those closest to them. They can pick you up and put you down with the greatest of ease. They are the holiest of all angels and have more then earned their title but I soon learned from the best that this stage is not final.

The hidden stage of an angel lies within the heart of a mum, whose beauty is captured in the heart of her child. Her perfection is quiet and graceful and you must feel to see that the love they give us is free of all strings. We are bound to them through loyalty, honour and respect but most of all we are bound to them through love that is purely heaven sent. A mum is a ten in the stage of an angel and a messenger from God is the one who told me that this is so because they taught me how to look for their perfect wing span and that is what our mummy has.

# Chapter Eight
# The Bright Side of Life

In every situation life hides something for you to find, be it a lesson learned, a trail, a clue to another piece of the puzzle or something to help you look on the bright side of life. As easy as it is to see misery and defeat you have to look harder for something to give you hope. This is usually where the little things come into play and a tiny bit of laughter can be carried with you forever. No matter what I went through I would always find something to make me laugh even if I had to tell myself a joke. Believe it or not when I was going through all my mental adjustments and could not figure out who I was I asked my brain to tell me a joke and it did. (I was so depressed I would have laughed at mooning myself.)

The joke went like this: You know how I have been taking art classes and have been studying really hard because finals are coming up? Well you're not going to believe this but I flunked the final. I could not figure out for the life of me how to draw a conclusion!! I was not depressed enough not to find that just freaking hilarious because I was not even signed up for any classes. Now when your brain can make up its own jokes because it just knows that you need one then Lord knows what else it's capable of if you would just give it the chance.

Just like when I rode in the basket, I did not do it so people would look at me I did it because I needed a break from hell and that sure gave me one. I still laugh when I picture everything because the car had two steering wheels and I got to handle both of them. Plus I was not even looking around to see if anyone was watching, this was for me. If anyone else had fun with it that was great but this was one of the few times I was not setting out to make someone else laugh.

If I cannot find anything to make me laugh then I can always remember something funny that has happened and go on from there. Laughter is the best medicine and an apple or two a day does indeed keep the doctors at bay. They say that the Lord works in mysterious ways and I agree because He made laughter contagious.

Working at the same place with my mum, I got the chance to work on the line where you get to use the intercom. This is great because only permanent people not temps get to use this thing and I was known as the permanent temp because I worked through another company for them. The thing about this intercom system is that the entire warehouse hears everything that comes across not just your department. One day I was talking to one of my co-workers and I heard this freaky laugh coming across the P.A. and listening to it made me laugh out loud. The more I would hear them laugh the more I could not stop myself from laughing. This went on for what seemed like a lifetime but that laugh of theirs would make anyone crack up. I looked all around me to see who had such a hysterical laugh but could not see every department to see where this was coming from. Then I looked down to see a finger on the intercom button and noticed to whom it belonged to….me. When this registered with my brain I just lost it and made a noise through my laughter before I hung the phone back up.

I asked my co-worker to call the person I needed because I was still rolling about the whole thing and you could still hear me laughing through her P.A. Everyone in that warehouse knew that it was me from the start, well that is everyone but myself. The most embarrassing thing is having to explain to your mum what happened and how you did not realize through your talking that you are the one who pushed your own intercom button. The great thing is that a lot of people had a good laugh hearing that over the speaker. Before I left I had members of other departments telling me how I made their day with that one. Then I made it even more when I told them that I did not realize it was my laugh, I just heard them and could not stop.

They said, "Yeah we guessed that when we heard you make that Homer Simpson noise, that's what made it even funnier. We thought that you were just laughing but when we heard that we know enough about you to realize you were the last to know it was coming from you."

256

A couple of people told me that my mum received a couple of phone calls, "You know that was your kid don't you." I was laughing to hard to be embarrassed about things.

I was working at another place that had a speaker and the sweetest boss you could ever ask for tells me, "You know it usually takes close to four months to get someone on that thing and you are the first person that I cannot get off of it." In between orders I would sing or see what noises I could get to come out of it. One day I got a wild hair to put my cheek up against it and just kind of blow. I thought that it was going to make this quiet little noise but that is so not what happened. The noise that came out sounded like the biggest and longest fart you have ever heard which would have been o.k. if nobody else was there or better yet if I had planned it to happen that way but Boss Lady came flying around the corner. "OH my God what were you thinking?! Now go and apologize to that customer for him having to listen to that." Every drop of blood that I owned was in my face way before my boss came around the corner. If you are going to try something like that, make sure you do it in private because you just never know about sound systems.

I walked up to him trying so desperately to apologize for what happened through my embarrassed laughter and told him, "Sir, I did not know that putting your cheek on that would make it sound like well you know what it sounded like. I really am trying to apologize even though I cannot for the life of me stop laughing."

He just smiled so big at me and replied, "I have been coming here for a long time because I like that every day something weird happens up here but that just topped them all."

When my boss heard him say that she just looked at him, "Don't encourage her."

"Oh, I think that sound surprised even her because I have never seen her turn red and I have seen her do a lot of strange things."

Every place that I have ever worked or to be honest anytime I am out in public I usually look for somebody to mess with. I love scamming people out of facial expressions. Now I will admit that sometimes my humour is more sexual in nature but not all the time, and this too has a way of coming back to bite you in the bum. What I mean by sexual in nature is how you can say one thing that sounds innocent but it is the underlying meaning that you're actually going to apply for. Oh you can tell from the look in my eyes that I am far from innocent but I try.

One day while working up there with boss lady and her crew an elder had come into my line and we talked for a second or two and then I told her what her total would be, so many dollars and a penny. Now she handed over the paper money but could not find a penny and I told her that I would spot it to her. "Oh, no I have always paid for my things." I looked over there at my partner in crime and was telling her through my eyes that she knows I would just give her a penny but the elder still searched. Then she did something that I never thought the elders would ever do, she got me big time and in such a way that I will never recover from it. "Honey, all I can find is a screw; would you take a good screw for a penny?"

The only thought that I had in my mind was, "Out of everybody here I am the worst one to do this with because you do not know how my mind works, oh please just let me give you that penny."

She continues, "I remember when you could get a good screw for a penny, I mean a really good screw. If I could find you a really good screw would you be interested in one if they only charged a penny?"

I looked over there at my partner in crime and now am trying to tell her through my eyes, "Oh, please help get me out of this. I really do not know if I can hold on any longer."

Believe it or not my partner in crime just looked at me and replied with her eyes, "No, you somehow have managed to get yourself into that one and I am staying clear."

Now the elder is still looking through her purse for that freaking penny that she is not in a hurry to find. "I remember back in the good old days when you could get a good long hard screw for a penny. They would always seem to hold you over until you could get your hands on another penny. Some days you could find long screws and some days just short screws but you always knew that for a penny long or short you were going to get a good screw."

I looked over at my partner in crime and was now begging her with my eyes, "Please, please help me." She just grinned real big and continued to wait on her customers but was still listening to what was going on. That is not helping me at all.

Now my elder was coming in for the kill, "You know not everyone would take a good screw for a penny, now a days its just hard finding a good screw and I do not mind if they're long or short screws I just want a good screw and if I can still get it for a penny then why not. No, any more all you ever seem to find are cheap screws and you just know that they're cheap screws just by the way they feel. I do not mind cheap screws if that is all they have but I sure do look forward to a good hard screw, one that you know will hold up. Yes, I come from a time when you could get a good hard screw for a penny but now a cheap screw that feels like a cheap screw will cost you more than a penny."

"My Lady, I will trade you your screw for a penny, that would not be a problem."

"NO, no, it's a good long screw and I sure would hate to trade it for a penny when I might need a good long screw later on." I looked over and now my so called partner is no where to be found, I finally realized after all of this that I was indeed on my own. She found a penny and gave it to me and told me, "If you have a good long screw you need to hang onto it because you never know when you are going to need one."

"Yes, my Lady. I will definitely keep that in mind the next time I am looking for a good screw."

"Well just be careful about taking screws for a penny because you never know if they're going to be good screws or just cheap ones. I myself do not like cheap screws because you just know that they are not going to last or be good and if I have learned anything in my life is that a good long screw is hard to come by. You could find good screws back in my day but now you have to look harder to find a good screw."

I handed her the order and she just calmly turned around and left like she did not have a care in the world. I was just about to try and catch my breath when Boss lady comes flying around the corner and starts attacking me. "Oh my God for someone who claims that they respect their elders how could you? Do you know that she could be on her way home and decide that what you did was inappropriate and call the company?"

"But I."

"But I what, never thought that it would be carried so far, but I tried to stop myself and just could not." Then boss lady looks over at my partner in crime who is literally on the floor laughing so hard that she is about to pee her trousers and is trying to tell boss lady something but cannot get it out. Boss lady turns her attention back to me who I will say was innocent in all of this, granted it was my first time to actually be innocent on something of this magnitude but I really was. "Of all the things that you have pulled while working for me this has got to top it off. She is one of your elders and…"

"No (laughing hysterically) she (still laughing) actually (Losing it) innocent. Her face, (will not stop laughing) Help me."

Somehow boss lady figured out that she was trying to tell her that I was innocent and that my elder started all of this. She just looks at me, "Oh, well I just know how you are," and turned around and walked off. I get embarrassed beyond belief, get nailed by boss lady, find out that my partner in crime will not help me if it brings her a good laugh and all I get to comfort me is, "Well, I know how you are." What are they trying to tell me, that just because I messed with people like that for as long as they have known me that it was o.k. for them to get me back all at once through one single elder?

After everything had settled down I talked with my supposed partner in crime. "How in the world did she just so happen to get into my line out of all the ones opened? And you! Why did you not come in and help me?"

"I have never seen you beg with your facial expression like that before. You are always the one sure footed and for you not to be was just priceless."

If you ask me the universe told on me and sent this lady in to get me back for everyone that I have ever messed with. They knew that if they sent in someone other then an elder I would have played it to my benefit but with an elder you do try and be on your best behaviour. The odd thing is every time I come across a screw of any kind I always remember the lady who taught me about good long screws that back in her day only cost a penny.

You would think that since you are aware that the universe takes notes you would stop messing with people, trying to scam them out of facial expressions but that is just not me. The universe did indeed get me really, really good, better then any one person has ever gotten me before. I did what I could to tone my sexual joking down for now (at least for a while anyway.) I could get customers to sing over the intercom for their food because I had convinced them that was the only way to get the company discount, (which was not true because it was a promotion thing that was just automatic but unless you worked there how would you really know.)

One time I asked a gentleman if he would prefer to sing Mary had a little lamb or if he wanted to do the twist for the discount. He picked the twist. I told him that I had to go get boss lady so she could witness it and know that I was not just saying you did it and give you the discount. "Boss lady, you are not going to believe this but I got someone up front who is willing to do the twist for you but you have to keep a straight face otherwise he is going to know that I lied about him having to sing or dance for the discount."

"What did you tell him?"

"I told him that without the discount he would have to pay twenty something dollars."

She just looks at me, "Even without the discount his total would not be over twelve dollars."

"I know but no one has ever noticed that or called me on it before. Please come up front so that he can do the twist for you."

We both go to the front and boss lady tells him that she has to be present for the dance because she can hear the singing over the intercom for the discount. He starts doing the twist and really gets into it. I mean up and down and down and up mixed in with side to side twisting. I was so proud of her because she kept a straight face the whole time. After a while she tells me, "O.K. go ahead and give him the discount while I go and make his order." I continued to talk with him like everything was fine but inside I was jumping up and down, he did the twist and never tried to do it half bum either.

After he left I ran back to boss lady, "Oh my God, I cannot believe that you kept a straight face, you rock."

"Now I know you're crazy."

"What? How am I crazy, he is the one who never looked up on the menu to notice I was doubling his order?"

"I know you're crazy because only a crazy person could talk a normal person into doing something like that." We both just died laughing.

She called the other stores and told them what had happened and none of them wanted to believe her. "So she told you that she got someone to do the twist?"

"No, she talked them into it and told them to wait until she could get me. I am the one who got to witness him dancing from the beginning to the end. She is not making it up, I saw him do the whole thing."

The funny thing is that when the other stores found out what our store could talk people into doing they tried it but needless to say they never could pull it off. I do things like that to get people to laugh, they were doing it to make people look and feel stupid.

Kids are great to mess with too because you just never know what their answer is going to be.

One time I was riding in the backseat with my mates two little grandkids and the oldest one and I got to talking. "My birthday is coming up soon."

"Really, how old are you going to be?"

"I am going to be three."

"Three wow. Have you ever renewed your birth certificate?"

She looks at me all serious like she did not know what on earth I was talking about, "No."

"You have never renewed your birth certificate?"

Now she looks worried, "No."

"You have never renewed your birth certificate. Did you not know that if you do not renew your birth certificate you cannot get any older?" She looks petrified.

Her grandmother jumps in, "Will you stop messing with her like that. Tell her how old you're going to be."

Her grandkid looks at me and says, "I am only three."

I look at her, "But don't you feel a lot older then three?"

She throws those little hands up, "Uh, uh yeah."

Everyone in the car lost it, I am just glad that I was not the one driving because I could not recover.

Another time when we were driving around I asked her who her best friend was. She tells me a name and I told her, "Well you might want to reconsider her being your best friend because she is going around telling everyone and I mean everyone that you have done went and lost your mind."

Without missing a beat she tells me, "Well she's the one who gave it to me."

'When her grandmother hears what happened she just looks at me, "How in the world do you get her to play with you like that?"

"I just ask her questions, she supplies the nutty answers." Although her little one did get me back without ever realizing it. For the little ones at Christmas I got them all big teddy bears and was in the process of wrapping up the third one when I heard a noise that sounded like a huge freaking rat. I looked around and went back to wrapping, I heard it beside me and went looking for it again because now it sounds really close. This went on for about twenty minutes with me trying to wrap and jumping every time I heard the rat rustling through the papers. I finally got up and moved the wrapped gifts up off the floor and still could not find that rat. I sat back down when I heard it coming from where I had just moved the gifts to and about the time I went to get up it jumped out at me. It would have been really embarrassing if I would have wet myself because it was not a rat, but rather a bear busting out of the wrapping paper. "Surprise!!!" Yes I was.

I looked around and found some bubble wrap and re-wrapped the bear in it. This time I made it secure enough that it was not going to break out again. The day comes to give little one her gift and she starts to unwrap it. When she sees the top of it she goes nuts, I literally mean nuts, and I was smiling so big because I knew that she was going to like the teddy bear. The more she unwrapped the more excited she got until she finally got the whole thing unwrapped. The next thing I know she is showing everyone what she got from me for Christmas and my mouth was on the floor.

"You do know that there was a bear that came with that freaking bubble wrap do you not?" and I picked up the bear. "It is o.k. once she realizes that you are the gift and not that bubble wrap she will be back to get you." Needless to say, I ended up holding the bear all night so it would not feel left out, poor thing. The weird thing is that one gift got me twice, once on its own and then through her.

I remember another time with Boss Lady. Before my mum straightened me out I had an ill-mannered temper and Boss Lady sometimes was there to see it. I knew that I had been more than rough on her at times so I would go out of my way to make her laugh. One day I came to work holding my stomach and looking like I was in pain. She asked me all concerned if I was o.k.

I asked her, "Can beans go bad?"

"Well I am not real sure how come?"

"Well my flatmate made some beans last night and ever since then my stomach has been hurting really bad," and I kind of softly moaned.

We go to the back to do prep and the next thing you know this big loud fart comes from my direction. Boss Lady is trying so hard not to laugh, "Well maybe that will make your stomach feel better?"

We both giggled and went back to work. I turn to get something when an even louder one came out and we both lost it. I looked at her all stunned, "I sure hope that I do not do that all day long when I am up at the front."

We start laughing some more and after a little while I tell her. "I am just playing my stomach does not hurt it was this whoopee cushion," and I bend down to pick it up.

She just looks at me and dies laughing. "The reason I had the look of such surprise the second time is because I thought when I stepped on it the first time that all the air was out of it." She just laughs and after a while goes back to her office. Everything is all quiet and then I hear her laughing again. (This happened way before I ever put my cheek up to the speaker.) Usually when I know that I have been more than hard to deal with I will go to what ever extreme necessary to make them laugh, not that it makes up for it, but like I said this is before I met my mum.

One time I was having someone look at some equipment of mine to see if they could fix it and their little grandkid that was about three stayed right beside me talking to me the whole time. (She had a lot to say.) They hear their mum call them into the living room and after a little while she came right back and started talking with me again, shortly after her mum calls her back and this time I hear her mum tell her, "Will you get out of her face."

And little one, "I am not in her face; I am standing next to her."

I told her mum that she was not bothering me because I was not paying attention to them repairing it so she was nice to talk with. We both go back to the shop and little one starts getting excited and jumpy and knocks the back of her head into the corner of a sharp object and lets out a holler and starts crying while she is trying to ask if it is bleeding. They look at it and tell her that its not and she looks at them and goes, "O.K." and goes right back to talking with me. Man I would have still been crying because even for a hard head like mine that hurt.

One time I was taking care of my mates little one who was also three and her dad brought her over and she just carried on and on with genuine tears and everything and you could so tell that her dad was feeling so bad. I told him that she would be o.k. after a while and that if not I would call him to come get her and that made him feel better. He leaves and I hollered her name really firm and she looked at me but still crying.

"Hey, you're not living here your just kicking it."

She stops just like that and goes, "I just kicking it?"

"Yes, you're just kicking it."

She gets the most priceless look on her face, "Oh!" and went about her business.

I get to work the next day and her dad tells me, "It broke my heart to leave her that way so I just stayed by the window to listen because I could not leave her like that. I heard you holler at her and it just broke my heart, then when I heard her say 'I just kicking it', oh I had to go to the car and die laughing."

I started laughing and told him, "You should have seen the look on her face when she said Oh. I was also trying really hard not to die laughing."

She comes over again only this time she is really having a bad day and I told her that if she was going to do that business to go to my room because she was hurting my ears. I go in after a while and ask her if she is ready to come out and she tells me no. I go back a couple of more times and she tells me no again. She falls asleep and when she wakes up I told her that she could come out because it had been a long time now and she tells me, "I fell asleep while I was taking care of my business so I forgot what I was taking care of." The funny thing is you could so tell that she was trying to remember just what it was. Her little hands were behind her head and she was in rather deep thought. After a little while she comes out and tells me, "I think I am too little to be taking care of my own business so can I just come out." Now how could you say no to that?

Kids are freaking hilarious especially if you just let them talk. They can tell you some of the best stories and all you have to ask them is, "What happened next?"

I have had people tell me, "Don't encourage them to lie."

"What! Do you not know the difference between real and make believe, or the difference between a lie and a good story?"

My mum will vouch for me, I can tell you a story that you can picture in your mind all the way to the end and be there when I say, "No, I am just playing with you."

Sometimes I get really wild hairs and nothing is planned it sort of just happens when I mess with someone. There was a lady who came up and asked if the placed I worked at smoked turkeys and I told her yes. I get the little pad book out and begin the usually routine of questions. I come to the part when I have to ask her if they had taken the insides out when I knew that they had not because it was frozen and she ever so politely said no.

"Did you want us to?"

She just looks at me, "Yes?"

"O.K. then since you need us to do it I will need you to sign a release form."

"For what?"

"To give us permission to put our hand up the turkeys bum because legally it is yours so the permission has to come from you."

She looks at me and laughs, "Your joking right."

And I shot her a firm look, "No my lady I am not. We cannot afford another sexual harassment lawsuit and this protects us from having to go through another one." She is searching my face for some kind of laughter when I became even more serious, "We were just like you and thought it was funny until we really had to go to court over this. We thought that it was going to be an open and shut case because it is part of our job to retrieve the insides through that means and laughed it off. That is until we found out that the judge is a vegetarian and found no humour in violating this turkey's rights by putting our hand up its bum without asking for permission. I have never in my life seen a turkey break down before while explaining to the judge that it would not have been so bad if we would have just asked but the fact that we did not just made him feel ashamed. He hid his face with a veil but everyone could hear his sobs in the court room. The judge fully understood and it almost cost us the business trying to pay off the lawsuit so this way by signing a permission form we lessen the chance of being sued again."

I asked her a straight question after that and she told me, "I do not know, it's not my turkey I have to ask."

"That would not be a problem; here you can use this phone behind me."

She walks back behind me and I looked up to see this news paper shaking and I just went about my business filling out the forms (I just forgot to make two copies.) The only thing I heard her say is, "No, I'm not playing she really is going to make me sign the form. I'm not playing." I have no idea what she was talking about but when she gets off the phone we went back to business.

"When you come in to pick up your turkey make sure that you bring in this paper otherwise we are not allowed to let you pick it up by law o.k."

She looks dazed, "O.K." and left with the signed paper that read: I do hereby give you permission to put your hand up my turkeys bum she signed it and I signed it as a witness or at least I think I did. The door closes and one of my regulars (I just love him and his wife) slowly pulls the paper down and dies laughing telling me that I was nuts.

I was the one who looked all confused now, "How am I nuts, she is the one who signed the paper?" (Oh that is right I do not believe that I signed it because that would have made me a witness.) The sad thing is that he does not keep what he had just witnessed to himself (and neither did I for that matter) and his wife comes in ribbing me about it then gave me grief because I did not make two copies. "I know I screwed up I was just trying really hard to keep my facial expression looking like no we almost lost the business this is not funny you have to listen to me before I have to start shaking you." She laughs and tells me that her husband almost lost it when you said that the judge was a vegetarian and kept right on adding to it. I told her, "Your husband was great because he never pulled that paper down and tried to ruin it with no she is just playing. I am not kidding you he never broke character and never tried to make me laugh so that I would break mine. She is supposed to bring the paper back when she comes to pick it up so I will show it to you."

There were several people who wanted a copy of that. The day comes to pick it up only it was her brother this time not her. I stayed straight, "Do you have that piece of paper so I can relinquish your turkey."

He too has a straight look on his face, "No, I do not."

I just looked at him mainly to study what I was up against. "Do you know what piece of paper I am talking about?"

"Yes."

"You do know that without that paper I cannot legally give you back you turkey correct!"

He still has a straight face, "Yes."

I looked at him all confused, "You do know that without that piece of paper I cannot give you back your turkey? Do you know what paper I am talking about?"

He just looks with the slight hint of a grin and replies, "You're never going to see that piece of paper again." Apparently it was more important to pass it around through their family than it was to give it back so that I could do the exact same thing. What cracked me up was he never broke his facial expression and I so desperately tried not to break mine because we both knew that this was serious.

She comes back after the pick up date, "Do you have it?"

"No and your not going to believe this but they will not give it back," and told her what was said and done.

"That is just not right, after all that they still refused to give me back the paper."

"Did you give them their turkey?"

"Yes, no sense in another frivolous made up lawsuit." Everyone had a great laugh over that one for different reasons but I laughed because I wanted the paper more so to prove that there are people stranger then I am if you just give them half a chance to be. My mum even laughed over this one, yes I tell her when I do weird things like that too. If I do not then somebody else will I have learned.

One time a lady came in to pick up her order and I looked at her all serious, "Oh, I have some bad news for you."

She looked, "Oh, did you drop my chicken on the floor?"

"I wish, this is worse." She looks priceless as I continue, "It all happened so fast that I mean. O.K. when you brought your chicken in we did everything that we are supposed to do. Then came the day to prepare him and he looked at my mate and I and asked us if we could grant him one last request because he knows what prepare them means. Well we thought that since he knew what that meant that the least we could do is go ahead. He asked my mate if we would let him try and be that chicken that crossed the road, he was going to get prepared anyway so it did not matter if a car hit him or anything but what a way to go. To get to be that chicken, the one who does cross the road. We looked at each other and neither one thought that that was too much to ask. So we walked him to the curb while holding his hands and helped him to look both ways and let him try it. He was a little unsure at first but got his legs working and made it across the street and was jumping up and down and so were we to be perfectly honest and we looked at him. O.K. it is safe to come back and he just looked at us flipped us the bird and ran off laughing. We were so stunned that we never thought to go after him."

She just looked at the both of us and said, "You know I pictured the whole thing in my head including him giving you the bird. Why would you tell me such a story?"

"Oh, because your order was not quite ready, and we were stalling for time."

The other people who were in there were laughing too. There are three great things that can happen at work, one you have other people who enjoy having a good time while they work too, second that you can make your customers laugh, and third that you can make the people not directly involved join in the laughter. I know that you can have a good time at work and still get your work done.

My sister ratted me out to our mum one time, well probably more than that but how was I suppose to know she would. When we worked together and I would have to count down their tills, I would tell them that they're for example sixty dollars short but give them ideas of where to look for it. Then I would go outside or stay in the office and make sure that nobody would see me break my facial expression. They would come back in all worried and I would help them with more advice like maybe it was a cheque that got caught up in the till. Then after a little while I would go out there and tell them, "You are not going to believe this but you are only six cents short. I am dyslexic so I accidentally flipped the numbers." I would start out laughing just to get the ball rolling while they're busy with the we will just say odd look in their face towards me.

Oh, this is a good one when you are a shirt, meaning management, the ones that you work with are the undershirts. The undershirts stay close to the skin and stay protected and the shirt goes over them but like I always tell them that does not mean that they are protected from everything. Anyway when you are a shirt you have better opportunities to play with your co-workers. We told one that her till was short and she thought we were messing with her like we did the others ones. She comes back into the office waiting for my partner in crime to laugh when she looks down at the desk and notices a write up sheet and looses the 'I am being played with look'.

I told her, "I have never in all the time I have been a shirt had to write anyone up before so I am not sure of how to go about it. I thought that if you wrote yourself up that you could go easier on yourself than any of us ever could. I know that you did not take the money but since it is over five dollars we have to call the main office and they may have to file charges."

"Let me go look again." Right after she hit the door we smiled because that was a lot to hold in and straightened up before she got back. She slowly walks back and my partner hands her a pen and she is shaking trying to figure out how in the world to write herself up.

I lean towards her and try to be helpful, "Maybe you could start it with something like they got me."

She starts to write and looks up to see two of the biggest grins you have ever seen. "OH, you two!"

"Well, we heard you say that we would never get you and your write up sheet should say that we did." She had to go home and tell her mum that we got her, we got her. It may have taken a little while to set it up but we got her.

One time someone handed me some money before she started her shift and there again I told my partner in crime of a scheme. "Tell her she is short exactly and it has to be exactly fifty dollars because that is what she handed me before she started. Now she will tell you that she gave me fifty dollars so make her get me to confirm it to you. Then we will and I whispered…" The moment comes and I see her come up to the front to start looking for the invisible lost money, I am in the lobby wiping off tables grinning from ear to ear. The next step she goes back into the office and then comes back out to try and look again. Here she comes and I have to turn my back because the next time she will be coming to get me and I cannot have this goofy grin all over my face so I am doing what I can to straighten up. She comes up to me all worried and I looked concerned, "What is wrong."

"My till was short."

"Calm down, you know that we will help you look for it. Did you look for a cheque or in the receipts?"

"No you don't understand I am short a lot and I have the money to pay for the short but…Well, I gave you the money before my till came up short. I need my money but I do not want my till to be that short either."

"Oh, your till was short more then five or ten dollars?"

"No, it is short exactly fifty dollars and I told her that I gave you….What am I going to do?" "Well, let's just go to the office and figure out what is going on." The crew is looking and you can only tell that something is wrong and nothing else. We get to the office and my partner has the same disturbed worried look on her face.

"This is not good. She told me that she gave you some money before she started."

"And she did she gave me fifty dollars before she ever came back here."

"Well the thing is that her till came up exactly fifty dollars short."

"You know that she did not take it, come on we know her."

"Oh, I know that she did not take it but."

Then the one we're getting says, "I can just give you that money even though it is mine so that my till does not come up short."

My partner, "But see it makes you look guilty because it makes it look like you took it yesterday to see if it would be missed today."

I looked perplexed, "Oh, that is how the company might look at it, I never thought about it like that. She was waiting to see if it came back around."

"Then because you gave it to a shirt before your shift makes it look like you were trying to leave her holding the bag if you got caught."

She just looked at me and I just looked at her and we both looked like, "What?!"

Then my partner, "Another probability could be is that she told me ahead of time about the money to mess with you."

Now when you do this please expect to get hit in the shoulder sometimes but no matter how hard they hit you it can never erase the smile plastered all over your face.

She just looks at us, "Why would you mess with me!"

"We mess with everyone that we like."

She just shakes her head and walks out of the office telling everyone what we just did for her. My partner in crimes tells her, "Before our shift started the people who even we call management because we do not like them either ticked us off and we did not want to take it out on all of you so it was a tension breaker." She did not like them either. Shirts works right beside their undershirts so respect goes back and forth. Management act like they're above their workers so only dirty looks gets passed around.

My boss lady taught me that, "Be the type of shirt you would want to work for. If you do not like working for people who just sit in the office all day bossing everyone around then do not do it when you work for that position. She rocked too and was always right there in the thick of it with us. My mum is a shirt, if you need help or have no idea of what you are doing when you come to her she will never make you feel daft.

I have had some good times at either the places I have worked or places where I am visiting someone while on break. I have had some good times in my life, some great times and some hysterical moments in my life too. I was telling our mum some of the things we used to do in front of some of the ladies she works with and one of them asked me, "What do you have to say for yourself."

I laughed, "Be glad that you're in charge of me and that I am not the one in charge of you otherwise I would be doing that to as many of you that I could."

Another great time that I had with my boss lady, partner in crime and our store supervisor was when I asked my partner in crime (I love saying that when it comes to stuff like this) "Do you want to help me pull off an April Fool's gag?"

She just looks all confused at me, "Do they celebrate April Fool's in October where you're from?"

I died laughing, "No, we celebrate it the same time that you do but if we plan it now and start the ball rolling by the time that holiday comes around nobody will think this has anything to do with that day."

The plan went into motion and all the stores tied to us started to freak out after a little while, my partner and I were not on the same page. We were fighting verbally and were not trying to hide it either.

Boss Lady, "I have never seen you two fight about anything before what is going on?"

"Will you talk some sense into her mum (Boss Lady was an aunt to me and a mum to her) when she comes in because she will not be reasonable and refuses to listen to me." I was clocking in later that same day and when I hit the front door all I heard was, "I cannot believe you."

I shot my partner a dirty look, "You just could not keep your mouth shut about it could you."

"Oh, like nobody will notice when you do it. See how stupid you're being and you have not even gone through with it yet. Talk to her."

The plot was that I was going to get some breast implants but could not decide on the size but that they were going to let me try some on to help. Everyone got into this one, some sided with my partner some were telling me what size they think I would look good in, the whole nine yards. The thing that only the two of us knew was I would go over to her house every day so she could help me with my lines. I had to find some props that I could use for the big day and that was not easy. I went back to my partners hide out and told her that I went and priced everything and I was not going to spend a hundred dollars on an April Fool's gag so we had to figure out something between now and then.

I thought about someone and went to see if they would help me, they would. They supplied the bra and the two boxes of poly fill that I would need for the falsies (Yes, I said two boxes and they wanted them back after it was over.) They went to work on making them, (Hint if you ever decide to do anything this funny do not, I repeat do not use velvet for falsies it is…it is just not a good idea is all.)

I always rehearse a couple of times with something of this magnitude to make sure that I stop smiling by the time I need to but no matter how many times I did I could not stop laughing. When I would put this thing on I kept looking up and down because now I have something catching my eyes. Mind you it took two boxes of poly fill to get them to stick out but now something is sticking out and I cannot stop my head from looking down to see what it is. My mates tell me that they would be expecting me to look at them just not as often as I have been. "Well, this is freaking me out, my shirt does not fit the same and oh. I never thought about that my work shirt." I went to the house and tried it on with these new things and it fit but now I could see my work pocket on it and then it dawned on me, "That is why they call it a breast pocket." To be honest I never really noticed the one on my shirt before because I never had anything to put in them before. Now please keep in mind that this one carried on for seven months and seven months is a long time to keep everything just going as smooth as you can so that nobody is the wiser. The longest who done it plot with two writers doing it as they go.

The big day comes; I jumped out of the shower and was getting ready. The neighbour said that she would help me with my costume and died laughing when she saw the originals. "Now you know why I do not know how to put one of these things on without getting it all twisted up. If I wore a training bra I would have to stuff it, maybe not with two boxes of poly fill but still. My motto is: If you have to stuff it then you should not bother with it." We get everything fixed so that I am not lop sided and she notices that I start moving my head up and down but that I have no idea that I am doing it.

"What's wrong?"

"They're distracting my eye sight, that maybe a good thing though to keep me from laughing. I never thought that I would live to see the day when I would be wearing breasts out in public." I get in my car and oh good night. Whatever size this was it was getting in the way. Have you ever been pulled over and was so distracted by your own April Fools gag that you had to explain to the officer what was wrong with you. I told her everything but even she noticed that my eyes were not accustomed to having something sticking out this far and kept moving my eyes to them.

"This has been going on for how long?"

"Seven months but this is the first time that I have ever worn them out in public and for all day long at that."

She cracks up laughing and asks me where I worked.

"Oh, they're coming out as soon as I clock out because we will tell them everything."

"No I want to see you pull this off."

I get to work and Boss lady is there and tells me that they look nice on me and not a bad size either. I told her that I was not too sure about the size.

"Too small?"

"NO! Too big."

"They do look nice on you."

We go to work and that whole freaking day was hysterical between the customers not knowing what if they were seeing was true and I never said a word either way. Some of them had the look of, "Didn't you always have them or…?"

Since I was distracted with taking their order and filling it I moved around too much for them to be the only distraction but when the rush was over even Boss lady saw me doing that head thing. "Boss Lady? Do your bobbies distract your eye sight?"

She smiled at me, "No, but I grew up with mine."

"Oh, I bet that would have a lot to do with it."

We have another rush and this time the cherry turn over lady comes by. (We nicked named the ones we like by what they order depending on our job.) "I cannot believe they let you wear that at work. They never said anything!"

Long story short she did not think I was getting a boob job, she thought I was a bloke all this time and was being a transsexual. That was funny and I told my partner in crime because for some reason they pulled her that day from our store and needed her to work in another one, of all the days.

That rush was ended and boss lady has me come to the back and talk with her. "I noticed you got them caught in the register a couple of times."

"Good thing mine are actually way back here when that happened."

She notices that if I stay busy my head is fine but when we are not waiting on customers I do get distracted by them. She laughs, "Are you going to be o.k."

"I am not sure, I mean mine are actually here and these come out to here and now they're hitting my paraphernalia vision and I am not use to anything moving right there."

Boss Lady just dies laughing as she watches me bob my head up and down trying to talk with her, "You mean your peripheral vision!"

I stopped looking long enough to look at her all confused. Then I cracked up laughing, "Well you hear one more then you do the other and I cannot think straight right now." I spaced out being pulled over that morning otherwise I would have told her that. She knew it too because I was not acting like myself even for me and I knew what was going on. "No wonder blokes loose their minds when they see a pair of these things, they really do keep you distracted from keeping your head picked up if you have not grown up with these things. I know why they call them booby traps now though Boss Lady."

She just looses it because I cannot keep my eyes off these things when I tell her that. The whole day was nuts with everything that went on, I think the universe had somehow gotten in on this too because it had seven months to listen in on our plans.

We get ready for another rush when the universe got me, (like getting them caught in the till in front of your customers is not bad enough and then having to act like it was a delay in your reaction time when you looked down to see what they were looking at in horror was not bad enough.) Now that my shirt is filled out a great deal more I notice a draft coming through the button holes, this had never been an issue before and I have no choice due to my job just to stay in the draft. You would think that since it was a tremendously warm day that this would feel so good. My chest was noticing the cool draft and was responding like it normally would when it gets cold but this was not ordinary by any means. This area is not a good place to wear velvet that is facing you and this was the wrong place and time to discover that problem. Oh man is that not a good idea. You walk around with a smirk and cannot tell anyone why but it did make me stop looking at them. I guess the universe knew that I needed help with that and blew right in to take care of it.

Guess who decides to show up and ask how things are going, my officer from this morning, "Everything seems to be going well I take it?"

"No. You know how I said that we made them?"

"Yes. Oh, is the material bothering you?"

"I would not say so much bothering, they're made out of velvet."

She lost it, "That explains the strange look on your face."

"Nobody here knows that they're homemade and I cannot take them out until after this is over."

"Looks like your April Fools gag is having fun with you."

"Yes, and I still have four hours to go."

I finally clock out and go back there to talk with Boss Lady and Our supervisor (they both are two of the sweetest ladies that you could ever work for and with.) "What did you think of the April Fools gag?"

Boss Lady looks, "When did you do it, we missed it."

I died laughing and pointed to the boob job. "You mean, but it started…that was it!!!" I rolled. "I cannot believe the extremes that you will go to just to get people to laugh. All this time?"

"All this time?"

"Does your partner in crime know?"

"She was in on it from the start. We had to figure out the argument we were going to have and get it down pat the night before so neither one of us would crack up laughing."

"So all those fights and you two going at it?"

"Was planned out ahead of time."

Everyone had a good time with that one, I am just glad that Boss Lady had the best time with it because I told her about the velvet and the two boxes of poly fill too. "I have to give my falsies back today because they need the two boxes that it took to fill these for their work."

"Two boxes!"

I was giggling but tried to sound proud, "A box a piece. I had borrowed one of her bras and he would fill them and hand them back and then I would have to hand it back and say no still not there. When it finally filled out he had went through a whole box so we knew what the other one would take. Everything I have on is borrowed."

To make it even funnier when I go back to work the next day some of the daily regulars were losing their minds and my partner in crime was there and said, "You can so tell that some of them want to ask you but they're not too sure what they want to ask."

That was fun, it may have taken seven months to thicken the plot and keep it all going but it was so worth it and now I have a better understanding of where not to wear something made of velvet, or at least not have that side of it facing such a sensitive area.

Sometimes like I said, the universe plays with you depending on your style of humour, as I have said mine is usually in the sexual department. One time I was ribbing one of my mates because I knew she liked someone and she was denying it. We are still talking as we are going in the store to get a coke and the clerk in the back hears what we are talking about.

"You know that you like him all you have to do is admit it because everyone else already knows and that includes your mum."

She has her cup under the dispenser and is talking to me and the lady who works there is wiping things down. Her cup was full and she let go of the button only it did not stop and I was laughing. She tapped it a couple of times and it finally stopped and I busted out laughing, "I wonder who you were thinking about to make that button stick and got it stuck, I saw it," and went to fill my drink cup still laughing about busting her. I let go and mine would not stop, then I remembered what she had done and did the same, only it did not stop pouring out. I tapped it a little harder but it kept coming out and I looked at the clerk and she is just standing there and I know the look on my face said, "HELP

ME!" I hit the thing and then hit it three more times and am now looking at the clerk with horror in my face and hit the thing again.

I finally knock the dung out of it and it finally stops and the first thing I did was look at the clerk as if to tell her through my eyes that since she worked there she should have known how to stop it and she just stands there and looks at me. "What happened? Did it get stuck?" The smirk that filled her face. I had so forgotten the conversation that led up to this up until those words came out of her mouth.

All I could do was hold my shattered dignity together as best as I could while thinking, "Did it get stuck? Did it get stuck?" You think that I would learn from all this that the universe listens to you carefully but no!

My mate asked me if I would go to the store with her, not a problem. She was shopping while I lag behind and looked at things. She goes to pick up some milk and I noticed the display of honey. "Ohhh, honey," and you saw goose flesh run up and down my arms and I heard a laugh but it was not coming from my mate. I looked up to see a lady standing there giggling and you could so tell from the look on my face that I was not thinking about honey in the tea sort of way. My face turned red and I just lowered my head a little and walked off. My mate is still picking up items here and there when we go in the area of the fruits and vegetables. "Ohhhh, Strawberries," and goose flesh races across my arms again. I hear laughter again and again it is not coming from my mate but it does sound rather familiar. I turn to look and it is the same lady once again and all I can do is turn a little more red then last time and tell my mate, "I am going in the ice cream department; I know that I cannot get into any trouble there."

I stand there while she is shopping and I am looking around and what have you when I notice a flavour of ice cream that I have never seen before, I look again, rub my eyes, look again, rub my eyes and yes it said what I thought I saw so I hollered for my mate to come over there and look quickly. "Come here, come here you are not going to believe this."

She walks over there and asks me what I was so excited about.

"Look."

"What?"

"Read the ice cream."

"Rocky Road?"

"No."

"Dutch chocolate?"

"No, read the one that would trigger me." She looks all around and then looks at me all puzzled.

I go up to point it out to her, "Right there, it says? Where did it go? I swear there was one right there that said panty-less and cream. I swear it did, I looked three times before I called you over."

"She did too, I saw her and she rubbed her eyes and everything before she called you over."

I ever so slowly begin to turn around and saw the exact same lady standing right there.

The only thing I could think of to save face was, "I am going to sit out in the car."

She finally comes out after she was through shopping and starts laughing as she is heading for me. "She got the biggest kick out of you. She told me she had never seen anyone get goose flesh over honey and strawberries before and had never seen anyone's face turn that red so fast. Then I told her some more stories about you along those lines."

"Yes, and I see you had to tell her what kind of car you drive too."

"No, I did not."

"Well when she came out she looked right freaking at me and was giggling just like you are now!"

"I swear I never told her anything except for stories about how things like this happen to you and sometimes I get to be there to be a witness to it."

"How did...but she looked...Man this is not funny." Have you ever tried to pout when you're trying so hard not to laugh and get embarrassed? Then it hit, "What do you mean you told her more stories!"

One time my mate, her son and I went to the store and I picked up a latex glove and he carried it out of the store and then proceeds to tell me, "I cannot believe that you took that glove!"

"Me, you are the one who walked out with it." His mum turns around fast and saw what we were talking about. We get in the vehicle and he asked me if I would blow it up and I was trying to tie it off when he made a grab for it. I lifted my arm and told him, "You need to wait until I hand it to you." I gave it to him and let the games begin, even his mum got into trying to think of new things to say about this glove.

We passed it back and forth between the three of us, she is driving and puts it on the steering wheel and sings, "I've been driving all night my hands wet on the wheel," then passed it on. We had raise your hand if you're sure and played with this thing for hours and hours on end.

Her son told me after a long while that enough is enough now and I cracked up.

"No, it is not. Do you realize how far and how many things we have come up with so far, we cannot stop now. See how far we can take it."

I was outside when he comes running out and looks at me, "Look a hand me down."

I rolled with laughter on that one, this was better than any board game because you had to think on your toes because you could not repeat. We never thought, "Oh, we should have a good time with this glove making something up as we go," it just happened and it just so happened to be a blast of a time.

No matter what you do in life you have to have some kind of tension breaker whether they are planned or not. I think that is the secret to kids not becoming stressed over life and hard times because they go out and play. Now sometimes I do things on purpose because I think that they are going to be funny and sometimes the universe gets people to play with me and then there are the times when I get to be the bum end of something that I really did not start. I have embarrassed myself before and act like I did it intentionally because I am trying to save my face from turning red and sometimes people around me buy it but other times my mum sees right through it.

One day my mum tells me not to let my humour become sexual, (like I let it become that way,) because I was going to be around workers who did not find that type of humour funny. I told her that I would be on my best behaviour and went to work. The people come to fix the equipment and apparently knew that my mum had me right where they wanted me. All I heard all day long was comments like: This is a tight screw, I do not know if I can back it out by myself we both might have to try breaking this screw loose together, I have never had a screw this tight before and on and on and for someone like me this was torture. I finally could not handle it any more and went to my mum's office to try and protest. "You did that on purpose, Mum." She just looks at me like she has no idea of what I am talking about and she did not so that was understandable. "You told them that I was going to be on my best behaviour and that is why they keep saying what they are," and I told her the comments that I had to endure.

She laughed and told me, "No, it is just coincidental," and then went back to laughing at my situation. Did I believe her when she said that, well I did not have any choice in the matter because I could tell from her facial expression that she was telling me the truth. The universe had indeed gotten me and used my mum's help without her knowing it to get me good.

One time I went to the airport with one of my mates so that she could pick someone up and did not want to go by herself. When we get to the airport it was pretty well empty and where we need to go is on the second floor. We walk around the corner and there was an escalator with nobody on it and I looked over there at my mate with a look that she knows all to well. "Do not even think about it."

"Nobody is here. Come on it will be fun," and I went running up the escalator in the opposite direction of the stairs while she on the other hand was going up the right one the correct way. I was laughing the whole time that I was running past her. I looked behind me and was laughing, "Ha Ha, I am beating you to the top. I am going to win," and I laughed even harder. I was just about to the top when I began to notice something rather strange. I was running up to the top but for some reason I could not get to the top. All I had left to clear was maybe four stairs that kept coming towards me but that was it, I kept having the same four stairs appear and I kept trying to get to that top that I was not getting any closer to. Meanwhile on the, "I am not going to do that in public escalator," she is now coming up fast and that caused me to run that much harder to the top. I look over there at her and she is just smiling but is not looking at me. I kept looking up to see the same four bloody stairs coming towards me and I am so close to the top that I can just feel it because Lord knows I am looking at it from where I am running in place.

She reaches the top and turns towards me and I was going to reach out for her hand when I noticed that she did not have it out for me to grab onto. She looks around and then looks right at me, "You know," and looks around again. "I would help you up to the top but," looking around even more now, "I do not want people to think that I know you," and with that she freaking walked off and just left me there running in place because by now I realized that is all I was doing. Some people would have stopped, went down the correct way and then went up the correct one the right way but by now you should know that that is not my style. I was so close to the top you do not understand, it was right there and all I had to do was clear these four never ending stairs that kept coming out at me.

I stopped, slid down a ways and then thought to myself, "No, I am to close too end it like this," and went back to running up the escalator the wrong direction and even though I slid down I was right back to those same four stairs in no time. Finally, I leaped for the top and even though it was not pretty by any means, I made it and went looking for her. Guess what, she had passed the metal detectors and was calmly sitting down waiting for the plane to arrive that had people she knew on board. I on the other hand was held up due to the fact that I cannot sew. I kept setting them off and cleaning out my pockets and setting them off to the point where they got their wand out and came to the bottom of my trousers where it went off big time. My face turned so beet red that I wished I was back on that escalator. I flipped my trousers so that they could see all the freaking safety pins around the bottom of my trouser leg.

The lady looks at me and I tried to tell her with dignity, "They are hand me downs and they were to long and since I do not know how to sew, this is the best that I could do so that they would not drag the ground."

She just looks at me, "Why not just cut off the excess?"

"Because, I could still grow at some time in my life and when I do I can let out my make shift hem."

They let me pass and when I finally got to my mate she kept looking straight ahead, I guess to prove to anyone watching that no she did not know me even though we came in the same car. "You never did go back down did you?"

"No."

"So tell me again how funny it will be when you beat me up to the top. Oh and by the way in your case they call it a mental detector that is why you set it off." She kept her face straight the whole time and never would let on like she knew me. "Do you know that it took you forty five minutes to climb four stairs?" Well that would explain why I was so winded. I was planning on that being extremely funny to me but it ended up being hysterically funny to her. I got her back though even though she is not the one who started this.

We went to the store so that she could pick up some items and she has her purse at her side. You know all those freebees that come in the form of free recipe cards and it says: Free Take One. Well that is what I did, I took every one that I could get my hands on and snuck them in her purse. I am not kidding you, you do not realize how many the store gives out until you take one of each and stick them in someone's purse without them knowing it. We go through the check out line and she goes to get her cheque book when she discovers she has a great deal of things in there that she does not know about. She actually thought that she has picked up somebody else's purse it was so full. She keeps digging them out and the more she does the more the cashier keeps looking at her because there were a lot, I never noticed how many I just kept sticking them in her purse.

I looked at the cashier all concerned and told her, "She is a freebee kleptomaniac and she is getting treatment but as you can see," and I made a jester towards the cards. My mate looks at the cashier and then pops me in the head right in front of her. I did let out a holler then asked, "Hey, I thought elders were supposed to grab us by the ears not go around smacking us in the head. How could you?"

"Only when they do not listen do we grab the ears, this is you getting me back for not being able to climb four stairs in less then an hour isn't it." The cashier just looks at the both of us like we had lost our minds but the good thing to come out from all of this is that she was included too so my job was done.

Another time one of my mates and I walked to the store to get a coke and I was grabbing a bunch of sugar packets and sticking them in my pocket. She just looks at me, "I know someone that does that same thing."

"I bet that we do it for different reasons though."

"I bet you don't."

"I bet we do," and we went through the line and left the store. We walked and I stopped and looked down and asked her, "What do you see?"

She looks down and answers, "Ants."

I look down and ask her, "Are you sure?"

She looks at them and then looks at me, "Yes."

"Are you sure that is what you see?"

She looks at me and asks, "Why, what do you see?"

"A bunch of uncles in drag," and we both started laughing. I then take the sugar packets out of my pocket and open them up and pour it all around the ant bed. "Have you ever seen ants eating sugar, they look like they're junkies."

We watched them for the longest time and when we got back to her house she tells her son what happened. "I never thought that I would ever be standing there watching ants eat sugar." The funny thing is one of her mates calls her a couple of days later from a pay phone and tells her that she has ants crawling around her feet while she is talking to her. My mate asks her the same thing, "Are you sure that is what you see?"

You would be amazed at what is all around you that you can have a good time with. I got into feeding ants when I worked at a food take-a-way place and would put things in front of them to see what they would like. (They will move meat away from their hole if something sweet is there.) One time I got one of my co-workers to come out there with me and even he got into it feeding the ants. "How do you keep them from biting you?"

"Easy, I tell them that if they bite me they will have to start paying for their own food and that if they think that a piece of grass is heavy try carrying around a dollar bill in their mouth. Tastes like crap."

"Oh," and went on looking at the ants until that comment hit and then he just looked up at me.

Yes, I do like doing strange things and getting other people to join in the madness, that too can be contagious.

One time I was by myself getting a coke and just standing in line with everyone else when a lady comes running in and asks, "Can anyone break this ten dollar bill for me real quick please?"

I told her that I could and she hands it to me. I look it all over front, back and even hold it up to the light. Everyone thought that I was trying to make sure that it was not counterfeit when I proceeded. "You know what you worthless scum you will never amount to anything more then a ten dollar bill. You may think that some day if you work really hard and save up that you could be something more like a twenty or a fifty but known truth all you will ever amount to is nothing more then a ten dollar bill. You heard me; all those dreams of becoming a hundred dollar bill are out the window. Oh, you could be two fives, ten ones but no matter how you add it you will always be just a stinking ten dollar bill. No more and no less so you had better get it through that paper head of yours." I looked at her straight faced, "I think that broke it. I do not think that it will ever try to be more then what it is at least for a while anyway," and I handed her back the ten dollar bill. She just has this stunned look on her face. "What! Do you think that I went to far trying to break it for you, is that why your looking at me that way because you feel I was being to hard on it? You did ask me to break it for you right?"

The cashier is more than accustomed to me and tells the lady, "Here, I will make change for you," and then looks at me when she shakes her head. The lady leaves and I go up to pay for my coke. "How have they not locked you up yet?"

"Oh, they tried to once but then they forced me out because they said that I was a bad influence on the rest of the crazy people. Their exact words were you're being too disruptive to be in here. Now how could you be a bad influence to crazy people, they were almost normal before I helped them make a come back to this side." You could hear everyone behind me giggling, at what exactly I will never know.

I remember something that I still find hysterically funny even though I did get the dung knocked out of me after it was done. I was getting one of those classroom massages where everyone is in the same room together. She was finished working on my back and asked me to turn over and re-draped the sheet. I have my eyes closed and everyone is going about their business. After a while she picks up my head and turns it so that she can rub my neck but when she did you heard my neck pop. Now it was not by any means a little pop but sounded more like a machine gun going off and she just froze still holding my head in her hands. The room is more than quiet because everyone heard what had happened. (It was kind of hard not to because it even surprised me and it is my neck.) I still had my eyes closed when I was wondering to myself, "Why is she not moving any more and why does it feel like everyone is raised up looking over at us?" I waited and waited and then it hit me, "Oh, I bet she thinks that she broke my neck the way it sounded off and so does everyone else in the room including the teacher." Since you could tell that is what everyone thought I did the only thing I could think of doing in a situation of that magnitude. I let my arm fall limp and let it drop out of the sheet and I could feel her freeze even more now. Quiet would have to be really loud if it was going to be heard in this room because the tension was so thick. Everyone had taken notice that she was still holding a head to a limp body that was not saying a word. The instructor ever so slowly walked up to her and I could feel her trying to check for a pulse. "Are, are you o.k.?"

I said, "Sure," and made the whole room jump and the one giving me the massage jump clean out of her skin causing her to drop my head on the table.

"Why did you not say something sooner, I thought...it sounded like...Oh my God I thought I broke your neck."

"I know that is why I pulled my arm out of the sheet."

"You did not pull it out you made it drop like....there is a difference you know."

The instructor was telling her that she should not make adjustments to someone's neck like that and that it really did sound like she had broken it. I told her while I was still getting a massage and laughing that my neck does that all the time and that it really had nothing to do with her except for the fact that she was holding it when it happened. Everything settles back down including the other people getting their massages, everything is nice and quiet again. Then she turns my neck the other direction and it does the exact same thing only this time I hear, "Don't even think about it."

Now I was told after I got dressed that that was not funny and I could not stop laughing. "You have a deranged sense of humour, you stayed quiet for the longest time, and what did you think we were going to think?"

Then I told them my side, "When am I ever going to be able to pull a stunt like that again. Plus, she is the one who waited so unbelievably long to ask me if I was o.k. so how is this my fault just because I was so relaxed that my arm dangled out?"

"She was in shock. Nobody's neck has ever sounded off like that before."

I have to admit, I really did know what I was doing when I let my arm dangle from underneath the sheet and just drop like that, plus I could feel everyone jump even though I would not open up my eyes but in my total defense, I did not plan for that to happen. It just did and I took full advantage of it. Who in their right mind could resist. You should try doing that and not laughing before you get everybody, it is harder than what it appears.

The universe let me play with everyone in that classroom all at once and I never even planned on that happening I really did not but sometimes you have to take advantage of something like that because up to date it has never happened again. I had someone who was getting a massage come up and tell me, "I sat up when I heard your neck pop and wondered why you were not moving. That freaked me out the way your arm just fell out of the sheet all limp like that, all I could think was oh my God she broke her neck, I am so glad that I did not get a massage from her." I just cracked up laughing when he says, "I would have never thought to do that. I would have been reassuring her that I was o.k."

"I know, and how funny do you think that would have been if you did not add the arm drop thing to it?" Even he just looked at me like I was nuts but I am not the one who started it. It was hard on me too you know, having to hold my facial expression while everyone is trying to figure out how they are going to explain this.

Another great time that I had was when I worked with my mum and I had to go into her office to ask my boss something and for the first time since I had been there I left the door open. My boss hollers, "Were you born in a barn," and started laughing.

I looked at her with the most horrific look I could come up with on my face and replied, "Yes as a matter of fact I was. What the hell do you mean by that?"

She just wants to look anywhere but at me. All I could really make out was, "That is just a saying of ours."

I left it at that and went back to work. She on the other hand cannot leave it alone and tells my mum, "I am so sorry I did not know that your kid was born in a barn I really did not. I was not trying to be insulting to her I really was not. I never thought that someone might actually be born in a barn I have just always said that when someone leave the door open." My mum just looks at her, "My kid was not born in a barn she just did that to mess with you." I could not stop laughing, how was I supposed to know that she was going to apologize to my mum for saying that to me after all she never apologized to me after she said it. As a matter of fact all she did was look everywhere but at me.

She tells my mum that my facial expression was what got her to believe that I really was born in a barn. "She just looked so hurt and shocked." I still get a kick out of that one.

There was one time that my mum got me and somehow I had helped her unknowingly. I was working (and yes I do work when I am playing) when my mum walks up to me and asked me, "What did you do?!"

I had to stop and actually think of what I did that she did not know about already and finally replied, "I did not do anything, Mum."

She just scans me and looks into my eyes, "Well, you're going to do something."

Now having heard that come directly from my mum you would think that I would be on my best behaviour but I went on and never kept that thought in mind. They have someone new starting and asked if I would train them. "Sure, not a problem." I give them the lay down and tell them, "Now at ten o'clock you are going to hear a bell go off, when it does drop to your knees wherever you are and put your hands on top of your head because it is a fire drill. I know what you must be thinking if it were a real fire then should we not be heading out the building but that is just what they do around here and it happens every day at ten so you might want to get used to it. Remember ten o'clock bell goes off, you go to your knees and put your hands on your head no matter where you are or what you're doing."

Then I went back to my work and forgot all about him because that happened at about six thirty in the morning. The bell goes off and I really did completely forget about looking for him and I go to break with everyone else. I get back and for some unknown reason my mum wants to see me in her office, I go like nothing is wrong because well nothing is wrong to my knowledge. My mum tells me that he is on his knees looking at everyone heading to the front door and it was not until then that I remembered what I told him. Then it hit even harder her words from that very morning.

I just looked so shocked at my mum when I replied, "This is what you were talking about huh, Mum?"

Yes, my mum knew that I was going to do something way before I did. Yes you would think that I would have listened to and paid attention to my mum coming straight out and telling me that she knew I was going to be up to no good that day but noooooo! That never occurred until after I had done the crime and still I had to wait for her to point it out. You know that your mum is freaking awesome and powerful when she can predict your crimes against laughter before you have anything planned.

Sometimes I do get wild hairs to do other things, we went to all the stores one time after Christmas and did a search and rescue operation of all the Teddy Bears that we could find because I had gotten it in my head that they were going to be destroyed if nobody wanted them. We rescued between thirty to fifty bears and they all ended up at my house, good thing they were always stuffed because they would have eaten me out of house and home. My partner kept one in the back seat as a sympathizer and to let the others know that they were going to be safe, they even buckled them up in a seat belt. I would take a couple to work with me and find good homes for them. Sometimes you just never know what is going to happen when you do something like this. All we wanted to do was find them good homes. One of my mates came up and I asked her if I could give her a bear hug and she said yes so I went and got one from the back and placed it in-between the two of us. After the hug I asked the bear if they liked it and got it to nod its head yes. (When you see a bear nod its head yes you cannot help but to fall in love.) I told her what we were doing but that I did not have room for all of them and asked her if she would mind giving them a kind and loving home. She grabbed it and had the biggest tears in her eyes when she was holding them. "I have never had a teddy bear before," and squeezed them even harder. To be perfectly honest that one got to me.

One of my regulars came up and I asked her if I gave her some petrol money if she would mind giving one of my mates a ride. She asked me how well I knew them and I told her that I would trust them with any secret that I had so she agreed. I went to the back and since she was the only one in there I made sure that she could hear the conversation from the back. "O.K. I got you a ride but you are the one that is going to have to ask her if you can stay at her place for a couple of days."

I could hear her gasp as if to say, "What did you get me into."

"She is really nice and has a big heart so I do not see why she would not plus I did vouch for you so that should give you some points. I know that you are shy that is why I asked her to give you the ride but you have to ask her for the rest because that would be me pushing it. O.K. now go and get your things because we do not want to keep her waiting like I said she is nice."

I held their hand and walked out with them. "My Lady, my mate would like to ask you something," and the bear scurried up into my arms and buried their face, but slowly looked over at her.

She is the one who asked, "So this is the mate that needs a ride," and she paused for a moment and then said, "And if I heard you correctly also needs a place to stay." The bear turned around and looked at her and slowly shook their head yes. "Well, I do not think that would be asking too much," and I walked the bear over to her. She holds them just like you would a baby on your hip and just starting talking. People would walk in and she would move back so that I could wait on them and then come back up to the counter just holding them close. If you looked close you could swear that there was a little kid standing at that counter holding her mate.

Every one of those rescued bears found a good home. There were a couple of times that we had to sneak them so that nobody would see them but they made it safely home. When that first started it was all about finding every bear that we could because we did not want any harm to come to them. Then it was all about finding loving homes for them but what it turned out to be was that year a lot of people were in need of a loving Teddy Bear. I actually had someone try and ruin the moment by saying, "I cannot believe that you would waste all that money on something like that just to give them all away, how childish."

I looked at them and asked, "Would you like to take a loving Teddy Bear home, just on a trial basses?"

"Yes, please," and I could not believe the look in their eyes. It went from all rough and grumble to the softest, "Yes please," you have ever heard.

The sweetest thing for me is when my partner picked one out and named him (He choose the sex of his bear) and then hinted around that he liked this one the best but I took him inside before I realized what he was asking. A couple of days later I brought him out and told him, "I apologize the bear had to explain it to me but he said that he wanted to go home with you too I just missed it because I was caught up in the rescue mission."

He took him and placed him in the car and now he is the ambassador of all bears. He is a grown man who knows how to keep his bear safe and to me that was one on the sweetest things I have ever seen. The sweet thing for me personally is that my mum and brother brought me up a bear from the whole family that very same year.

There was one time that I was at work and a lady came up with her daughter and I noticed little ones eye brows and I told her, "Oh baby I just love your eye brows they are awesome." Her mum snaps at me and goes, "She cannot help it, she is on medication and it causes them to grow like that," and was about to come unglued when I stopped her.

"My Lady you do not understand," and I lifted up my hat and pulled my hair back to expose my unibrow, "I love her eye brows. Mine is an heirloom from my grandfather."

Her eyes got real big, "Oh, it is just that so many people make fun of her."

I looked at the little one and smiled great big, "Sweetie, the reason that they make fun of you is because they do not have one. Plus they cannot be real smart if they're making fun of a little baby. Moreover, they're just jealous that they cannot grow their own. You be proud of your eye brows because they make you look distinguished." Oh I wish that you could have seen the smile that covered that little baby's face as well as her mums.

I was teaching my mates little one words and I was getting them to say words like, Epiphany, ostracized, sesquicentennial, galvanize, dissipate, garrulous just to name a few. She brings him over and has the funniest look on her face. "I had a little party last night and you know that when he gets tired he starts to get cranky so I told him that he needed to go to his room. He slowly starts heading that way but he has the most peculiar look on his face and you can tell that he is working on something. He stops and looks at me and cocks his head then looks back to the ground and then back to me again. I was about to tell him to go to his room again when he looks at me again and says, Am I being ostracized?"

I lost it. I told her, "I never taught him the definitions I just taught him the words, that little guy is smart." Then she laughs and tells me that some of the people at the party had no idea what that word even meant.

I love getting little kids to play word games with me and the trick to teaching them big words is not to tell them that your teaching them big words. I myself would rather hear a little one say big words than hearing them say cuss words.

My mum got me real good one time over the phone. I was telling her about dog sitting while they went out of town and I was telling her about the animals. "Mum, they have one that is huge even for me I mean he is big and he thinks that he is a little bitty lap puppy and makes his way into my lap. Then they have one who is so tiny but thinks that she is a huge dog."

Without missing a beat my mum replies, "Who else do you know that suffers from little doggie syndrome?" I could not stop laughing because my head was bobbing as if trying to dodge the comment that was coming right for us. My mum just cracks up and says, "I knew that you would catch that one." How could I not, it felt like I was being held in place so that I could not dodge or jump out of the way. I am telling you straight, my mum is good and never misses a beat.

Sometimes something happens to me that is completely unexpected but still hysterically funny none the less. I went over to my mate's house for the first time and we get to talking and after a while I have to borrow their facilities so he told me where it was. I was laughing so unbelievably hard that they came by the door to ask me if I was alright. "You know I would tell you what I am laughing about but this is just something that you have to see for yourself," and with that I told him to open up the door.

I was sitting on the throne at the time but that was not it. When he saw how far off the ground my legs were he could not stop laughing either. "I cannot believe that you would show me something like that I really cannot. Your legs are like four feet off the ground, how on earth did you get up there?" I was still laughing when I told him that I had to climb onto the bath tub and then flip myself over onto the throne. I thought about going back in there with them and ask someone to pick me up and put me up there but that I had to go too bad. "I have never seen anyone be able to swing their legs back and forth while sitting there." The hardest part was not letting everyone see this, no the hardest part was jumping down with your trousers around your knees. The cool thing is that the next time I went over there and had to use the facilities there was a step stool that I could put in front although I could still swing my legs back and forth with no worries. Sometimes you just have to enjoy an awkward moment and share it with someone who will laugh at you while you're laughing at yourself.

When I had to go take care of some business and it was all serious and it was getting to me, I waited for her to tell me how much it was going to cost and she was getting everything run through the computer and told me the total. I patted myself down a couple of times and looked so worried and told her, "You're not going to believe this but I am short."

She looks at her other co-worker as if to say, "What am I supposed to do everything is already logged in," and then looks back at me.

"Oh, I have all your money, I am just short."

Apparently neither one had heard that line before because they both thought it was funny and in their line of work nobody brings them a good laugh so I thought that they needed a tension breaker even though I was going to be the one under stress. See, now when I have to go back I can remember them laughing and feel a little easier about having to go through something of that magnitude.

One-liners are great they really are and those I know I am going to do ahead of time. The way I see it is if people do not want me to play with them then they should run before I get close enough to mess with them. You can tell a joke but after a while everyone has heard all of yours and one-liners seem to fit anybody. For example I love coming up to a line and tapping the person in front of me and asking them, "I am in such a hurry. Is it o.k. if I cut in line behind you?" They just look at you like you do not know that you're nuts, little do they know that I am very much aware that I am nuts.

Sometimes you have to make your own fun but you did when you were a kid so what would be the difference. No matter what road your life is on you have to take some laughter with you otherwise you will stay miserable when you do not have to be. We really do need to learn to let go and move on and laughter can do just that for you. Anything can be made to bring you a laugh as long as you're not too serious about how it comes to you. You can be a little bit of everything throughout life but the best thing to be in the end is your own comedian. I for one got tired of hearing that so and so is the life of the party but they were never there so I learned how to make myself my own life of my party and I have never looked back. I have been told by more then one person, "I just do not understand how you can act like you do when you're out in public." When I asked them if they have ever seen a comedian and they say yes then I ask them what the difference is. "I am paying to see them." You would think that since I was not charging them that it would have been better but that is not how they choose to see it.

I have also been asked, "Why don't you try and be a stand up comedian."

My reply, "I tried but it was standing room only and since everyone in the room was taller than I am they never could see who was the one being the comedian."

Somebody saw a picture of my mum and dad and told me that I look exactly like my mum but that I did not look anything like my dad and I told them that I beg to differ. She looks at me and then looks at the picture, "Your dad is built like a brick shit house no offence but you are not."

I laughed, "Ha Ha Ha. I look like both my parents thank-you very much. It is true that I do gets my looks from my mum but I do get my build from my dad, I am built just like a port-a-potty and we are just as sturdy," and I inflated my chest so that I would look bigger. She just looks at me and knew I believed everything that just came out of my mouth and I do too. Yes I told my mum what I had said and she asked me how I managed to pull that one off and I told her and she did the same thing that I did, she laughed.

No matter what, all of us should learn to be our own tension breakers so that life itself does not drive you mad. No matter what your philosophy is in life please let it include laughter of some kind because nothing is better than hearing yourself laugh when you feel like you're at your wits end.

# Chapter Nine
# Your Wit's End!

The more I listen to my mum the more I realize how true she is about life, family and all that it entails. She knows her stuff and the one thing that echoes in my ear is when she said, "You need to respect your mum." To be truthful I never gave mums a second thought until I was given one of my very own and there is a difference between not disrespecting your mum and showing and giving her the respect that she has earned and more than deserves. I know that my mum makes it look easy loving all of us the way that only she can do but being a truly great mum is one of the toughest jobs there is.

I never realized how great a mum's love is until I searched the world over for her, then when she found me I thought that I was not worthy of such a great love. She cleaned me up, fixed all of my hurts and showed me what I look like in her mirror with her. My grandfather taught me not to cry because it was not safe and now my mum has taught me that if I need to cry I will always be safe but I no longer feel the need to cry. The greatest gift a kid can ever have is the gift of a mum and even though we can never repay them for all the gifts of love, hugs, courage and refinement that they bestow on us the best thing that we can do as their kids is just like my mum said, "Respect your mum."

I have always heard that the word "mum" was another name for God on the lips and heart of a child but I never wanted to believe it simply because I did not have one of my own. Now I know in my heart how true those words really are. Mum is another name for God (A really good reason not to disrespect your mum because it shows the utmost disrespect for the both of them,) and I understand now why Dad says for us to Honour thy father and thy mum because they truly are one in the same and they pass onto you part of her soul. Your job is to build your own holy spirit and find the path that leads you into pulling yourself together.

I cannot remember for the life of me who said it to me but they grabbed me and looked me dead in the eye to make sure they had my attention because they knew how head strong I am, "You have got to get a hold of yourself and pull yourself together. I know that you can do it." I felt like laughing but I did not even grin I just kind of smiled because something told me that it was just to deep for me at the time. I wish I could remember who it was because I would like for them to look me back in the eyes and see if they can tell if I have done it or not. If you ask me, honestly if I have not I sure feel like I am pretty close. I have always been in touch with my mind, brain and anything tied to it. I think that is the reason I freaked out when the door shut, it made me realize that I have always spent my life inside my head and very seldom came out to play. I could always figure things out because I never added anything else into it, no heart or soul.

When you start to pull yourself together you realize that there is more to you then meets the eye especially if you're anything like me and keep your eyes closed or just so narrowed that they might as well be closed. (I guess when your head is up your bum it is better to you have your eyes closed. See I was onto something with all of that corn and potato theory after all.) Some of us only see what we want to and some of us only hear what we want to and if we would switch them out we will find that we indeed have a sharper picture of that clear rain drop. We keep our eyes opened and can decipher everything that we hear between what is real and made up. The pieces that we pick up are our head, heart, body, soul and spirit. Since I went head first into everything I have always had that part of me and I backed it up with a spirit that was on fire but it went out in front of me not inside of me.

Now that my journey has ended and my life has begun I find that all of my answers to life lies within the heart of my mum who is extraordinarily genuine. When I first set eyes on my mum I wanted to be over there with her but I knew in my mind I was elsewhere. My spirit never had to come out in front of my mum because I knew better than to go head to head with her from the start but the soul I was meant to be was with her and somewhere inside of me I could feel it. I had a hard time going to my mum because I knew that I had not completed my puzzle and I learned that all of us have been working on the same one together. The first time I met my mum she held my hand but I did not want to look up close because I was scared of what I was going to see. When I finally went home I felt my mum hold my heart surrounded by my Family and we looked at the puzzle together. The puzzle was a portrait of our entire family and she showed me through their love that I was not at the bottom or in the corner but together in the circle with all of them.

I realize that in order to close a chapter or to finish a book you need to turn the page. My life started out in the wrong puzzle box and I keep going back to find my pieces. It was not until I looked up close at our family portrait that I saw where the heart of the family is held. Our mum holds the heart of the entire family because we are all connected to her and together we surround our heart through her. I more than agree with my mum about respecting your mum when you are given a good one but I also feel like you should adore and idolize her too. The reason being is that you would not be worshiping a false idol. To idolize means to feel great admiration and respect for and be forever devoted to and after everything that a mum's loves and heart feels for us you would be a fool not to.

I would never feel that way about the one that I had to come through in order to return home and we both knew it because to me they would have made me worship them as false idols and Dad said that you should not do that and left it up to each individual to their decisions. Worship a false idol or idolize your mum for the great admiration that she has for our Dad and shows us through her teachings? I was born to man but I will stay with my mum because I respect her way of life far more. I will always hold my family in the highest of regard but my Honour will always be held through my mum's heart and head of office.

Sometimes you do have to let your kids hit rock bottom out of love for them because they have to want help and they have to want to better themselves. Rock bottom for me was when I had to decide between life or death and the conflict I was having was between my spirit and my soul. One firmly believed that today was a good day to die for what ever cause and my soul is the one who felt and finally spoke out and said, "Screw that, we want life with our mum and you had better start including us if you ever want to see her again." (Did you know that you could mentally bitch slap the dung out of the other side of your brain into coming around? Remember when I said about them walking around rubbing their head so you know that they have been put in their place!! I felt me getting put in mine. Karma did not slap me on the fanny, it full force head butted me for my mum. Now do we have your full attention? You need to admit that you cannot do it all by yourself and that you desperately need help but you need to get it through your thick head that you need the kind of help that only comes from a mum's heart. If you do not comply the universe is going to help us head butt you the next time and even your head is not strong enough to take the blunt of that blow.) When I came to I decided to choose life instead of surviving a slow death, the choice was firm by both my spirit and head we just could not find our heart to go home, where did we put it. That is when I realized what my mum is the true keeper of, souls be they lost or found she knows where they are and where they want to be and she guides us home with the beat of her heart. (Yes it is finally sinking in; I should have told you way before now that I am rather slow on some things.)

I remembered something that Lady Legs said to her son, she so lovingly said, "How about next time we use our eyes when we are looking for something o.k." I was not using my eyes when it came to finding my family. My grandfather taught me that when you're in total darkness to use your ears in place of your eyes because your eyes cannot see everything in the dark. I heard my mum's voice and they say that you recognize the voice of your Parents but I kept trying to use my ears to find her. (A real life version of Marco Polo.) Now that they're opened I can hear with better understanding because I can see what my mum is talking about now instead of having to picture it in my head first. I can feel her words instead of having to picture everything, my mum broke into my realm of undisturbed thinking and derailed my completed train. My mum knows how my brain works and talks with me accordingly and I am learning how to listen to the feelings in the words by listening to her with my heart.

I learned about the saying that if your friends all jumped off a cliff would you follow? I think it would be better worded if it were put if you were pushed up to the very edge of a cliff would you jump, allow yourself to be pushed or dared over by the word chicken or would you simply learn to turn around and walk through the fiery pit of hell to come out a better person for it. I learned that that is where my mum has always been standing, on that very same cliff edge with me, trying to get me to open my eyes because I had fallen over but managed to somehow hang on. When she pulled me out she tried to get me to turn around and see that although it may be a rocky road to elsewhere at least you know for sure that you will fall on solid ground you will not have that far to fall which is more than anyone can say about hanging on the edge of a cliff.

I also learned that my mum got tired of waiting on that same edge of a cliff with me as I watched the horrors of people I had met go over. All I had to do was turn around and open my eyes and I could have walked home with her together. I never noticed how much tunnel bum vision and being an autistic dyslexic can really mess with your reality and logic all at the same time. I went through life looking forward but was walking backwards the whole time but because my mind was moving forward I thought I was too. That could be why my mum made me jump so high that day, to forewarn me that I was about to go over and was never going to realize it on my own. My mum allowed me to drive her up the wall but she was not going to allow me to drive her over the edge to come and save me and she should not have to. I had not hit the bottom of the cliff yet and there was still time to grab her hand since she has the whole family holding onto her. The reason none of them could pull me up was because I was carrying too much dead weight. I could either hold onto the dead weight with one hand while holding onto a twig about to snap with the other or I could let go and reach out my hand while still holding onto that same little twig. Since I never told my left hand what my right one was doing they both let go without realizing it and I screamed the whole way….but I never felt myself hit the bottom. I opened my eyes to see that my mum had grabbed me and had me safely in her arms the whole time as I screamed. Freaking nightmares, I am just highly grateful that my mum woke me up before I hit the ground. I was truly petrified and my mum could see through all that battered armour that I was and took hold of me until I could get a hold of myself. Some say that when a baby is born that they have a spirit animal and if that was the case I had broken the heart of mine. I had come to the hard realization that it was not me who was out in the cold; in reality I had put my family out in the cold because I have always had to do things alone. My spirit knew we had screwed up trying so desperately hard not to. I could not have felt any lower when I broke down to my mum and she never made me feel bad for it not one drop.

I wrote something long ago but sadly an evil villager stole it but it starts out Dear World, (Just to the people in it,) I just wanted to let you know just how bad you suck. You gave life to a mere thought and now you made me an outcast. The last lines was, if I have to face reality is it yours or mine? Sometimes I think that some of us are living in the wrong realm of reality, I know for myself I would not even acknowledge that reality existed and the truth of the matter is it really does even if you choose not to see it. To me reality was interfering with my realm of thinking and I had put a do not disturbed sign because they already are up long ago. My mum got me to not only wake up to reality she got me to face it and to pick once and for all this is for all the marbles because I know that you have lost yours choice, jump or walk away.

I learned how to just let things go and walk away and learned that I should not be ashamed of what they did to me but that I should be ashamed at the hell I put my mum through. It finally dawned on me what my grandfather had done all those years ago for me, he got me to believe that he was playing solider with me but in reality what he had done was taught me how to survive out in the wild for as long as it took. When I look at things now, I really was a wild child when my mum found me. I went wild anytime she hugged me and went wild with excitement when she claimed me. I had been left alone for so long having to fend for myself that I forgot what human contact was of any kind. My mum knew that I was free of corruption to a certain point just not free from all the pain that put me out here in the wild. My mum never forced me into anything and she never told me how I felt or what was going on through my mind. She did not want me so that she could parade me around in front of her society friends and become, "Look at the noble savage I took in and flaunt around anytime I need to feel good about myself." My mum fooled me when she said that every kid needs their mum, she had known all along that I was indeed just a lost child who thought they were a kid and because nothing was governing me I had indeed become wild. It finally dawned on me that I have always been a wild child and the great thing is my family found no fault in surviving alone. They taught me that even though I did not throw childish tit fits I was still going off to sulk by myself and that is what my family could see, an abandoned child sulking because we were taught nothing else before being left.

My mum taught me a lot, how to walk up right, how to communicate with words instead of growling. How to talk when something is bothering us and more than that she taught me where my home has always been. I guess that is why I fought so hard to stay wild because I knew that all the villagers wanted to change me into something corrupt be it somebody who looked down on others because they're different or somebody they could use and then discard again. My mum knew that I had it in me to be one of her kids if I could just get it through my head that I was a child.

That is what my rocky road through hell was for, learning to shed that snake skin of childish behaviour, going off to sulk because something was way beyond my thought process. I noticed something amazing, my mum has never said and she says a lot to me but she never once told me that I thought too much, I guess she knew before I did that that was all I had. I have always thought about feelings but not enough to have any for myself. Having feelings when you're living out in the wild will get you hurt, thinking when your out in the wild will make sure that you live to see another day. My mum never attacked me when I came in for supplies either; as a matter of fact she would pack some extra things for me for free because she knew that I would use everything. The one thing that she packed extra of is love from the family and when this feeling started seeping into my thoughts I actually pictured a life out of the wild with them and that is what made me feel like I could go through the rest of hell for them. I did not want to be childish in any form any more and honestly I did not know that I was but yes I was. I did not want to hide behind trees while looking into my mum's heart and I sure did not want to live out in the wild any more. My mum never did try to take that wildness out of me, she gave me enough free things so that I would have something to compare. I am the one who decided that I did not want to live out in the wild any more. My mum knew that with time, a little understanding and a tremendous amount of patience I would grow from her wilderness child into her kid. I had to learn to stop going back to the only place I have ever known and now I do not even know where the wilderness is any more.

My mum did not change me she changed my surroundings and therefore my environment and knew in her heart that I would always adapt to my surroundings. I did not want to treat my family the way others have treated me and I learned that that is part of the childish skin once it is finally shed. A mum helps you to build your heart while using your head and the dad teaches you how to use your head without losing your heart and you connect the two through your backbone giving you perfect balance.

Some people are unbalanced before they start a family and they just keep the cycle going. Dads are not supposed to be emotionally distant from their families and mums are not meant to be the entire backbone for their kids. Parents should want their kids to be both mentally and emotionally strong because not only will they be able to stand on their own two feet they will be healthier and more well rounded for it. If more people were created this way then there would be less broken marriages and fewer of us would be coming out of broken homes trying to start families. I did not want anything to do with broken homes and emotionally wrecked people and that is why I stayed out in the wilderness. My mum got me to open my eyes to a world that had been closed off to me for so long. "Look, the family that we want you to be a part of has its ups and downs and goes through hard times but if you can use your minds eye to look past that you will see that above all else we do love each other and we know that you have it in you to be a part of it too." The sweet thing is she instilled it inside of my nature and that caused me to want to shed my skin of being childish when something was beyond me.

I went through hell a wild child and came out on the other side my mum and dad's kid, a member of the family and now I realize that I have parents. I may not be as big as my grandfather taught me to believe I was but I have a big family who makes up for what I lack in actual size. I also realize that I may not be built exactly as big as my dad meaning that I am not tall enough to be built like a port-a-potty, I am built more like a urinal but they're strong too so I am more then o.k. with that, it also gives you more chances to flush your Karma so look how well that worked out. The important thing that I keep in mind and heart is that I get something from both my parents, my looks and my solid build. Now when I look at my body it is built pretty solid, thanks Mum and Dad.

My mum knew that I had spent my whole life wanting her and never needing anything else, but what she did was teach me how to make my wants more complex. She taught me that at the time I was not being selfish by surviving a war I never started and trying to help others survive that feeling of abandonment, which is what kept me a respectable child. I just got lost when I saw others going over the edge of a cliff because I had helped others before they went over and could not understand why I could not reach all of them. She held my hand as she taught me the reason behind them going over and she knew that I would feel it in the one place I did not want to, my heart. "Those people have nothing to loose, nothing to live for and nothing to fight for, and nothing to keep them going," and I finally remembered feeling like that too and that is why I was put out in the wild. That is why I jumped over the edge but my mum was quick to grab me by the hand. She knew that logic had led me everywhere including over the edge so in reality logic was going to be the only thing to get me to want to come back to the top. "Look at everything you fought for and lived through. Look at how hard you fought to stay alive and the conditions you endured and if you will turn around you will see that you indeed have everything to loose if you choose to let go." Logic had held onto our mum's hand for dear life and it finally let us become not only scared but it allowed us the feeling of sheer terror when it allowed us to remember that before we did have nothing to loose and without realizing it we had gained everything we had ever wanted we just never saw it. I had went over before I had realized this and my mum knew that I did not know that I was standing on a little piece of an edge the other side of the cliff. She never told me to worry or that she would be back to come and get me. She got me to jump high enough to where she could grab me by the hand because she knew that I would fight like mad to get my little bum back up there with her.

I never noticed the view from way up here before, I made it to the top of that all seeing pyramid and used the wisdom I had obtained from my elders and they're right, this is a great place to live. I had hit the mummy load of all hidden treasures, a complete family and the one who led me there was my mum. I realized the all seeing eye belongs to her, she sees everything and knows a great deal more then you could ever comprehend on your own. She allows you to look through her eyes at a world that is peaceful and full of love. All I had ever seen is destruction in massive amounts and the worst things imaginable. The one thing that I did not want to witness: I never wanted my mum to mourn the loss of a soul that belonged to a child she once met and knew. I realized that I was nothing more than a skeleton that my mum had found but I was too weak to unlock my own mental door. You know what I learned a real mum has no need to pick locks because they truly are the Master Key. I was on deaths door and knocking hard but she never freaked out. She stayed with me and gave me a piece of her heart, a soul, put meat on my bones and did the greatest thing anyone has even done for me, she covered me with clothes made of close knitted family. I have travelled a great many places but these are the finest clothes I have ever seen, they're a perfect fit, they're so unbelievably warm and they allow you room to move and grow. I finally grew into my clothes when I went from being a child to growing into my parent's kid and I will never go back to hand me downs ever again. I went from being abandoned and unwanted to being chosen as a member of an awesome family and to me that is a treasure all in itself.

I realize now why I had stayed on the end of that cliff looking over after my mum had pulled me up, it was my way of trying to say good-bye to a world that never wanted me but allowed me to stay until someone found me. My mum had helped me to pull myself together by giving me all the parts that I had been missing I just stuck my head up the wrong body part. When my head was finally put on my shoulders Karma knocked reality through my head and got me to see that logically my family has always been and always will be a part of who I am. The thing that I had gotten screwed up was that in reality they could not be a part of me if logic did not let go and let them become part of my reality. Life had used the wind to blow the smoke screen away and I finally saw what was so overwhelming, I am part of something bigger then myself and never had the heart to realize I could be.

A part of me was sad for the first time in my life, I was actually saying good-bye instead of just leaving and I was saying good-bye to everything, all the loss, all the people, I was saying good-bye to everything that was no longer there but had once been. I did not just let go because I knew that all of them, even the villagers helped me to get this far by making me fight for a better life and I was giving the ghosts of their skeletons a proper burial as my way of saying thank-you for all that they taught me to survive. I went back to that very same edge to pay my respects to the lives that were lost, to the souls that were never found and to the life I was never meant to be a part of but made it mine. I went back to tell them all thank-you for making me tough enough to survive the hell that their lives had become but the main reason I went back was to tell their memories good-bye, that this was going to be the last time I come here any more. I could not be a part of their spirit world any more because my mum had given me a human form and therefore I could not come and play and visit with them any more. I have never went to anyone's grave site before and this was a first for me although I never shed a tear because I knew in my heart too many had been shed before. I had to go back because I made a massive grave and just threw everyone in without so much as leaving a head stone to honour the memory of them.

I went back through time not to dig my own grave but to dig one for each one of them because the soul that my mum had given me knew that what I did was wrong and that it was time to make things right again if I was ever going to be free. This time my mum was not the one who was going to be there with me, instead it was my spirit animal helping me to separate their graves and helped me to put something respectable on their head stones. "Here lies someone that the only drop of good they had in their body they saved to give to me. They made me fight for it but to them because I had won it made that drop belong to me. Thank-you and I hope that your life is easier on the other side." I felt my spirit animal holding my hand as we knelt on one knee and said a prayer for all that had passed for us to come here. I stood up on the legs that my mum had given us and I realize that they're the ones that I was walking on when I came back on this visit. They were strong enough to walk out here alone, strong enough to bend on one knee and strong enough to stand me back up. They were strong enough to keep me from dropping to the ground and mourning the loss of all that I have ever known. I told them all a final good-bye because each of them gave me something to live for and I told them all thank-you for making me strong enough to find my way home. I felt my spirit animal squeeze my hand and I squeezed theirs before we became one and I felt my honour return.

I had to go back and make everything right because I had it all wrong in my head, I had to go back to show them that I had the heart to come back and let them go. My spirit was now inside of me and my soul was leading us home so they could rest easy now because I was not lost any more. I told my grandfather thank-you for being my father but that everything was going to be o.k. because I have a real dad now. I went back to show them that I was a big kid now and not that child that found a way to live in the spirit realm. I went back to tell them about my family as I was telling my family about them and together they helped me to find the middle between their two worlds but I knew both in my heart and head which one I needed to be a part of. My past did not come back to haunt me, I was indeed a spirit that learned to haunt my past. I realized that none of them could rest because I was the one holding onto them. I should have let go long ago but their ghost is all that I had to hold onto. I learned that by holding onto their ghost and locking them in my mental closet they are the one who could not find their way home, I was becoming a part of their world thinking that they were still a part of mine and that is what was indeed killing me. A part of me had died when my grandfather left me because I knew of nothing else and I never noticed.

I learned that what my mum did for me was to give me the heart to go back and to tell them all thank-you, to apologize, to be grateful and to restore my honour that I had lost long ago and to give me legs strong enough to walk there and back all on my own. My mum was never there for that life, I was and I am the one who had to go back and pay what would be my final respects and to let my grandfather go home to finally rest. I was not scared any more and I was not a child any more and I was not alone any more. The child my grandfather had sent out into the wild was found by the mum he knew I was looking for and together they turned me into a kid who would honour how I came to be. I went back to say good-bye and it caused me to greatly reflect back on my journey but not on my journey home but on my journey back to here because it made me realize that this is the place I have always called home my memory of them.

I went to the edge and came back and then went back to the edge to pay my respects so that I would never return to this place again, the need is not there any more. My mum did not go with me but she gave me everything that I would need not to become lost trying to say good-bye. She gave me an echo that I would hear all the way there and back. "Every kid needs their mum so respect her enough not to stay out to long and know who your mum is and always will be."

"I need to go home now because I can hear my mummy calling for me and she sounds worried because I have been gone a while but she knows where I am but I am going home to stay with her now. I learned that a child does not know what they want or need but the kid that she raised does need their mum and I need my mummy because I know that my Life is with her but do not worry because even though I am way out here saying good-bye I know the path that leads me home to her."

I realized that I let to many people pick me up and claim me as their child when I told them that I had a mummy now and that was showing my mum total disrespect because she is the one who claimed me as hers and I had to stop being everyone's child and start realizing that I am only my parents kid so the rest had to let go. My mum knows that I am slow in some things because I have had so many blows to my head and that I should have never allowed anyone else to pick me up but because my eyes were closed I only heard family but never would open my eyes to see that the ones who held me were not my real family. She let that child wander off because that was the only way I was going to force my own eyes open. Now the only one who can pick me up is my family and I know them.

I know that I hurt my mum by wandering off and making her worry about me and this made me realize that sometimes things happen in life that you cannot change you just have to learn not to do it again. I learned that no matter how many people want to act motherly to you they are the ones who leave you out in the cold and lead you there every time claiming to be your mother and I fell for it every time just because of that word. My mum never set a trap, she just got tired of every time she got me out of one that I would walk into another one so I had to learn the hard way to get myself out. That was the hidden agenda that separated my mum from the other ones. They both knew that I needed my mum but one was trying to make sure that I would never find my way back. The hardest thing I learned is the worst thing you could ever do to your mum is call someone else by her name and giving them the feelings that rightfully belong to her. I was not respecting my mum nor did I realize that my actions were the cause of it. I took a journey to tell all the villagers that I have a mum in my head and because I told them they went through my head to keep me away from her, they had outsmarted me because that is not where your mum belongs. She does not belong in your heart either, she belongs in your life and I had somehow excluded her trying to tie up loose ends.

I have learned, I have been taught, I have come to realize and I have been shown that there is no greater love in the world than that of a mum and for everything that I have learned I know who My mum is and the struggles that she has to endure keeping the family together. She gave me the world to see if I wanted to be a part of it and I left to see if I did but now I know beyond the shadow of a doubt that there is no greater place than the one you have with your family and I will never wander off again. My mum is not just versatile or unbelievable she is also incredible because she took the time to re-teach a wild child and allowed them to become her child and watched as they grew into one of her kids. I took a lot of hard knocks while in her arms but she always made everything better for me. People, mums are the heart and we really do need to learn not to break theirs just because we know how and that we can. Mums have to go through so much for us and we need to realize that they are so much and go through so much and we need to stop acting like childish shit-heads because none of us want to grow up and help take some of that pressure off of her. We have to show our intelligence and not make her figure everything out for us. We as their kids need to learn how we can make their life as great as they have made ours because without them we will never be anything more then a mere thought left to our own accord. My mum did not just take in a wild child, she took in and loved an angry stubborn wild child who was too hardheaded to realize they were hurt. I was living in a world without pain and my mum knew it was going to hurt like hell when I learned to feel so she gave me time. When I talked with my Circle of Elders and they were counseling me the strangest thing occurred, she had shown me something and I had smiled great big and they had tears of horror in their eyes because they could see like my mum. They could see what I could not cover and it was time for my Elders to step in and intervene and there was no avoiding them. One of the younger elders told me that my heart and mind were not the same and this was an intervention to make me face reality. A lot of bad things happened to me and I had to feel that if I was ever to get past it in order to feel my mum who has been waiting all this time. Life made me go to counseling and because I had lived a strange life it had to find strange ways of getting me to go there. My Elders grabbed me by the ears and after the shock was over and the terror set in and the tears began to flow I realized that my mum was finally getting to break through to me. My mum took me out of the wild and knew that I was going to need a great deal of counseling to deal with what happened and now I realize it too.

I now know that I hurt my mum in ways that I did not mean to all because I could not admit to myself that I did not have a good start in life. I was the one who had lied to myself all those years and because that had become my life I could not figure out how to get out because I did not want my mum to be a part of it. When someone needed my help they stepped in and stood in front of my mum and I allowed them to do it. I allowed everything to come up in place of them so that I would not have to face what my life actually was and Karma got tired of me being disrespectful to my mum and the family so they finally drew the line and shoved my bum over it. I got help and I am proud to say I made a break through as well as a come back. I went through a tremendous amount of tragic moments and thought that if I did not give it a second thought that I could just get over it. If you do not use your feelings they will use you against your own better judgment. I realized that since my mum was not going to let me go I was doing stupid things to make her let me go because it made it easier then dealing with the hurts of my past until Karma got them all together and had life at the trigger. "Face your past and let go of it or loose your family and yes that does include your mum and your world will be completely empty. Is that not what you want?" It had never been put to me like that and yes it hurt like hell for my heart to grow up that quickly and that rapidly but my mum never let go, even when I was kicking and screaming. I had learned to block a great deal out and it was coming up full force but my mum was there to close the door after everything was through.

My mum dealt with a tremendous amount of my dung, somebody else's and then the rest of what I was letting in but she never gave up on me. I may be slow about some things and not extremely smart in some areas of life but I learned the hard way that you should respect Your mum and not someone else's. I was allowing everyone to take my mum's place because I knew that they would treat me like crap and then drop me and I had to realize why this was o.k. with me. When I realized how this came to be I was the one who said, "Screw this, my mum thinks I am better then this and has always wanted me. Moreover she never has treated us badly." I got tired of being treated like dung I really did and I was the one holding onto all of their guilt. I got fed up with all of it and was way beyond tired of it and I am the one who had to see it for myself, I was a bloody fence rider, dang it. Those are the worst ones and I was being the worst of their kind. Crap, no wonder Karma did not smack me on the fanny there were far too many splinters to get a clean shot. Sitting on a fence and spinning is not a good idea.

The wrong person who claims you as their child can severely damage you and that is not something I say lightly or take lightly for that matter. They can take the life right out of you and so many of the wrong ones had gotten through and my mum dealt with that crap too and stayed through all my night mares and terrors. A mum's job is not easy but you never hear them complain, I put my mum through a lot of crap and I was given one of the good ones. I was respecting everyone but my mum and she knew it.

If I had not have gone through all of this and had not have gone to my Spiritual Circle of Elders for counseling I would not have grown up to realize that I was not loving my mum by staying away and only checking in when I thought it was a good time. I was being a spoiled brat and was sulking that I did not need therapy until the universe showed me the toll it had taken.

I cannot for the life of me understand how in the world a mum puts up with the things that she does for her kids but thank the good Lord that they do but we really do need to grow up and start learning how to help take care of our family too. I realize that I need my family if I am ever going to be anything deep and some people need family if they are ever going to be anything more and it is my firm belief that the kids need to get off their bum and start helping out and stop being so bloody selfish, (Yes this does include me.) We are a part of the lost generation gap because we come from the ones who told us that we were smart enough to figure it out for ourselves. I learned that I was taught a tremendous amount about respecting my Elders but due to the fact that I did not have any parents at the time I was not taught anything about them. I told my mum that all I wanted from her was a hug and when she gave me one I thought, "This is the best hug I have ever gotten in my life, Thank-you so much I will always cherish this moment," and I left. I thought that if I asked for more, then that would make me appear greedy. What the hell did I know, I wanted a hug she gave me one so to me there was no need in standing around looking daft because I had gotten what I had wanted. I had no idea that a larger-than-life mum has more then one hug to give her kids and so much love that it over flows. I had no idea about parents and what they add to your life. Elders I knew about, screwed up children I knew about, parents what in the world are parents? I know that my elders tried to teach me everything that they could but what are they supposed to do point at somebody else's parents and say, "Now when you find your own set this is how you should act and treat them and they are your lifetime boss."

You would think that since my mum grounded me and told me the reason for it that I would have looked at them as the authority figure but all I knew is that I got into trouble from the one person that I was so desperately trying to impress. I liked my mum from the moment I saw her but I did not know what to do after that. Kids do not come with a rule book and I learned that neither do parents. Would that not be funny, "O.K. here is the book on me and I need the book on you. O.K. Wait all of your pages are blank, how am I supposed to figure you out, just make it up as I go along or what!" I learned that I was not taught squat about being someone's kid and I was taught even less about the role of a parent and when you become a member of a family there should be some kind of notes on the subject but since there is not I will share with you what I have slowly figured out with the help of my family.

I found out that parents come from our elders, (I had no idea because I did not come from a family tree. You should have seen the look on my face when I found out that my mum and my sister are related, that took a while to sink in. My brain is the one who had to explain it to me, "You know your sister well that is one of mum's kids."

My brain could feel my thoughts going, "Huh."

"Your mum has kids and those kids are her children."

My thoughts were still going, "Huh."

"You're related to your siblings dip-shit."

"Oh, cool."

I noticed that my brain did not say the word parents because they did not know about that word either so I do not feel so bad.) What does all of this mean, to me it finally hit that your parents are the younger of the elders but they are still your elders. The one thing that my elders instilled is that no matter how smart we become we will never be their equal, we are not dogs sitting at our masters' feet but we are not their equals. We are equal to everyone else and to other people's parents but never to our own.

"I cannot stand it when a child talks to their parents like they're the kid and acts like they're the adult." I agree with my parents whole heartedly on that one. I can stick my head up to my mum's head when we talk because she is my mum and knows that I am not trying to go head to head with her. I can put my heart up with my mum's and the same rules apply and no matter how smart I am my mum has the greater intelligence and always will. I will never outsmart my mum and it would show great ignorance if I thought that I could. Parents are elders and nothing should be taken away from them just because they're the younger version. I went pretty far because of my elders but look at how lost I had become because I did not have my parents. We have all been taught in some form by someone that we can do it on our own and what we should discover is that we can do so much more and accomplish a great deal more together. (Elders, parents, kids and grandkids.)

We exiled our elders by taking their respect away making them feel less than feeble and now we are doing the same thing to our parents. They are not our kids, they are our parents and we are not their elders they are ours. No wonder everything has gone to hell in a hand basket. Nobody is raising anything but Cains, where did the Abels go? Apparently I am not the only one going bum backwards through life. I have seen people give their employer the utmost respect, "Yes sir, no sir, yes my lady," and the whole nine yards. When it comes to our parents however, all they receive is, "Yeah what. You don't know what you're talking about so shut up. Whatever, give me some money." None of the younger generation knows what they are doing and the backlash is coming up fast kids. It is not the generations that we need to separate; I think that we need to get villagers out of families and the family members out of the villages. We have learned how to separate everything and look where it has gotten us; we have learned how to combine everything and did not get any further. When are we going to admit that we have no idea of what we are doing and that we need our parents to guide us through the wisdom they had obtained through their parents, the ones called the elders? Yes, I have learned a great deal through my elders but I soon found out that it does not mean squat without my mum and dad so really how useful is all that knowledge without them? It's worthless, absolutely worthless without my Parents to filter it all through and this is coming from a reformed angry wild child people.

I know that things got screwed up when the big brothers of this day and age took the role of the parent and put it in the hands of the kids so please do not think that it is all your fault because they need to step up and take some of the responsibility for screwing things up but since we all know that that is not going to happen then that leaves it up to us to fix this. My question is how in the world did big brother lock out their parents and ostracize the elders to keep themselves in charge? There is not a fine line between discipline and abuse there is a world of difference between the two. "Oh, you poor baby, your parents told you no." Suck it up; they are trying to teach you that you cannot have everything handed to you. What is really nuts is that the generation that got everything handed to them expects their parents to hand everything to the kids that come out of them because they're not going to give anything of theirs up. They blame everything on their parents and then expect their parents to bail them out every time while still telling them that they are no good.

If wild children can survive and be grateful for leftovers then how come babies who came out normally cannot be grateful for everything being handed to them? (I know it was a silly question that answered itself but I thought that I would put it out there anyway.) All big brother knows how to do is steal, lie and get others to be the scapegoat, nothing in any of that is honourable. They steal from our elders, our parents and then convince us that it is not only ethical but morally correct to do so. The government is on the front of money and Dad is on the back so what does that tell you. My parents do not put themselves in front of Dad but the ones that I came from sure did and look who I call the evil ones, the ones I came from, why do you think I left. They wanted to be my master which made me their dog; I do not believe that is how Dad treated us. My parents on the other hand treat me as their kid, that is why I had such a hard time adjusting because I was accustom to looking for new masters and they refused to treat me like a dog.

When big brother put the kids in charge of the parents they created a world full of wild children instead of dealing with the ones that were already there now look at where that has gotten us. Where in the world is it moral to tell your parents that you are the boss of them, and why are parents allowing their children to boss them around? Somebody needs to put their foot down and since we have doped up the elders I think it should be the parents. Our employers are not our parents and therefore should not talk to us like we are school children, and we should not be giving our employers the respect that is rightfully our parents and that is all there is to it. A job is a job and nothing more and despite contrary belief they are not your family no matter how many times they call themselves that. Just because more than one person says something is so does not make it true. Hell I had an entire village call me an evil no good bastard, but it did not make it true and half the crap that we are being told is just that, crap. Any government is supposed to protect its citizens and all they are doing is helping themselves to someone's hard earned money. They justify this by telling people that they need to work harder and to start saving up for their retirement because they spent it all. Get your damn hand out of the cookie jar, that money is not yours and you are not entitled to a dime of it. Tell me how something that is always being added to, can run out? There is a thief in the chicken house.

The thing is that none of this is beyond fixing but the thing is we have to get not only our priorities straight but our morals as well. That is sad when we have to have two different sets of laws, one that deals with morals and one that deals with ethics and then a set of laws for the ones who have no morals or ethics.

We become outraged at same sex marriages and people who do drugs and we cannot get enough rumours about who is sleeping with who but we do not have a task force to protect our elders from being taken advantage of and none for parents about to go over the edge. You can molest a child while stealing from the elderly as long as you're not smoking a joint because that would be wrong. Look at the crap we teach the younger ones. Drugs are bad; drugs are no good unless there prescribed. Where are the commercials for, "Disrespecting your elders and your parents is pissing Dad off and Karma is about to come unglued." I do not care who is sleeping with whom because if they are anything like the rest of us then they have problems of their own and really do not need our nose in their life. We have more important things to worry about here and if kids are our future then Lord help us because we are not going to have one. How are they going to protect our elders if they do not even know anything about them? How are they supposed to take care of a world that does not care enough to protect them? If you take care of the little things the rest will follow, if not you can always go back and fix what did not take care of itself.

We need to start coming home because our parents cannot do it all on their own and they should not have to. They should be able to rely on us because we spent years relying on them. We should be taking care of our families and not the ones at work that claim their employees as families because they make them live at their jobs. I do not see anything wrong with family members supporting their families and not their bosses getaway home. If we do not start taking care of our family now there is not going to be anything left to go home to. Man has allowed everything to break down the family and Dads kids need to start stepping up and bringing it back. This has nothing to do with your gender, colour or how you pray because we need to get over that ignorance, break it all down and we are all human but we are being inhumane to those we claim to love. I met someone who thought the world of themselves because they had made their fortune while their parents supported them and now they could afford a good nursing home for their parents. I asked them why they did not think enough of their parents to share their made fortune with the ones who helped them achieve it. Their response, "It is my money, I worked for it not them. It is mine." The sad thing is more people in that restaurant agreed with them. How! If someone supports you as you're trying to make it then you should do the moral thing and share or you should be made to spit out your candy since you're too greedy to share.

We cannot wait for the world to change because it is not going to until we do. Remember the world is our environment and before our environment can change we have to start with ourselves first. We have to stop waiting for someone else to take care of things or wait for someone to get tired of looking at it and let them clean up our mess. My family cleaned up someone else's mess and then I had to clean up the one that I made but we both did it and now its done. If you do not know where to start just start anywhere all you have to do is begin for the ball to start rolling. Nothing worthwhile is going to happen over night but it is not going to happen at all if we all wait around for someone to start. My parents started my ball rolling for me and I took it around the block and lost my temper in the process. There are too many people in the world for us to stay as miserable as we feel our lives have become.

We have to find our own happiness, I found mine in my family, some may find it in a hidden passion but when you find yours you will notice that depression goes knocking on somebody else's door until after awhile nobody answers it any more. My family is just like everyone else's, we have our problems but we talk them out and work through them and before you know it there is no problem any more. The only way for any of this to occur is for respect to be present. I thought that I was being respectful by keeping my problems from my parents and as you know everything got worse. I was under the misconception that I was being respectful to them by dealing with everything on my own. It was not until I heard somebody tell me about their kid and how they were not taking sides. It finally hit my family has always been on my side, I was just never on theirs and I had to fix a lot of what I did wrong. My mum has always been on my side even though I was not on my side. They may not agree with me and they are honest enough to tell me so but they are still on my side.

Your family does not always have to agree with you but that does not mean that they are against you when they disagree. What has ever happened to conversation or has it really become a lost art? We have to have open conversations and text messaging will not cut it. "This is how I feel and these are the emotions that stirred from it," and then let them tell you the same thing. If we will learn to start respecting our parents just as the good Lord intended then the respect for our elders will come into play. You cannot disrespect your kids and think that they will show you anything more and the same rule applies to the kids. My family has always been respectful to me and I was not showing the same to them and I took the advice that I gave to the lady in the bakery, I cut myself loose until I could straighten up. I did and my family took me right back in. I lived a hard life and then had to go through counseling to get past it because my demeanour was causing harm to those I was learning to love. My family has never held a grudge and taught me to do the same because I learned a great lesson; I have great parents who are Heaven sent role models which helps me get over things faster. Plus my family has never given me leftovers of any kind; my mum is such a great cook that she does not have any leftovers. I do love my dad and my siblings but my mum will always be my hero because she took the time to jump in and save my scrawny little bum.

Now sometimes there are thoughts that never cross my mind but I try not to think about them enough to give them much thought. What I do know for sure is that if we do not start respecting our parents we will never learn to respect our elders which in turn will give us respect for ourselves.

I personally think that what separates us from the animals is the ability to pleasure ourselves.

Printed in the United States
122387LV00004B/93/A

9 781424 184965